THE PSYCHOLOGY MAJOR

Career Options and Strategies for Success

R. Eric Landrum
Stephen F. Davis
Teresa A. Landrum

Prentice Hall
Upper Saddle River, New Jersey 07458

Library of Congress-in-Publication Data

Landrum, Eric.
    The psychology major: career options and strategies for success/
Eric Landrum, Stephen Davis, Teresa Landrum.
        p.   cm.
    Includes bibliographical references and index.
    ISBN 0-13-083753-9
    1. Psychology—Study and teaching (Higher)   2. Psychology—
I. Davis, Stephen.   II. Landrum, Teresa.   III. Title.
BF77.L26 2000
150'.23'73—dc21

99-35067
CIP

Editor-in-Chief: *Nancy Roberts*
Executive Editor: *Bill Webber*
Assistant Editor: *Jennifer Cohen*
Managing Editor: *Mary Rottino*
Production Liaison: *Fran Russello*
Production Editor: *Kerry Reardon*
Manufacturing Manager: Nick Sklitsis
Prepress and Maufacturing Buyer: *Tricia Kenny*
Art Director: *Jayne Conte*
Cover Designer: *Bruce Kenselaar*
Cover Art: *Kamalova, Stock Illustration Source, Inc.*

© 2000 Prentice Hall, Inc..
Upper Saddle River, NJ 07458

This book was set in 12/14 Times New Roman
and was printed and bound by Victor Graphics.

Printed in the United States of America

10   9   8   7   6   5   4   3   2   1

ISBN 0-13-083753-9

Prentice-Hall International (UK) Limited, *London*
Prentice-Hall of Australia Pty. Limited, *Sydney*
Prentice-Hall Canada Inc., *Toronto*
Prentice-Hall Hispanoamericana, S.A., *Mexico*
Prentice-Hall of India Private Limited, *New Delhi*
Prentice-Hall of Japan, Inc., *Tokyo*
Pearson Education Asia Pte. Ltd., *Singapore*
Editora Prentice-Hall do Brasil, Ltda., *Rio de Janeiro*

Contents

Preface

Why did we write this book? We wrote this book because we saw a need for a resource in our classrooms, a resource that was not available elsewhere (demonstrating, once again, that necessity is the mother of invention). Our goal for this text is to provide strategies for success that will allow students to achieve their career goals, whatever they may be. Also, we wanted to provide some fundamental tips and advice that can be useful to *all* students, but especially useful for psychology majors.

Our basic approach to writing this book was to provide immediately useful and helpful information to students majoring in psychology or thinking about majoring in psychology. The approach of this book is both functional and applied—to provide students with practical, timely, up-to-date information that helps them. We think there are a number of benefits to be gained by using this text. First, it fulfills a need—to our knowledge no book exists that presents this mix of knowledge in such an easy-to-read and easy-to-use format. This text standardizes and catalogs much of the practical advice that professors often give to students on a one-to-one basis—this book does not replace that interaction, but it helps to supplement it. We provide tips on how to do well in all classes, how to find research ideas, and how to write papers in APA format. Also, the book contains up-to-date career information that professors might not normally have at their fingertips, including the latest salary figures for a number of psychology-related jobs and occupations. Other benefits include the coverage of ethics for undergraduate students, and the sections on self-reflection and an overview of disciplines related to psychology. These are important perspectives that may not often be shared with the new or prospective psychology major.

Who might use this textbook? As a primary text, it is appropriate for courses such as "Careers in Psychology," "Introduction to the Psychology Major," "The Professional Psychologist," or courses with similar titles and content. This book provides a thorough overview of the discipline, career options (both with and without a graduate degree), strategies for success in and out of the classroom, and coverage of critical issues in psychology. It is also an excellent complimentary text for a number of courses in the psychology curriculum. For any course that requires students to conduct research and write papers in APA format—this book will be helpful. For any course that discusses potential careers and earnings in psychology—this book will be helpful. For any course that covers the opportunities for psychology majors and the ethical implications for being a psychologist—this book will be helpful. Specifically, this book makes a good supplemental text for research methods/experimental psychology courses, any capstone course, introductory courses, careers courses, etc. The unique mix and coverage of topics makes this text useful in a variety of teaching situations.

Projects such as this one do not occur in a vacuum. We would like to thank Bill Webber at Prentice Hall for having the foresight and faith to support this project. We would also like to thank Tamsen Adams for her perseverance and attention to detail that helped keep us on track. Additionally, we are grateful to our families for their patience while we worked on this book. For those reading these words at this moment, this book will be successful only if YOU find it to be useful and helpful.

R.E.L., S.F.D., & T.A.L.

Chapter 1
WHAT CAN I DO WITH A DEGREE IN PSYCHOLOGY?

Are you the type of person who might be interested in any of the following?

- Would you like to study the mental processes that help us acquire and remember information so we can improve our everyday memory?
- Would you like to help people with behavioral disorders help themselves to achieve a better quality of life?
- Would you like to work with communities and neighborhoods to help them deal with growth and plan for the future?
- Would you like to understand those factors that facilitate teaching so that teachers can be taught techniques to improve student learning?
- Would you like to be able to assist the legal profession in understanding criminal behavior, improving lie detection, or understanding the problems with eyewitness testimony?
- Would you like to use the information we have about health and behavior to *promote wellness and prevent illness?* Would you like to improve the coping strategies of persons under stress?
- Would you like to study the brain and begin to understand the changes that occur with the use of drugs or the onset of brain injury or trauma?
- Would you like to better understand why people behave differently in a group from how they behave when alone, and why personal decisions are affected by the context in which they are made?

If any of these questions interest to you, then psychology may be a good fit as a major! In fact, a general interest in and a passion for the understanding of human behavior go a long way in motivating many people to explore whether or not psychology is the major for them.

Congratulations! If you are reading this book, the odds are that you are in an elite group. This book is primarily intended for three audiences: (a) high school students thinking about going to college and majoring in psychology; (b) college students thinking about majoring in psychology; and (c) college students who have already declared psychology as their major. Less than 50% of all Americans ever attend college, and only 13% attain a bachelor's degree. Plenty of people try to reach this lofty goal, however, and there are ample opportunities to do so. In 1997, there were 12.3 million undergraduate students and 1.7 million graduate students attending the 4,009 colleges and universities of higher education in the United States. Of those students, 55.8% were women, and 44.2% were men; 57.8% attended full-time, whereas 42.2% attended part-time (Chronicle of Higher Education, 1998a).

The focus of this book is to look at the opportunities and limitations associated with majoring in psychology. We will examine different career paths and options, explore undergraduate opportunities, focus on the development of skills and abilities, and conclude with some self-reflection and self-assessment. However, before exploring the options specific to psychology, let's look at why students choose to go to college, how they choose a college, and what happens after they get to college.

GOING TO COLLEGE

In a survey of Fall 1997 freshmen, the top four reasons for attending college were: (a) to be able to get a better job, (b) to learn more about things that interest them, (c) to be able to make more money, and (d) to gain a general education and appreciation of ideas. After studying this book, we think you'll agree that (b) and (d) are often achieved by those students studying psychology, and that (a) and (c) can be achieved with an advanced degree in psychology. As students enter college, what is the highest degree they plan to attain? From the survey of Fall 1997 freshmen, 25% indicated that the bachelor's degree was the highest degree they planned to achieve; 39% reported the master's degree, and 15% stated the Ph.D. or Ed.D. (doctoral degrees, or doctorates) as the highest degree they planned to attain. The remaining 20% reported various other degrees and less than 1% indicated that they did not intend to achieve a higher degree (Chronicle of Higher Education, 1998b).

As you think about your own choices, you may be interested to know some reasons students cite for selecting a particular college or university. The top five reasons they rated as "very important" in selecting a specific college were (a) college has a very good academic reputation; (b) graduates get good jobs; (c) size of college; (d) offered financial assistance; and (e) low tuition (Chronicle of Higher Education, 1998b). As a recipient of a college degree, you will be in an elite group, but you're not alone: In 1997, over one million students received their bachelor's degree (Chronicle of Higher Education, 1998a). Over 72,000 of those students were psychology majors (Chronicle of Higher Education, 1998c). This figure represents a 34% increase in the number of psychology graduates over the past five years, by the way.

THOUGHTS ABOUT THE PSYCHOLOGY MAJOR

At the undergraduate level, many students select psychology as a major because of their interest in someday becoming a psychologist. If you study this book carefully, talk to students majoring in psychology, and listen to your psychology professors, you'll quickly understand that you will not be qualified to be a psychologist at the conclusion of your undergraduate training. It's best to think of your undergraduate education in psychology as learning about psychology, not learning "to do" psychology. McGovern, Furumoto, Halpern, Kimble, and McKeachie (1991) made this point clear when they stated that "a liberal arts education in general, and the study of psychology in particular, is a preparation for lifelong learning, thinking, and action; it emphasizes specialized and general knowledge and skills" (p. 600). A quality undergraduate education in psychology should prepare you to be a citizen and a critical thinker—the professional functioning of a psychologist comes after specialized work and training at the graduate level. Studies of students majoring in psychology have found that "psychology is selected as a major because of its overall appeal as a discipline and not on account of the courses offered in psychology or the occupational aims of the student" (Quereshi, Brennan, Kuchan, & Sackett, 1974, p. 70).

Even though the bachelor's degree in psychology is not a professional degree, it is still a good choice to produce a well-rounded, well-educated citizen and person. Why? Although psychology departments and colleges and universities differ, McGovern et al. (1991) identified common goals for undergraduate students to accomplish. These goals include:

- **A knowledge base**—there is a wide array of information in psychology that you need to understand to truly be a student of human behavior.
- **Thinking skills**—critical thinking and reasoning, analysis of outcomes through experimental methods and statistics give psychology students the tools to make reasoned decisions.
- **Language skills**—as scientists, psychologists must be able to communicate findings to the broader scientific community; students must develop reading, writing, and presentation skills.
- **Information gathering and synthesis**—psychology students need to be able to gather information from a number of sources (e.g., library, computerized databases, the Internet) and be able to synthesize this information into coherent lines of reasoning.
- **Research methods and statistical skills**—the development of quantitative and qualitative methods of data analysis and interpretation is central to the discipline.
- **Interpersonal skills**—psychology students need to be sensitive to the diversity of the environment in which they live and be able to use this increased sensitivity and self-knowledge to monitor their own behavior.
- **History of psychology**—psychology majors need to understand the contexts out of which popular ideas and people have emerged—George Santayana once said, "Those who do not know history are doomed to repeat it."
- **Ethics and values**—psychology majors need to understand the ethical treatment of research participants, to understand conflicts of interests, and to generate options that maximize human dignity, human welfare, and the maintenance of academic and scientific integrity.

AREAS OF SPECIALIZATION WITHIN PSYCHOLOGY

As you can see, the skills and abilities that a student can attain in the major are impressive. These skills and abilities help to explain, in part, the growing popularity of the major. Students seem to be initially attracted to psychology by courses in the areas of abnormal psychology, personality, developmental psychology, and educational psychology. At first they are less interested in courses such as statistics, physiological psychology, and experimental methods (Quereshi et al., 1974). Students are also attracted to the major because of the applicability of the subject matter—human behavior! What could be more basic to human life than the desire to understand human behavior? Also (you may or may not agree with this), it has been our experience that a variety of interesting people are drawn to the field of psychology, and sometimes it is the intellectual attraction of these people that, in turn, attracts majors. For instance, although some students enter college declaring psychology as their major, often psychology departments see increases in the number of majors following completion of the introductory/general psychology course. This is a challenging course, and many departments have very talented instructors teaching the course. Talented instructors can make interesting subject matter really come alive—perhaps another reason for the popularity of psychology.

In the introductory course, students are introduced to the various areas and specializations in psychology; the options are truly staggering. As a psychology major, you'll receive a good grounding in the basics of psychology, taking courses that emphasize the development of skills and abilities (e.g., research methods and statistics) while also accumulating a knowledge base (e.g., developmental psychology, social psychology, history and systems). Even if you recently completed an introductory course, it's hard to remember all the options. Table 1.1 describes the major areas in psychology. To our knowledge, there is no "official" list of the major areas of psychology; we compiled this list from a number of sources. Within most of these areas, there are opportunities to specialize even further—more on this later.

Table 1.1: SOME OF THE AREAS IN PSYCHOLOGY

Clinical psychologists assess and treat mental, emotional, and behavioral disorders. These disorders range from short-term crises, such as difficulties resulting from adolescent rebellion, to more severe, chronic conditions, such as schizophrenia. Some clinical psychologists treat specific problems exclusively, such as phobias or clinical depression. Others focus on specific populations: youngsters, ethnic minority groups, gays and lesbians, and the elderly, for instance.

Cognitive psychologists are interested in thought processes, especially relationships among learning, memory, and perception. As researchers, they focus primarily on mental processes that influence the acquisition and use of knowledge as well as the ability to reason, the process by which people generate logical and coherent ideas, evaluate situations, and reach conclusions.

Community psychologists strengthen existing social support networks and stimulate the formation of new networks to effect social change. A goal of community psychologists is to help individuals and their neighborhoods or communities to grow, develop, and plan for the future. They often work in mental health agencies, state governments, and private organizations.

Counseling psychologists help people accommodate to change or make changes in their lifestyle. For example, they provide vocational and career assessment and guidance or help someone come to terms with the death of a loved one. They help students adjust to college and help people to stop smoking or overeating. They also consult with physicians on physical problems that have underlying psychological causes.

Developmental psychologists study the psychological development of the human being that takes place throughout life. Until recently, the primary focus was on childhood and adolescence—the most formative years. However, as life expectancy in this country approaches 80 years, developmental psychologists are becoming increasingly interested in aging, especially in researching and developing ways to help elderly people stay as independent as possible.

Educational psychologists concentrate on the conditions under which effective teaching and learning take place. They consider a variety of factors, such as human abilities, student motivation, and the effect on the classroom of the diversity of race, ethnicity, and culture.

Table 1.1: SOME OF THE AREAS IN PSYCHOLOGY (continued)

Engineering psychologists conduct research on how people work best with machines. For example, how can a computer be designed to prevent fatigue and eye strain? What arrangement of an assembly line makes production most efficient? What is a reasonable workload? Most engineering psychologists work in industry, but some are employed by the government, particularly the Department of Defense. They are often known as *human factors specialists*.

Experimental/general psychologists use the experimental approach to identify and understand basic elements of behavior and mental processes. They focus on basic research issues, and their interests often overlap with fields outside psychology (e.g., biology, computer science, mathematics, sociology). Areas of study for experimental psychologists include motivation, thinking, attention, learning and memory, sensory and perceptual processes, physiology, genetics, and neurology.

Forensic psychologists apply psychological principles to legal issues. Their expertise is often essential in court. They can, for example, help a judge decide which parent should have custody of a child or evaluate a defendant's mental competence to stand trial. Some forensic psychologists are trained in both psychology and the law.

Health psychologists are interested in how biological, psychological, and social factors affect health and illness. They identify the kinds of medical treatment people seek and get, how patients handle illness, why some people don't follow medical advice, and the most effective ways to control pain or to change poor health habits. They also develop health care strategies that foster emotional and physical well-being. Health psychologists team up with medical personnel in private practice and in hospitals to provide patients with complete health care. They educate medical staff about psychological problems that arise from the pain and stress of illness and about symptoms that may seem to be physical in origin but actually have psychological causes. Health psychologists also investigate issues that affect a large segment of society, and they develop and implement programs to deal with these problems. Examples are teenage pregnancy, substance abuse, risky sexual behaviors, smoking, lack of exercise, and poor diet.

Industrial/organizational (I/O) psychologists apply psychological principles and research methods to the workplace in the interest of improving productivity and the quality of work life. Many I/O psychologists serve as human resources specialists, who help organizations with staffing, training, and employee development and management in such areas as strategic planning, quality management, and coping with organizational change.

Neuropsychologists explore the relationships between brain systems and behavior. For example, neuropsychologists may study how the brain creates and stores memories, or how various diseases and injuries of the brain affect emotion, perception, and behavior. Neuropsychologists frequently help design tasks to study normal brain functions with new imaging techniques, such as positron emission tomography (PET); single photon emission computed tomography (SPECT); and functional magnetic resonance imaging (fMRI). Neuropsychologists also assess and treat people. With the dramatic increase in the number of survivors of traumatic brain injury over the past 30 years, neuropsychologists are working with health teams to help brain-injured people resume productive lives.

Table 1.1: SOME OF THE AREAS IN PSYCHOLOGY (continued)

Quantitative and measurement psychologists focus on methods and techniques for acquiring and analyzing psychological data. Some of these professionals develop new methods for performing analysis; others create research strategies to assess the effect of social and educational programs and psychological treatment. They develop and evaluate mathematical models for psychological tests, and propose methods for evaluating the quality and fairness of the tests.

Rehabilitation psychologists work with stroke and accident victims, people with mental retardation, and people with developmental disabilities caused by such conditions as cerebral palsy, epilepsy, and autism. They help clients adapt to their situation, frequently working with other health care professionals. They deal with issues of personal adjustment, interpersonal relations, the work world, and pain management. Rehabilitation psychologists have also become more involved in public health programs to prevent disabilities, especially those caused by violence and substance abuse. They also testify in court as expert witnesses about the causes and effects of a disability and a person's rehabilitation needs.

School psychologists work directly with public and private schools. They assess and counsel students, consult with parents and school staff, and conduct behavioral interventions when appropriate. Some school districts employ a full-time school psychologist.

Social psychologists study how a person's mental life and behavior are shaped by interactions with other people. They are interested in all aspects of interpersonal relationships, including both individual and group influences; they seek ways to improve such interactions. For example, their research helps us understand how people form attitudes toward others, and when these attitudes are harmful—as in the case of prejudice—they suggest ways to change them. Social psychologists are found in a variety of settings from academic institutions (where they teach and conduct research) to advertising agencies (where they study consumer attitudes and preferences) to businesses and government agencies (where they help with a variety of problems in organization and management).

Sports psychologists help athletes refine their focus on competition goals, become more motivated, and learn to deal with the anxiety and fear of failure that often accompany competition. The field is growing as sports of all kinds become more and more competitive and attract younger children.

Note. From *Psychology: Careers for the Twenty-first Century*, 1996, Washington, DC: American Psychological Association, adapted with permission; *Psychology* (6th ed.), by L. A. Lefton, 1997, Boston: Allyn & Bacon.

As you can see, it is quite a list! Typically, you will not specialize in a particular area at the undergraduate level. There may be "tracks" or "concentrations" for you, but your bachelor's degree will be in psychology; it will not be a bachelor's degree in experimental psychology or neuropsychology. Additionally, as you pursue your undergraduate degree, you will be exposed to ideas from the history of psychology. It is important to us as scientists to understand our past as prologue to our future. See Appendix A for a brief history of psychology.

As you will see in Chapter 3, your area of specialization becomes much more important if you elect to attend graduate school. In fact, if you decide to pursue a graduate degree in psychology, not only will you probably specialize in one of the areas presented in Table 1.1, but your degree may come from a program that specializes even further. For a sense of those different levels of specialization, Table 1.2 presents a listing of master's degrees and/or doctoral degrees that can be earned in psychology in the United States.

Table 1.2: AREAS IN WHICH A MASTER'S DEGREE AND/OR DOCTORATE CAN BE EARNED	
adolescence and youth	comparative
adult development	computer applications
aging	conditioning
AIDS intervention or research	consulting psychology
animal cognition	consumer
applied	counseling
applied developmental	counseling and guidance
applied social	counseling psychology
art therapy	counseling—colleges and universities
behavior therapy	counseling—elementary school
behavioral analysis	counseling—marriage and family
behavioral genetics	counseling—secondary school
behavioral medicine	counseling—vocational
behavioral neuroscience	developmental
behavioral science	developmental psychobiology
behavioral science—applied	developmental—comparative
child development	developmental—exceptional
child psychopathology	doctoral preparation
clinical	early childhood education
clinical mental health counseling	ecological
clinical neuropsychology	educational
clinical respecialization	educational administration
clinical—child	educational measurement
clinical—community	educational research and evaluation
clinical—school	engineering
cognitive	environmental
college counseling	evolutionary/sociobiology
college counseling and administration	experimental psychopathology
college teaching	experimental—animal behavior
community	experimental—general
community rehabilitation counseling	forensic
community—clinical	general
community—rural	group psychotherapy
community—school	health psychology

Table 1.2: AREAS IN WHICH A MASTER'S DEGREE AND/OR DOCTORATE CAN BE EARNED (continued)	
history and systems	personnel and guidance
human development and family studies	phenomenological
human factors	physiological
human relations	preclinical
human services	primate behavior
human services administration	professional
humanistic	program evaluation
individual differences	psychobiology
industrial/organizational	psycholinguistics
law and psychology	psychological assessment
learning	psychology of women
learning and instructional technology	psychometrics
learning disabilities	psychopharmacology
learning—animal	psychotherapy and psychoanalysis
learning—human	public policy
life-span development	quantitative (including measurement)
marriage and family	quantitative methods
marriage and family therapy	reading
mathematical	rehabilitation
medical psychology	research methodology
mental health	school
mental retardation	school psychometry
minority mental health	sensation and perception
neuropsychology	social
neuroscience	sociocultural perspectives
organizational	special education
parent education	sports
pastoral counseling	statistics
pediatric psychology	substance abuse
personality	supervision

Note. From "Index of Program Areas of Study," in *Graduate Study in Psychology* (31st ed.), 1998, Washington, DC: American Psychological Association.

Table 1.2 also shows there are specializations within specializations in psychology. For instance, if you have always wanted to become a clinical psychologist, which type? Will it be clinical, clinical mental health counseling, clinical neuropsychology, clinical child, clinical community, or clinical school? (Clinical respecialization is a special degree for those who already have a Ph.D. but want to go back to school to get a degree in clinical psychology.) Even areas such as developmental, education, and experimental have subspecialties. At this point, it is not necessary to know exactly which area of psychology you want to study—what is important is that you begin to understand the vast opportunities and diversity that psychology has to offer. With all of the choices available you may ask, "Where do I begin in selecting courses as a psychology major, and what can I do with a bachelor's degree?" Those questions sound like ones that you might ask of your academic advisor.

THE IMPORTANCE OF ADVISING

At some universities, advising is divided into categories: academic advising and career advising. Academic advising focuses on the curricular demands of the major and addresses such issues as course scheduling and availability, student success in academic courses, meeting prerequisites, and graduation requirements. Career advising emphasizes the student's short- and long-term goals and takes the form of multiple discussions between the student and advisor over the course of an academic career. It is during these career advising sessions that much of the information provided in this book would be imparted. For example, questions about employment opportunities with a bachelor's degree and graduate school options are often discussed during career advising. The advising function should not be overlooked or taken lightly, as Quereshi et al. (1974) remind us that "a substantial number of students are either misinformed or uninformed as to the occupational value of a bachelor's degree in psychology. Thus there is a definite need for a careful and thorough system of academic and occupational advisement" (p. 70). This book helps provide resource information to the psychology major and will help you prepare for meetings with your academic advisor.

Lunneborg and Baker (1986) described four types of advising models that exist on college campuses:

- **Central model**: centralized, all-campus advising office completes advising for all majors; no psychology faculty formally involved in advising.
- **No-faculty model**: undeclared majors are advised at a centralized office; after declaring a major, majors are advised in psychology department in the departmental advising office; advised in department, but not by faculty (e.g., peer advisors).
- **Part-faculty model**: undeclared majors advised at centralized office; then majors declaring psychology are assigned to all psychology faculty members.
- **All-faculty model**: almost all psychology faculty advise majors from the first year through the last year.

Regardless of the model used in your psychology department, it is important to determine yours. Academic and career advising-based decisions are ultimately your responsibility; the institution shares some responsibility in providing accurate information about academic and career choices, satisfaction with the major, progress toward the degree, and interest in the profession. It is hard to imagine a psychology department in any college or university where you won't be able to find someone to help you—the key may be in finding out *whom* to ask. By the way, Lunneborg and Baker (1986) found that students preferred the all-faculty model with smaller numbers of majors.

In order to maximize your gain when meeting with your advisor, Appleby (1998a) suggests the following:

- Learn your advisor's name, office location, office hours, phone number, and e-mail address.
- Meet with your advisor regularly to plan next semester's schedule (academic advising) and to discuss future plans and how to accomplish them (career advising).

- For academic advising sessions regarding registration, be aware of the courses you have to take, the courses you have already taken, and the courses offered for next semester. Have prepared a tentative schedule of classes you think is feasible.
- Be open and honest about your career goals with your advisor.
- Consult with your advisor when you are in academic difficulty, when you want to add or drop a class, when you might be thinking about changing your major, or when you might be thinking about withdrawing from school or transferring to another college or university.
- Accept responsibility for the academic and career decisions that you make.

At times, you may be surprised by the reactions of your advisor(s); he or she has your best interests at heart. That is, if your best option is to withdraw from school, your advisor will probably not try to talk you out of it. In making that big a decision, however, an advisor may suggest that you seek additional input, such as from trusted friends, a career guidance center, counseling center, etc. If you are miserable as a psychology major, why remain in the major. As academics, we really do have your best interests in mind—we want you to be satisfied with, and successful in, your college experience. Many students fail to take advantage of the advising opportunities afforded them—be sure that you are not one of those students!

RECAP: WHY THE PSYCHOLOGY MAJOR IS A GOOD CHOICE

According to the American Psychological Association (APA, 1996), "psychology is a discipline with a bright future. Among fields requiring a college degree, it is expected to be the third fastest-growing field in America through the year 2005 and to continue to grow steadily for at least another dozen years after that" (p. 3). Completion of a rigorous undergraduate program in psychology affords the student with a host of developed and honed skills that can be applied to the marketplace (with a bachelor's degree) or to graduate school (for a master's degree or a doctorate). Successful graduates of undergraduate psychology leave with many of these skills and abilities (Landrum, 1998):

- Scientific literacy in reading and writing
- Strong analytical skills and statistical/computer familiarity
- Interpersonal awareness and self-monitoring/management skills
- Communication skills and the ability to work in groups
- Problem-solving and information-finding skills
- Critical thinking and higher order analysis capabilities
- Research and measurement skills

More than likely, the opportunities to acquire these skills exist in your psychology department. Some of these skills will be honed and sharpened in the classroom and by performing class-related tasks, but others are better learned outside the classroom from experiences gained as a research assistant, intern, or teaching assistant. This book is designed for one primary purpose—to help you get the most out of your undergraduate psychology major experience. If *you* don't take advantage of the opportunities that surround you, someone else will.

Chapter 2
CAREER OPTIONS WITH A B.A. OR B.S.
IN PSYCHOLOGY

When students think about becoming a psychology major, they often think about becoming a psychologist. However, one does not necessarily lead to the other. Early in your undergraduate career, it is important to think about your future career goals—those goals for the future influence the decisions you make today. If there is a particular area in psychology that you would like to work in after graduation, the coursework you take now should be related to the skills and abilities you'll need on the job. This chapter is about the options you have as a bachelor's-level psychology graduate. You may be surprised at the opportunities that are available, but you also need to recognize the challenges and limitations.

A bachelor's degree in psychology is presently a popular choice in the United States. The Chronicle of Higher Education (1998d) reports that in the 1997–98 academic year, there were 72,083 bachelor's degrees awarded in psychology, with 72.8% of those degrees awarded to women. This figure represents a 34% increase over the number of degrees awarded 5 years earlier. In the same time frame, 13,921 master's degrees (72.0% women) and 3,822 doctoral degrees (Ph.D.'s and Psy.D.'s; 62.5% women) were awarded (the terms Ph.D. and Psy.D. are covered in more depth in Chapter 3). As with any career decision, you must consider the supply and demand of the marketplace and make your skills and abilities as attractive as possible to potential employers. This chapter provides you with some of the information you need to prepare.

THE UNDERGRADUATE CURRICULUM

As you think about selecting a particular college or university, or as you ponder the decision you have already made, how much did the curriculum (the courses required and recommended by the psychology department) influence your decision? Although the reputation of the institution overall probably influenced your decision, your choice of psychology as a major was probably not made on the basis of a particular course offered by the department. You may be surprised, but psychologists care deeply about the undergraduate curriculum! This interest has a long history (Holder, Leavitt, & McKenna, 1958; Menges & Trumpeter, 1972; Wolfle, 1947), and psychologists continue to study and tweak the curriculum to meet the needs of students and employers (Perlman & McCann, 1998a,b). This research on curriculum offerings specifically addresses current practices, and what skills and abilities students need to succeed after college. Although students may not give the curriculum much thought, it provides the intellectual foundation on which you can achieve a career in psychology. A good curriculum meets the needs of students who want to work as a bachelor's-level psychology graduate as well as students who go on to graduate school.

So what are the skills and abilities employers want in bachelor's-level psychology majors? First, let's be clear about the terminology. According to Lloyd (1997a):

- **Abilities** are the activities or processes that come relatively easy to you, without much effort: intellectual ability, problem-solving ability, musical ability, or athletic ability. "Ability" is a generic term.
- **Interests** are those activities or events that we are intrinsically motivated to seek out and participate in. Your abilities and your interests may not be synonymous. That is, you might end up in a particular job because you are good at completing the required tasks, but you might not be very interested in that job.
- **Skills** are specific types of abilities. You can have great computer skills, or public speaking skill, or other types of specific skills. Often, the terms "skills and abilities" are used together and synonymously.
- **Traits** are the characteristics you possess. They do not relate to a certain skill or ability, but rather address your general approach. Skills and abilities are more easily acquired than traits; traits represent longer term behavior patterns that exist in addition to your skills, interests, and abilities.

So what are those skills, abilities, and traits that employers want you to acquire en route to your baccalaureate degree? Table 2.1 is an attempt to summarize some of the current key beliefs in this area.

Table 2.1: Confluence of Skills and Abilities Desirable in Bachelor's-Level Psychology Graduate

Skill or Ability	Examples	References
Utilizing resources	Scheduling, using a budget, assigning space and managing a staff	United States Department of Labor (USDOL), 1991a
Working effectively with others	Demonstrating teamwork, teaching new skills to others, fulfilling customer needs, leadership, negotiation, sensitivity to diversity	Appleby, 1998b; Butler, 1997; Edwards & Smith, 1988; Lloyd, Kennedy, & Dewey, 1997; USDOL, 1991a
Acquiring and using information	Acquiring, interpreting, organizing, maintaining, and evaluating information; knowing how to learn	Landrum, 1998; Lloyd et al., 1997; USDOL, 1991a
Utilizing technology to solve problems	Familiarity with new and emerging technologies, awareness of applications to work use	USDOL, 1991a

Table 2.1: Confluence of Skills and Abilities Desirable in Bachelor's-Level Psychology Graduate (continued)

Skill or Ability	Examples	References
Communication	Reading and comprehending complex materials, clear writing, listening carefully and accurately, speaking articulately and persuasively	Appleby, 1998b; Butler, 1997; Edwards & Smith, 1988; Landrum, 1998; Lloyd et al., 1997; USDOL, 1991a
Computation/ numeracy	Ability to perform mathematical operations, measurement skills; possess analytical skills, ability for word processing, e-mail, internet	Butler, 1997; Landrum, 1998; Lloyd et al., 1997; USDOL, 1991a
Problem-solving	Decision making, learning, reasoning; understanding symbols, tables, and graphs	Appleby, 1998b; Edwards & Smith, 1988; Landrum, 1998; USDOL, 1991a
Personal qualities/traits	Responsibility, self-esteem, appropriate social skills, self-management and awareness, integrity, hard-working, tolerance for stress and ambiguity, outgoing personality	Appleby, 1998b; Edwards & Smith, 1988; Landrum, 1998; Lloyd et al., 1997; USDOL, 1991a
Flexibility	Use of creative thinking, adaptable, ability to be a critical thinker	Appleby, 1998b; Butler, 1997; Edwards & Smith, 1988; Landrum, 1998; Lloyd et al., 1997
Proficiency in field of study	Good grades, understand psychological ideas and how they are applied	Appleby, 1998b; Butler, 1997

What is the benefit of knowing this information? As you pursue your undergraduate career, try to arrange your curriculum choices to give yourself the opportunity to acquire these skills and abilities as necessary (and as possible). You won't be able to achieve every one of them—at least not during your undergraduate years. These are skills and abilities you might aspire to—your undergraduate courses (i.e., curriculum) should be designed so that, as you complete the coursework, you acquire proficiency in many of the above areas. Realize, however, that some of these items are more "teachable" or "learnable" than others. With the right coursework, I can improve your computational/statistical ability, but I am less able to influence some of your traits (e.g., your personality).

The list of skills and abilities in Table 2.1 is impressive. As an undergraduate, it would be difficult to achieve all of those skills and abilities to any significant level of proficiency. So which ones are the *most* important? If you have to choose certain skills and abilities to concentrate on, what should they be? First, you might want to honestly evaluate your current strengths and weaknesses. Seek out opportunities to improve on your weaknesses. We sometimes tell students: You need to have good oral communication skills before you leave this university. Where and with whom do you want to hone this skill—with us, where the absolute worst thing that can happen in a supportive environment is that you get one bad grade, or on the job, where a bad performance might cost you your job, your security, your home, your car, etc.? College is the place to improve what you are not good at—not the place to avoid your weaknesses altogether. Students who fear math courses often take the minimum number of credits required when they should be working to strengthen their math skills. A similar pattern often occurs with writing but if you have difficulty in writing, or are not confident, the last thing you need to do is avoid all courses that involve writing. You might be able to graduate that way, but you may not be very employable.

A study conducted by Edwards and Smith (1988) surveyed 118 different organizations and asked the organizations what skills they want to see in psychology graduates, as well as what knowledge areas are most useful when hiring psychology graduates. Think about this second point for a minute—*at some point in your future, someone is actually going to expect you to know something about your major!* The curriculum and your study strategies need to be designed with this in mind. In other words, whereas a cramming/rote memorization session may be a stop-gap measure to get you through an exam, these techniques often do not lead to long-term retention of the material (Rickard, Rogers, Ellis, & Beidleman, 1988). Table 2.2 presents in rank order employers' ratings of usefulness of skills. Note that the response scale answers were *very useful, somewhat useful, not at all useful*, or *not sure*; the higher the score (mean), the more useful the skill.

Table 2.2: Usefulness of Skills	
Item	**Mean (Standard Deviation)**
1. Writing proposals and reports	2.62 (.63)
2. Being able to identify problems and suggest solutions based on research findings or knowledge of human behavior	2.44 (.75)
3. Conducting interviews	2.40 (.76)
4. Doing statistical analyses	2.37 (.70)
5. Knowing how to design and conduct research projects	2.26 (.81)
6. Job analysis	2.17 (.75)
7. Coding data	2.11 (.72)
8. Using computer programs to analyze data	2.05 (.82)
9. Systematically observing and recording people's behavior	1.84 (.86)
10. Constructing tests and questionnaires	1.82 (.79)
11. Administering standardized tests	1.43 (.66)
Note. From "What Skills and Knowledge Do Potential Employers Value in Baccalaureate Psychologists?" by J. Edwards and K. Smith, 1988, in *Is Psychology for Them? A Guide to Undergraduate Advising*, P. J. Woods (Ed.), Washington, DC: American Psychological Association. Copyright © 1988	

The value of this table is that it prioritizes those skills that employers find most useful in psychology graduates. If you look carefully at the list, some of the topics students tend to dislike the most appear at or near the top of the list! Edwards and Smith (1988) also asked employers what they expected psychology major graduates to know and understand. Table 2.3 should reinforce the notion that at some point in your future, someone is going to expect you to know something about your major!

Table 2.3: Usefulness of Knowledge Areas	
Item	**Mean (Standard Deviation)**
1. Formation and change of attitudes and opinions	2.19 (.75)
2. Principles and techniques of personnel selection	2.19 (.78)
3. How people think, solve problems, and process information	2.16 (.68)
4. Structure and dynamics of small groups	2.08 (.68)
5. Effects of the physical environment on feelings and actions	2.06 (.79)
6. Organizational development	2.05 (.75)
7. Principles of human learning and memory	2.03 (.81)
8. How people sense and perceive their environment	2.00 (.71)
9. Theories and research on individual personalities, differences	1.98 (.79)
10. Principles of human needs and motivation	1.92 (.74)
11. Theories and research about organizational behavior, work, and productivity	1.89 (.65)
12. Theories and research about human development life stages	1.69 (.75)
13. Symptoms, causes, and treatment of mental illness	1.51 (.69)

Note. From "What Skills and Knowledge Do Potential Employers Value in Baccalaureate Psychologists?" by J. Edwards and K. Smith, 1988, in *Is Psychology for Them? A Guide to Undergraduate Advising*, P. J. Woods (Ed.), Washington, DC: American Psychological Association. Copyright © 1988

Hopefully, we've convinced you of the importance of the curriculum and its connection to what employers want in bachelor's-level psychology graduates. Next, see if there is a careers course available at your institution. For example, at Boise State University, two courses available that orient the student to the major as well as career opportunities are called "Introduction to the Psychology Major" and "Psychology Seminar: Careers and Graduate Study in Psychology." At Emporia State University, the course is called "The Professional Psychologist." Buckalew and Lewis (1982) called for such courses to be made available to let students know about the career opportunities and choices available to them. Kennedy and Lloyd (1998) completed an evaluation of Georgia Southern University's "Careers in Psychology" course and found that students in the course clarified career goals and were most satisfied with the topics tied to careers and graduate school. Dodson, Chastain, and Landrum (1996) also evaluated the psychology seminar course at Boise State and found that students changed their way of thinking about psychology because of the course. For instance, students often changed the terminal degree they were planning to pursue (e.g., from a doctorate to a master's degree), and they changed their strategies for seeking financial aid for graduate education (they became aware of more opportunities for funding). If your university has a careers course, seriously consider taking it—if it is not available, suggest it to a student-friendly faculty member (perhaps it can be taught as a special-topics or one-time offering).

CAREERS WITH AN ASSOCIATE'S DEGREE

At some colleges and universities, students can graduate with an associate's degree in psychology. Unfortunately there is very little national information about this degree, jobs available to associate's degree holders, salaries, etc. A comprehensive review found only a handful of published works (e.g., Kerchhoff & Bell, 1998; Taylor & Hardy, 1996). Taylor and Hardy's (1996) study was of associate's degree holders from one university. They found that the types of jobs held with this degree include "human resources worker, crisis intervention associate, rehabilitation worker, child welfare worker, psychiatric technician, correctional officer, police officer, child care assistant, mental health technician, aide to geriatric clients, and social welfare worker" (p. 960).

The information about salary levels of associate's degree holders is extremely limited, also coming from the Taylor and Hardy (1996) study of one institution's associate's degree graduates. They found that entry-level salaries for holders of the associate's degree ranged from $9,600 to $14,000, with salaries $4,000-$8,000 higher in the eastern and western coastal states. While the associate's degree is a popular option for some students, unfortunately there is very little national data collected on this topic that might be helpful for students considering this option.

CAREERS WITH A BACHELOR'S DEGREE

You may be surprised to discover the variety of opportunities available to you with a bachelor's degree in psychology. For some reason, faculty sometimes frame this career path as a bleak alternative (as compared with going to graduate school); the majority of most graduates, however, *do not* pursue graduate training. However, we do want to be realistic about the opportunities. You will *not* be able to be a practicing psychologist without an advanced degree in psychology. With your bachelor's degree, you can obtain jobs both within psychology (usually in a support staff–type of role) and related to the discipline of psychology. There are also a number of opportunities to apply your undergraduate training in psychology in areas that are not directly related to psychology but that involve some component of human behavior. If you stop to think about it, there are very few, if any, jobs or careers that do not involve or would not benefit from a greater understanding of human behavior.

What can you do with a bachelor's degree in psychology? Before we address some of the specific job opportunities available, here are some of the general areas and percentages of jobs that you might consider. This information is based on the 1994-95 Psychology Baccalaureate Survey conducted by the American Psychological Association (APA,1997a).

- Education and teaching (15%)
- Consulting/statistics (6%)
- Administration/clerical (19%)
- Professional services (19%)
- Sales (5%)
- Health and health related services (23%)
- Research and development/research and development management (9%)
- Other management (5%)

The future is reasonably bright for persons with a bachelor's degree in psychology. A National Science Foundation (1995) survey found that of 1994 psychology baccalaureate recipients, 70% were employed, 23% were full-time graduate students, and 7% were not employed and not enrolled full time.

Employers have different expectations about what you can do based on your level of education. Pinkus and Korn (1973) found that "BA-level employers expect their applicants to be generalists, with favorable personality traits and some type of field experience, preferably a supervised situation. MA-level employers, on the other hand, expect skill, competence, and intensive practicum experience" (p. 712). Later chapters in this book will discuss the types of field experiences often available to undergraduate psychology majors and how to gain the most from those opportunities.

Experience is important! You need to take advantage of the opportunities available to you in your psychology department. Even at the bachelor's level (and especially if you have intentions of going to graduate school), being a good (or even great) "book-student" is not enough. Straight A's and a 4.0 GPA are not enough to convince an employer to hand you a job. Although people will be somewhat interested in what you know, they also want to know what you can do and what you have done.

What are the careers related to psychology that are available to the bachelor's level psychology major? Often, psychology graduates work in a paraprofessional role (i.e., a support role that overlaps with job duties and responsibilities of a psychologist); however, the paraprofessional does not have the education, responsibility, nor salary of the psychologist. For example, some job titles for psychology paraprofessionals might include counselor, aid, or psychology technician (Erdwins, 1980). Who do paraprofessionals work with? Erdwins (1980) found that they most often work with adolescents and adults (but sometimes children). They also work with clients who have mental health problems (e.g., emotional disturbance, psychosis, antisocial disorders, mental retardation, and neurological impairments).

What do paraprofessionals do? According to Erdwins (1980), most paraprofessionals are involved with the implementation of a therapy program for patients or clients. Their duties may involve some counseling, gathering background information from family members, interviewing/intake processing, record keeping, receiving training from professional staff, and some custodial work (such as transportation of clients). Occasionally, paraprofessionals are asked to administer psychological tests or assessments. The most frequent problems that paraprofessionals reported were (a) burnout, (b) lack of recognition and support from professional staff, and (c) having little input in shaping the policies and procedures of the agency. Interestingly, 42% of the paraprofessionals surveyed were enrolled in a graduate program (going part time), and another 20% were planning to start graduate school within a year. Erdwins concludes that "the paraprofessional role as it currently exists in most settings may represent a satisfactory temporary work alternative for many individuals desiring employment in mental health settings while undertaking or planning for graduate study. As a long-term career choice, the paraprofessional role appears less rewarding" (p. 112).

More recent work seems to echo Erdwin's (1980) sentiments. Murray (1998) reported that, based on national surveys of bachelor's-level psychology graduates, 30% would like to find more challenging jobs. Some of the more desired positions, such as a full-time research consultant or program coordinator, typically go to applicants with an advanced degree. Murray reported on recent surveys of bachelor's-level psychology majors that 20% were in administrative positions such as coordinating community volunteers or supervising a small staff in a health service agency; 20% were in public affairs and social services positions such as dealing with community relations or conducting intake interviews; and 20% were in business management and sales. The 1998 Occupational Outlook Handbook (OOH) states that social and human service assistants (i.e., paraprofessionals) rank among the top ten fastest growing occupations, and that although job opportunities should be excellent (especially for those with a bachelor's degree), the pay is low. The OOH (1998a) found that starting salaries for social and human service assistants ranged from $15,000 to $24,000 annually in 1997, whereas experienced workers could earn between $20,000 and $30,000 annually; the exact figure depended on their education, experience, and employer.

As you explore your opportunities for employment with a bachelor's degree, it would be helpful to know some of the choices available and what some of the more common job titles are. Table 2.4 below lists job titles for those positions more directly related to psychology.

Table 2.4: Job Titles Directly Related to Psychology		
Academic advisor	Director of volunteer services	Public information specialist
Alcohol/drug abuse counselor	Eligibility worker	Public relations specialist
Behavior analyst	Employment counselor	Publications researcher
Career counselor	Family services worker	Radio/TV research assistant
Career planning and placement	Gerontology aide	Rehabilitation advisor
Counselor	Group home coordinator	Residential counselor
Case management aide	Housing/student life coordinator	Residential youth counselor
Case worker	Life skill counselor	Secondary school teacher
Child care worker	Mental health technician	Social service assistant
Child protection worker community	Mental retardation unit manager	Social services director
Outreach worker	Parole officer	Social work assistant
Community support worker	Political campaign worker	Urban planning research assistant
Corrections officer	Probation officer	Veteran's advisor
Counselor aide	Program manager	
Day care center supervisor	Public affairs coordinator	
Note. From "Entry-Level Positions Obtained by Psychology Majors," by M. A. Lloyd, 1997, [online], retrieved March 30, 1998, at http://www.psych-web.com/careers/entry.htm; *Occupational Outlook Handbook*, January 15, 1998, Social and human service assistants, [online], retrieved September 20, 1998, at http://www.bls.gov/oco/ocos.059.htm. "Employment Opportunities for Psychology Majors," by B. Shepard, February 12, 1996, [online], retrieved March 30, 1998, at http://www.cs.trinity.edu/~cjackson/employ.html#employ-top.		

As Chapters 1 and 2 indicate, the psychology major can obtain a number of valuable skills, abilities, and knowledge over the course of an undergraduate education. This education qualifies you for a number of job opportunities, not limited to those directly related to psychology (see Table 2.5).

Table 2.5: Job Titles Not So Directly Related to Psychology, but Appropriate for Bachelor's-Level Psychology Graduates

Administrative assistant	Energy researcher	Marketing researcher
Advertising agent	Fast food restaurant manager	Media buyer
Advertising trainee	Film researcher/copywriter	Newspaper reporter
Affirmative action representative	Financial researchers	Occupational analyst
Airline reservations clerk	Historical research assistant	Park and recreation director
Claims specialist	Hospital patient service	Personnel worker/administrator
College admissions officer	representative	Public information officer
Community recreation worker	Human resources recruiter	Public relations
Community relations officer	Insurance agent	Sales representative
Congressional aide	Intelligence officer	Small business owner
Customer relations	Job analyst	Staff training and development
Customer service representative	Law enforcement officer	Statistical assistant
Director of alumni relations	Loan officer	Store manager
Director of fund raising	Lobbying organizer	Technical writer
Employee counselor	Management trainee	Vocational rehabilitation counselor
Employee relations assistant	Marketing representative	Warehouse manager

Note. From "Entry-Level Positions Obtained by Psychology Majors," by M. A. Lloyd, 1997, [online], retrieved March 30, 1998, at http://www.psych-web.com/careers/entry.htm; "Employment Opportunities for Psychology Majors," by B. Shepard, February 12, 1996, [online], retrieved March 30, 1998, at http://www.cs.trinity.edu/~cjackson/employ.html#employ-top.

There are numerous employment opportunities for psychology majors with a bachelor's degree! In fact, the variety and diversity are staggering, reflecting the diversity and variety of psychology itself. How satisfying are these career options? Lunneborg (1985) surveyed the satisfaction of bachelor's-level graduates in a number of areas. The job areas with the highest level of dissatisfaction were organizational jobs, such as bookkeeping, small business owners, executive secretaries, administrative assistants, and department supervisors. Lunneborg (1985) strikes a reasonable balance when she concludes, "to say you can do 'anything' with a BA in psychology is as irresponsible as saying there is 'nothing' you can do with it" (p. 22).

Salary information at the bachelor's level is sometimes difficult to come by. According to the most recent statistics from the Bureau of Labor Statistics (1998), the median earnings for *all* full-time workers with a bachelor's degree was $35,672 annually; with work experience plus a bachelor's degree, the annual salary (all disciplines) was $40,872. Appleby (1997) cited the 1993 starting salary for psychologists with a bachelor's degree as $18,300; with a superior academic record, that starting salary increased to $22,800.

The most comprehensive information available comes from the APA's (1992) Baccalaureate Survey. Table 2.6 provides starting salaries for full-time employment positions.

Table 2.6: Starting Salaries for Psychology Baccalaureates, 1992			
Position Type	**Median**	**Mean**	**Standard Deviation**
All activities	$20,000	$21,054	8,396
Administrative	$20,500	$20,265	7,200
Clerical	$18,000	$17,973	5,305
Consulting	$27,000	$26,071	7,022
Education/teaching	$21,500	$21,196	8,272
Health, health related	$20,000	$20,784	7,143
Research and development (basic, applied)	$21,000	$21,452	8,180
Management, other than research and development	$21,000	$26,059	11,605
Sales	$18,000	$22,000	14,856
Professional services (Other than health related)	$19,000	$19,914	6,002
Reporting/statistical work/computing	$25,000	$23,667	6,892
Other services (e.g., Trades, Hotels, Law Enforcement, Military)	$19,000	$19,780	8,193

Note. From "Starting Salaries for Full-Time Employment Positions: 1992 Baccalaureate Recipients in Psychology," American Psychological Association, 1992, [online], retrieved November 20, 1998, at http://research.apa.org/95survey/table7.html.

TIPS TO HELP YOU FIND A JOB

The remainder of this chapter is designed to offer some general job-finding tips (e.g., securing letters of recommendation, creating a resume, interviewing tips, and writing your cover letter). This material is not designed to provide complete information about every job application situation—there are a number of good books and other resources available that are dedicated to each part of this process (e.g., writing a resume, being interviewed).

In some situations, you'll be asked to fill out a job application. Be sure to take every step of this process seriously. Your application tells the employer about (a) your work habits, (b) how well you follow instructions, (c) your character, (d) your personal achievements, (e) your job performance, and (f) your potential (Idaho Department of Labor, 1998). Even Ann Landers (1997) offers advice for job hunters; here are her seven rules:

Rule 1. Bring your own pen.
Rule 2. Dress properly.
Rule 3. Fill out the application completely and correctly. Answer all questions. Have all the necessary numbers with you before you apply.
Rule 4. Grammar, penmanship, and spelling count.
Rule 5. Ask to see the job description.
Rule 6. Be enthusiastic.
Rule 7. Be ready to work.

Instructions from the Idaho Department of Labor (1998) also emphasize that neatness counts, be completely accurate and honest, double-check your application, and be sure to notify those persons whom you plan to use as references. The information available about psychology baccalaureates in particular suggests that the three most successful methods of finding jobs were through classified advertisements (21%), a family member or friend (9%), or submitted unsolicited resumes (7%) (Waters, 1998). Landrum (1998) suggests that you tap into connections that you might already have. Former employers, family connections, and others can be extremely helpful in getting your "foot-in-the-door." Internships often lead to possible job opportunities after graduation; you get a look at how it would be to work in that environment, and the employer gets a sneak peek at your work habits, skill, and potential. It is also important to remember that you are not going to get the perfect job with the perfect salary the first time you apply. You need to be patient as you build your own set of skills and abilities, establish your track record, hone your work ethic, and develop your work history.

In many job application situations, you may be asked for one or more letters of recommendation (and letters of recommendation are a more typical requirement for graduate school applications, covered in the next chapter). Plous (1998a) suggests that you should ask for recommendations from people who (a) have worked closely with you, (b) have known you long enough to know you fairly well, (c) have some expertise, (d) are senior and well-known, if possible (e.g., department chair), (e) have a positive opinion of you and your abilities, and (f) have a warm and supportive personal style. Landrum (1998) and Wilson (1998) also emphasize that when you ask a faculty member or other professional for a letter of recommendation, ask for a *strong* letter of recommendation. Most faculty members would rather not write a letter than write a weak letter of recommendation.

Plous (1998a) also recommends that you give your letter writers plenty of lead time, at least three or four weeks. Then, about one week before the deadline, give your letter writer a gentle reminder about the upcoming due date for the letter of recommendation. You'll want to provide your letter writers with a complete packet of materials—this packet needs to be well organized in order for all the letters to get where they need to go and get there on time. Ask your references if they have any special requests before they begin writing. Some of the items you might be asked to provide include the following:

- Current copy of your academic transcript; usually an unofficial or "student" copy is fine.
- Copy of your academic vita that lists your achievements and accomplishments in the discipline (see Chapter 3) or a resume that summarizes your job history, skills, and abilities (see this chapter).
- Pre-addressed (stamped) envelope for each letter, whether it goes back to you (the student), or goes directly to the place of employment (or graduate school); does this envelope need to be signed on the back? Remind your letter writers if it needs to be sealed and signed.
- Any forms that the letter writer might be asked to submit with the letter.
- Cover sheet to the letter writer that includes contact information if your letter writer needs to reach you, when you will submit your application (you don't want the letters to arrive before your application), the deadline for each letter, your career aspirations (i.e., personal statement will do), and information you would like emphasized in the letter (Plous, 1998a).

How do you secure those strong letters of recommendation? You must be more than a good book student. Being involved outside of the classroom gives you well-rounded experiences; it also gives your letter writers something to write about. Chapter 4 highlights many of the ways you can become involved in your psychology education outside of the classroom. Table 2.7 lists two sets of ideas on how to secure a *strong* letter of recommendation.

Table 2.7: Strategies to Secure Strong Letters of Recommendation	
Strategy 1 **(in order of importance)**	**Strategy 2** **(not in order of importance)**
• Deal effectively with a variety of people. • Display appropriate interpersonal skills. • Listen carefully and accurately. • Show initiative and persistence. • Exhibit effective time management. • Hold high ethical standards and expect the same of others. • Handle conflict successfully. • Speak articulately and persuasively. • Work productively as a member of a team. • Plan and carry out projects successfully. • Think logically and creatively. • Remain open-minded during controversies. • Identify and actualize personal potential. • Write clearly and precisely. • Adapt to organizational rules and procedures. • Comprehend and retain key points from written materials. • Gather and organize information from multiple sources.	• Have a positive attitude. • Get involved in your major. • Demonstrate your capacity for independence and creativity by conducting your own research project. • Exhibit you leadership skills. • Take an interest in the profession of psychology. • Be dependable. • Be a self-starter. • Take responsibility for your own actions. • Be self-confident but modest. • Be polished and professional in all that you do. • Be genuine. • Be a model of perseverance. • Prove that you can work effectively with others. • Display initiative and motivation by doing more than is expected of you.
Note. a. From "The Teaching-Advising Connection: Tomes, Tools, and Tales," by D. Appleby, 1998, G. Stanley Hall Lecture, Meeting of the American Psychological Association, San Francisco. b. From "It Takes More Than Good Grades," by D. W. Wilson, 1998, *Eye on Psi Chi*, Winter, pp. 11-13, 42.	

One last note— Bloomquist (1981) as cited in Appleby (1997) lists those strategies on how to receive less-than-enthusiastic letters of recommendation. As Appleby (1997) states, the theme that emerges here is that "you cannot expect your teachers and adviser to write you good letters of recommendation if you do not treat them with courtesy and respect" (p. 68). So, if you want a *less-than-great* letter, follow these tips; for a *strong* letter, do the opposite:

- Treat your instructors and classes as though you are barely able to tolerate them.
- Be consistently late to class.
- Never ask questions or contribute to class, even when asked.
- Complain when instructors provide extra learning opportunities.
- Do not read assignments before class.
- Always try to be the exception to the rule.
- Disagree with instructors in a haughty and condescending manner (especially in public).
- Call assignments that you do not understand *boring*, *irrelevant*, or *busy work*.
- Be a classroom lawyer.
- Never do any more than is minimally required in class.
- Never help to plan or participate in departmental or campus activities.
- Avoid using an instructor's office hours.

In addition to good letters of recommendation, you're going to need a resume for your job application process. Because there are many resume preparation books on the market, as well as a Web site dedicated to this process (http://www.his.com/~rockport/resumes.htm), we'll provide some general tips and ideas to help you prepare a superior resume.

A resume continues to be an important tool in determining whether a job applicant gets an interview with an employer (Coxford, 1998). Lore (1997) found that only one interview is granted for every 200 resumes received by the average employer. Lore goes on to suggest that resumes are typically scanned in 10 to 20 seconds, not thoroughly read. Thus, an employer's decision is going to be made on the first impression of the resume, which means that the top half of the first page is critical. If the first few lines don't catch the interest of the reader, then the opportunity is lost.

Lore (1997) suggests two general sections of the resume. In the first section, make the claims and assertions about your abilities, qualities, and achievements. In the second section, present the evidence in support of the statements you made in the first section. Within these two sections, you will have multiple parts of the resume. Some of these parts (Coxford, 1998) should include the following:

- Name, address, city, state, phone number, and e-mail address where you can be reached
- Position objective statement and summary of qualifications
- Employment and education history
- Professional training and affiliations
- Military service history (if appropriate)
- Licenses and certificates (if applicable)
- Knowledge of foreign languages
- Publications and professional presentations
- Special accomplishments
- Statement that references and work sample are available upon request

CareerMosaic (1997) offers some general preparation resume tips. These ideas echo and reinforce some of the earlier ideas.

1. Make the first impression count. A good resume may get you to the next stage of the process. A poor resume may stop you from going anywhere.
2. Be concise—try to limit yourself to one printed page. Much more than that is too much.
3. Make sure others proofread your resume before you show it to potential employers. Typographical and grammatical errors are **unacceptable**. Mistakes in your resume will cost you the opportunity to advance in the employment process.
4. Keep your resume current. Make sure it has your new phone number, e-mail address, etc.
5. Electronic resumes have different formatting demands. Many Web sites can lead you in the process of preparing a Web-friendly resume. It probably is worth noting that it is the *student's* responsibility to make sure that the company's equipment is compatible with theirs when sending an electronic resume.

If you've just received your bachelor's degree in psychology, you may have a relatively short resume. That's OK—take that opportunity to go into some detail about the experiences you have had. Table 2.8 contains a list of action verbs you can use to accurately describe the types of duties and responsibilities you held as an undergraduate (and before, if applicable).

Table 2.8: Action Verbs

accelerated	carried out	demonstrated	financed	isolated	placed	responded	traced
acclimated	cast	depreciated	fit	issued	planned	restored	traded
accompanied	cataloged	described	focused	joined	polled	restructured	trained
accomplished	centralized	designated	forecasted	judged	prepared	resulted	transacted
achieved	challenged	designed	formalized	launched	presented	retained	transferred
acquired	chaired	determined	formed	lectured	preserved	retrieved	transformed
acted	changed	developed	formulated	led	presided	revamped	translated
activated	channeled	devised	fortified	lightened	prevented	revealed	transported
actuated	charted	devoted	found	liquidated	priced	reversed	traveled
adapted	checked	diagrammed	founded	litigated	printed	reviewed	treated
added	chose	directed	framed	lobbied	prioritized	revised	tripled
addressed	circulated	disclosed	fulfilled	localized	probed	revitalized	uncovered
adhered	clarified	discounted	functioned	located	processed	rewarded	undertook
adjusted	classified	discovered	furnished	maintained	procured	routed	unified
administered	cleared	dispatched	gained	managed	produced	safeguarded	united
admitted	closed	displayed	gathered	mapped	profiled	salvaged	updated
adopted	co-authored	dissembled	gauged	marketed	programmed	saved	upgraded
advanced	cold called	distinguished	gave	maximized	projected	scheduled	used
advertised	collaborated	distributed	generated	measured	promoted	screened	utilized
advised	collected	diversified	governed	mediated	prompted	secured	validated
advocated	combined	divested	graded	merchandised	proposed	simplified	valued
aided	commissioned	documented	granted	merged	proved	sold	verified
aired	committed	doubled	greeted	met	provided	solved	viewed
affected	communicated	drafted	grouped	minimized	publicized	spearheaded	visited
allocated	compared	earned	guided	modeled	published	specified	weighed
altered	compiled	eased	handled	moderated	purchased	speculated	welcomed
amended	complied	edited	headed	modernized	pursued	spoke	widened
amplified	completed	effected	hired	modified	quantified	spread	witnessed
analyzed	composed	elected	hosted	monitored	quoted	stabilized	won
answered	computed	eliminated	identified	motivated	raised	staffed	worked
anticipated	conceived	employed	illustrated	moved	ranked	staged	wrote
appointed	conceptualized	enabled	illuminated	multiplied	rated	standardized	
appraised	concluded	encouraged	implemented	named	reacted	steered	
approached	condensed	endorsed	improved	narrated	read	stimulated	
approved	conducted	enforced	improvised	negotiated	received	strategize	
arbitrated	conferred	engaged	inaugurated	noticed	recommended	streamlined	
arranged	consolidated	engineered	indoctrinated	nurtured	reconciled	strengthened	
ascertained	constructed	enhanced	increased	observed	recorded	stressed	
asked assembled	consulted	enlarged	incurred	obtained	recovered	structured	
assigned	contracted	enriched	induced	offered	recruited	studied	
assumed	contrasted	entered	influenced	offset	rectified	submitted	
assessed	contributed	entertained	informed	opened	redesigned	substantiated	
assisted	contrived	established	initiated	operated	reduced	substituted	
attained	controlled	estimated	innovated	operationalized	referred	suggested	
attracted	converted	evaluated	inquired	orchestrated	refined	summarized	
audited	convinced	examined	inspected	ordered	regained	superseded	
augmented	coordinated	exceeded	inspired	organized	regulated	supervised	
authored	corrected	exchanged	installed	oriented	rehabilitated	supplied	
authorized	corresponded	executed	instigated	originated	reinforced	supported	
automated	counseled	exempted	instilled	overhauled	reinstated	surpassed	
awarded	counted	exercised	instituted	oversaw	rejected	surveyed	
avail	created	expanded	instructed	paid	related	synchronized	
balanced	critiqued	expedited	insured	participated	remedied	synthesized	
bargained	cultivated	explained	interfaced	passed	remodeled	systematized	
borrowed	cut	exposed	interpreted	patterned	renegotiated	tabulated	
bought	debugged	extended	interviewed	penalized	reorganized	tailored	
broadened	decided	extracted	introduced	perceived	replaced	targeted	
budgeted	decentralized	extrapolated	invented	performed	repaired	taught	
built	decreased	facilitated	inventoried	permitted	reported	terminated	
calculated	deferred	familiarized	invested	persuaded	represented	tested	
canvassed	defined	fashioned	investigated	phased out	requested	testified	
capitalized	delegated	fielded	invited	pinpointed	researched	tightened	
captured	delivered	figured	involved	pioneered	resolved	took	

Note. From "Action Verbs to Enhance Your Resume," TMP Worldwide, 1998, [online], retrieved September 28, 1998, at http://www.aboutwork.com/rescov/resinfo/verbs.html.

So you've written your resume, the resume did its job, and now you have landed that valuable interview. Before the interview, you need to do your homework—learn as much as you can about the company and about the job. What should you know about your potential employer? Appleby (1998b) suggests that you should know about the relative size and potential growth of the industry, the product line or services, information about management personnel and the headquarters, the competition, and recent items in the news. Also, you should know about training policies, relocation policies, price of stock (if applicable), typical career paths, and potential new markets, products, or services.

The U.S. Department of Labor (1991b) suggests the following for the interview:

- Dress for the interview and the job—don't overdress, don't look too informal.
- Always go to the interview alone.
- Find common ground with the employer, and if possible, with the interviewer.
- Express your interest in the job and the company based on the homework you did prior to the interview.
- Allow the interviewer to direct the conversation.
- Answer questions in a clear and positive manner.
- Speak positively of former employers or colleagues, no matter what.
- Let the employer lead the conversation toward salary and benefits—try not to focus your interest on these issues (at least not during the initial interview).
- When discussing salary, be flexible.
- If the employer doesn't offer you a job or say when you'll hear about their decision, ask about when you can call to follow up.
- Be sure to follow up at the appropriate time.
- Thank the employer for the interview, and follow up with a thank-you note.

What type of questions might you be asked during an interview? Below is a sampling of the type of questions you might be asked. It's a good idea to do a mock interview with someone and think about your answers to these questions. Practice having surprise questions asked of you by your practice interviewer. Often, the type of answers you can come up with "on the fly" impresses your potential employer as to how you can handle yourself in pressure situations, such as a job interview. Think about these questions when prepping for an interview.

- What do you hope to be doing five or ten years from now?
- What made you apply for this particular job with us?
- How would you describe yourself?
- What are your strengths and weaknesses?
- What do you see that you can offer to us, and what can we offer to you?
- What are the two or three accomplishments in your life that have given you the greatest satisfaction? Explain.
- Do you work well under pressure and in stressful situations?
- What did you learn as an undergraduate that you think will be helpful on this job?
- Have you ever been in any supervisory or leadership roles?

- What types of activities and extracurricular interests do you have? What do you like to do in your spare time?
- If you don't mind telling me, what other jobs are you applying for?
- Tell me something I should know about you.
- Is there anything else we should know about you?

What if the interview doesn't pan out? Think of each interview as a practice trial toward the next opportunity. If you can identify certain reasons why the interview didn't go well, work on those problems. In some cases, you can contact the interviewer and ask for constructive feedback about the interview process: Was it the way that you handled yourself during the interview, or was it qualification and experience? Appleby (1998b) expands on these potential explanations, by providing a list of 15 "knockout" factors:

- Lack of proper career planning—didn't match job applying for
- Lack of knowledge in field—not qualified
- Inability to express thoughts clearly and concisely—rambles along
- Insufficient evidence of achievement or capacity to excite action in others
- Not prepared for interview—no background research on company
- No real interest in the organization or the industry
- Narrow geographical location interest—not willing to relocate
- Little interest and enthusiasm—indifferent, bland personality
- Overbearing, too aggressive, conceited, cocky
- Interested in only the best dollar offer
- Asks no questions or poor questions about the job
- Unwilling to start at the bottom—expects too much too soon
- Makes excuses, is evasive
- No confidence, lacks poise
- Poor personal appearance, sloppy dress

We've spent the bulk of this chapter discussing the career options for individuals holding a B.A. or B.S. in psychology. As you can see, the options are wide but limited. A psychology education provides valuable skills and abilities, and if you are willing to be flexible, you can make a career for yourself starting with a bachelor's degree in psychology. It is an underlying assumption throughout this book that a degree in psychology provides you with skills, insights, and knowledge about human behavior that allow for the general improvement of the human condition. Unfortunately, although many of the career options with a bachelor's degree can make a great deal of difference in people's lives, they often do not pay well. Better pay typically comes with more education, as can be seen in Chapter 3. However, to be clear and balanced, if pay is your primary consideration, it is fair to point out that you can have a top-paying job without a bachelor's degree at all. Banerji (1998) reported the median salaries of occupations that do not require a degree: millwrights ($60,000), electrical equipment/household appliance repairers ($52,000), tool-and-die makers ($50,000), advertising and business salespeople ($45,000), and rail- and water-transportation workers ($45,000). Banerji points out that although most of these occupations do not require an advanced degree, some do require formal training beyond a high school education.

If financial considerations are your primary objective, many areas of psychology may not satisfy your needs. Serious career exploration and an understanding of your own value system will help you find a suitable career match. Other chapters of this book also help you to find where your "niche" might be. Our suggestion—be as honest as you can with yourself from the start, and you'll probably have less grief in the long run. Contrary to the opinion of some, you are employable with a bachelor's degree in psychology!

*"Looks like your fears of people, speaking,
computers, and all forms of transportation
might limit your career opportunites."*

Chapter 3
GRADUATE SCHOOL OPPORTUNITIES, CHALLENGES, AND CHOICES

You've decided that your interest in psychology is going to take you beyond the bachelor's degree in psychology. You've heard some of the upper division students in the psychology department talk about graduate school. You've heard some of your classmates complaining about all the time they spend studying for the GRE, and you don't even know what the GRE is. All you want to do is help people. Why do you need to go to graduate school to be able to do this?

WHY GRADUATE TRAINING?

It all comes down to how you define "helping people." Psychology is one of those professions where an additional, professional degree is required to practice the craft. This requirement is similar to the additional training that you need to become a doctor (i.e., physician) or lawyer. You don't get your M.D. (medical doctor, physician) or J.D. (juris doctor, lawyer) after completing your bachelor's degree. This situation is unlike other undergraduate majors, such as teacher education or engineering, where the bachelor's degree (and usually some type of licensing or certification, often included as part of the undergraduate instruction) is adequate preparation for employment.

In psychology, there are basically three broad career paths or models that most graduate school students pursue: the *scientist model*, the *practitioner model*, and the *scientist-practitioner* model. Under the scientist model, graduate students receive training in a specific content area, as well as intense instruction in research methods, statistics, and those methods of basic and applied research that further our understanding of human behavior. The trainee under the scientist model typically has a teaching and/or research emphasis, advancing our knowledge of human behavior. In the scientist model, the graduate receives the Ph.D. (doctor of philosophy). In the scientist-practitioner model, the graduate student receives similar rigorous training in the creation and comprehension of scientific information but receives additional training in the helping professions. Thus, the student in the scientist-practitioner model typically has the goal of becoming a therapist (or a psychologist, in the strict licensing sense of the word). This person is trained in various therapeutic theories, conducts therapy under supervision, and completes an internship prior to receiving the Ph.D.

The newest of these three career paths is the practitioner model. In the practitioner model, there is less emphasis on the science side of psychology, but there is additional training on the practitioner side. In this model, the person is trained to become a full-time practitioner, with usually little interest in pursuing the scientific aspects of generating new knowledge in psychology. In this program, the graduate receives a Psy.D. (doctor of psychology). Training in a Psy.D. program is modeled after other professional degrees (M.D., J.D.) in that it is oriented toward being a practitioner in the field rather than the researcher (Keith-Spiegel, 1991). Some people in the profession have expressed concern about the Psy.D. and some of these concerns are summarized by Keith-Spiegel (1991): (a) the Ph.D. is a known quantity, whereas the Psy.D. is the newcomer; (b) many scientist-practitioner Ph.D.s end up never doing independent research, begging the question "Why make the degree distinction anyway?" and (c) some fear that the Psy.D. is seen as a second-class degree or a lite version of the real doctorate (the Ph.D.). If you're confident that your future is in becoming a practitioner, then it is a safe bet to consider a Psy.D. program. The only disadvantage may be if you earn the Psy.D. and then apply for jobs in research or academic settings. For the helping professions, the Psy.D. appears to lead to successful training, and Scheirer (1983, as cited in Keith-Spiegel, 1991) suggests that the Psy.D. may offer a slight advantage in the service delivery job market. It is important to note that the American Psychological Association (APA) accredits both Ph.D. and Psy.D. degrees. Accreditation asserts that a graduate program operates under certain practice and training principles that are believed to be beneficial to the training of future psychologists. Accreditation does not guarantee that you'll have a good experience in the program, and many good graduate programs are not accredited. Accreditation is APA's seal of approval. The APA does not accredit master's degree programs.

At this point, we hope you are still interested in graduate school. Good. Even before we discuss the occupational opportunities available and the entire graduate school admissions process, there is much to think about when considering the graduate school question. Consider the following questions from DeGalan and Lambert (1995):

- Are you postponing some tough decisions by going to graduate school?
- Have you done some hands-on reality testing (e.g., an internship—see Chapter 4)?
- Do you need an advanced degree to work in your particular field, would a bachelor's degree do?
- Have you compared your expectations of what graduate school will do for you compared to what it has done for alumni of the program you are considering?
- Have you talked with people in your field to explore what you might be doing after graduate school?
- Are you excited by the idea of studying the particular field you have in mind?

As you get more and more serious about pursuing a graduate degree in psychology, you may want to consult additional resources. There are a number of good books that can give you more insight into a degree in psychology. Although we recommend these books, they do not replace talking to your faculty members. Not only will faculty members be able to relate their own graduate school experiences, but discussions with them also give you an opportunity to build a relationship that might lead to later opportunities (such as serving as a research assistant or obtaining a letter of recommendation).

Opportunities in Psychology Careers (Super & Super, 1994) looks at the fields of psychology, the prospects, the rewards, and career-related issues. This book is oriented toward persons with an interest in a doctorate in psychology. *Great Jobs for Psychology Majors* (DeGalan & Lambert, 1995) addresses the interests of bachelor's-level graduates who are either pursuing jobs or graduate school. After covering topics such as self-assessment, resumes, networking, interviewing, job offers, and graduate school choices, this book presents five possible career paths. The career path theme is expanded upon in Sternberg's (1997) *Career Paths in Psychology*. This book contains chapters that are dedicated to tracing out potential career paths in psychology by presenting career paths of current psychologists. These career paths are organized into sections, such as academic careers, clinical, counseling, and community psychology, careers in diverse organizations, and careers in diverse areas of psychology.

The emphasis on graduate training in psychology exists because of the skills and abilities required to function as a professional psychologist. Although some of these skills and abilities are addressed in your undergraduate education, the idea is that these skills are mastered in the process of obtaining a higher degree (such as a master's degree or a doctorate). Just what these skills are that may be mastered in the pursuit of a graduate degree are listed in Table 3.1.

Table 3.1: Attainable Skills in the Pursuit of a Graduate Degree in Psychology	
Skill Category	**Examples**
General	action oriented, take initiative, bright, energetic, learn quickly, understand and know how to deal with people, can work on several problems at once, good team player, dependable, can negotiate effectively
Literacy	ability to write, can write in more than one literary format, accustomed to writing essays that allow the exploration of issues in detail, familiar with the techniques of concise writing in a particular format
Numeracy	statistical reasoning and analysis skills, ability to draw appropriate inferences from numerical data, computer literacy and familiarity with statistical software, ability to present data to nontechnical audience, seeks to understand the issue through the examination of the data rather than avoiding the data
Information finding, Measurement	can conduct literature searches, structure conversations to obtain information, avoid bias and preconceptions in information searches, design experiments (e.g., surveys, questionnaires) to obtain information, use observational techniques, prepare and deliver oral and written reports, organize program evaluations
Planning	identify steps in a project from beginning to end, identify potential problems ahead of time, identify needed resources, mobilize team members.
Research, Computer literacy	ability to detect confound variables and design settings for appropriate comparisons and conclusions, able to conceptualize in terms of cause and effect, understand the limitations of particular methodological approaches to the conclusions that can be drawn, understand the design of experimental and quasi-experimental research studies, knowledge of survey and sampling techniques and qualitative analysis

Table 3.1: Attainable Skills in the Pursuit of a Graduate Degree in Psychology (continued)	
Interpersonal awareness	knowledge of the capabilities/limitations of people from many viewpoints (cognitive, perceptual, physical, motivational, social, developmental, personality, emotional)
Problem solving	identify central issues and key questions, experience in identifying the most important problem(s) to be addressed from ambiguous information, can solve general problems and focus on details, understand that there may be more than one method for solving the problem, understand that there can be more than one right answer
Critical Evaluation, Higher-Order Analysis	read critically, synthesize and summarize information from multiple sources, interpret qualitative and quantitative data, deal with inconsistent/uncertain information, extract key pieces from information in a rapid manner, impose structure on ambiguous, messy data, translate information into meaningful conclusions and recommendations
Perspectives	understand that people trained in different disciplines may see the same problem differently, understand the advantage to understanding different perspectives; understand the perspectives of others (i.e., empathy), coordinate or facilitate action among people with different perspectives
Note. From "The Distinctive Skills of a Psychology Graduate," by N. Hayes, June 1996, [online], retrieved March 30, 1998, at http://www.apa.org/monitor/jul97/skills.html; "Skills (That May Be) Obtained During Graduate Study in Psychology," American Psychological Association, 1998, [online], retrieved March 30, 1998, at http://www.apa.org/science/skills.html.	

OCCUPATIONAL OPPORTUNITIES

In this section, we discuss the options and opportunities you will have with a master's degree (M.A. or M.S.) and the options and opportunities you will have with the doctorate (Ph.D. or Psy.D.). Some of the areas that we will cover include the outlook for the future of these positions, perceptions of the future, actual employment figures, different work settings, and relative salaries. The diversity of opportunities with a graduate degree is reflective of the diversity in psychology, as discussed in Chapter 1.

Opportunities With a Master's Degree. Master's degree psychologists and counselors are predicted to be among the fastest growing occupations; they are expected to have the greatest increases in employment for the period 1996–2006 (Occupational Outlook Handbook [OOH], 1998b). When master's degree recipients are asked about their perceptions of the job market, 31.0% percent report that it is fair, 25.3% report good, and 5.2% report excellent (APA, 1998c). In 1998 the APA conducted a survey of 1996 psychology master's degree recipients (APA, 1998d). The APA found that 67% were employed, 27% were full-time graduate students, and 6% were not employed and not enrolled full-time in school. Where are master's-level psychologists employed? According to the APA 1996 survey of master's degree recipients, 3% reported full-time employment in an independent practice, 12% in colleges and universities, 15%

in business, government, or nonprofit organization, 20% in education/schools, and 50% in full-time employment in other human services avenues (APA, 1998e).

According to the OOH (1998c), about 6 out of 10 counselors have only a master's degree. The differences between a master's-level psychologist and a master's-level counselor are subtle. Master's-level psychologists probably received their education in a department of psychology, and although their degree is from a psychology department, they may call themselves a counselor depending on the state rules and regulations concerning the title. (For instance, in some states "psychologist" is a legally protected term, often reserved for persons with a Ph.D. or Psy.D. who have also passed a licensing examination.) Master's-level counselors may or may not have received their degree from a psychology department; they may have earned the degree in a counseling department, guidance department, educational psychology department, etc. In many states, the term "counselor" is not legally protected; hence in some situations almost anyone can advertise as a counselor.

How much do master's-level counselors and psychologists earn? The OOH (1998c) reports that the "median earnings for full-time educational and vocational counselors were about $35,800 a year in 1996. The middle 50 percent earned between $25,600 and $48,5000 a year. The bottom 10 percent earned less than $18,600 a year, while the top 10 percent earned over $60,100 a year" (p. 6). The average salary for public school counselors was about $44,100. In APA's 1996 Master's Employment Survey, salary information was gathered on specific areas of master's graduate education (APA, 1998f). These data are presented in Table 3.2.

Table 3.2: Median Starting Salaries for Full-Time Employment Positions With a Master's Degree

Area in Psychology	Median Starting Salary
Research positions	$29,000
Director of human services, clinical psychology	$26,000
Director of human services, counseling psychology	$27,000
Director of human services, school psychology	$32,000
Administration of human services delivery	$33,000
Educational administration	$30,000
Other administration	$35,000
Applied psychology	$35,000
Other	$28,000

Note. From "Data on Education and Employment--Master's," American Psychological Association, 1998, [online], retrieved November 28, 1998, at http://research.apa.org/mas5.html.

Master's-level counselors and psychologists help people in a number of ways, such as evaluating their interests, abilities, and disabilities, and dealing with personal, social, academic, and career problems. You should know that there are related disciplines that also address some of these similar issues—professions such as college and student affairs workers, teachers, personnel workers and managers, human services workers, social workers, psychiatric nurses, clergy members, occupational therapists, and others (OOH, 1998c). There are a variety of options available for helping those who need help; more on this topic is presented in Chapter 9.

Opportunities With the Doctoral Degree. The doctoral degree in psychology (e.g., Ph.D. or Psy.D.) is generally required for employment as a licensed clinical or counseling psychologist. (Some states have limited licensure for master's-level psychologists. So you need to check the laws carefully.) Interestingly, over 40% of all psychologists are self-employed, five times the average for all professional workers (OOH, 1998d). In what areas do graduate students earn a doctorate in psychology? If you'll refer back to Table 1.1 in Chapter 1, psychologists earn Ph.D.'s in all of those areas, and more (see also Table 1.2). In 1996, there were about 143,000 psychologists employed in the United States (OOH, 1998d).

What degrees are being awarded? In a 1995 study of new doctorates conducted by the APA (1998g), Ph.D.'s accounted for 76% of the degrees awarded, Psy.D.'s accounted for 22%, and Ed.D's (doctor of education) accounted for 2% of the degrees awarded. In what fields were they awarded? Clinical psychology doctorates account for 40% of the total. In a different survey (APA, 1998h), APA surveyed Ph.D. degree holders in 1995 and found that, of the 82,150 Ph.D. holders at the time, 90% were employed and 10% unemployed. Of those who were employed, 79% were employed full time and 11% were employed part time. Of those not employed, 2% were pursuing postdoctorate work, 5% were retired, 2% were not employed and not seeking employment, and less than 1% were unemployed and seeking employment. This type of result speaks to the diversity of employment opportunities and the value of the skills attained by the completion of the doctoral degree. Although the doctorate is more difficult to obtain, persons who obtain it provide themselves more opportunities for employment in a variety of settings.

What are some of there diverse employment settings? According to the 1996 Doctorate Employment Survey done by APA (1998i), 30% were employed in academia (colleges and universities), 18% were employed by business or government, 7% were employed by education/schools outside of academia, 10% were employed by managed care, and 35% were employed in other human services settings. It should be noted that with respect to the *job outlook* (OOH, 1998d), "employment of psychologists is expected to grow more slowly than the average for all occupations through the year 2006" (p. 5).

What about the salaries for doctoral-level psychologists? The APA has completed the most recent surveys of doctoral employment and salaries reported in OOH (1998d). Table 3.3 below presents median starting salaries for full-time employed doctorates based on the 1996 survey, and the bottom half of Table 3.3 presents the median salaries for full-time doctorates.

Table 3.3: Median Starting Salary and Median Salary for Full–Time Employed Psychology Doctorates

Employment Area	Median Starting Salary
Associate professor	$49,000
Assistant professor	$43,000
Lecturer/instructor	$37,000
Adjunct/visiting faculty	$37,000
Research position	$40,000
Director of human services, clinical psychology	$38,000

Table 3.3: Median Starting Salary and Median Salary for Full–Time Employed Psychology Doctorates (continued)

Employment Area	Median Salary
Director of human services, counseling psychology	$38,000
Director of human services, school psychology	$43,000
Administration of human services	$45,000
Other applied	$54,000
Faculty position	$48,000
Research position	$50,000
Administration of research	$70,000
Independent practice/clinical	$74,000
VA hospital/clinical	$60,000
Independent practice/counseling	$70,000
Applied psychology (I/O)	$80,000
Director of human services/other	$60,000

Note. From *Occupational Outlook Handbook*, January 15, 1998, Psychologists, [online], retrieved September 20, 1998, at http://www.bls.gov/oco/ocos.056.htm.

As you can see, the starting salaries for psychology doctorates are impressive compared with those of master's-level psychologists. Also, it is important to note for Tables 3.2 and 3.3 that these are median salaries (the median is the score that divides the distribution in half). In looking at Table 3.3, the median salary of a full-time employed clinical psychologist in independent practice is $74,000—that means that 50% have salaries *above* $74,000, and 50% have salaries *below* $74,000. For access to more detailed information about psychologists' salaries, the best resource is probably the American Psychological Association (750 First Street, NE, Washington, DC 20002; www.apa.org).

Before we turn our attention to the graduate school admission process, let's draw a general salary comparison across all the options available to those with an interest in studying psychology. The top half of Table 3.4 presents salary data from the federal government (an employer of psychologists at all levels). The relative comparisons are interesting. The bottom half of Table 3.4 presents more information about the different levels of salary for master's and doctorate holders in different areas of psychology (OOH, 1998d).

Table 3.4: Salary Summary for Federal Government Psychologist Positions and Selected Positions from APA Salary Survey

Federal Government Salary Psychologist Positions	Median Starting Salary
Bachelor's degree	$19,500
Bachelor's degree with superior academic record	$24,200
Master's degree, 1 year of experience	$29,600
Doctorate (Ph.D., Psy.D.), 1 year of internship	$35,800
Doctorate with experience	$42,900
Average, nonstarting salary (across nonsupervisory, supervisory, and managerial positions)	$62,120

Table 3.4: Salary Summary for Federal Government Psychologist Positions and Selected Positions from APA Salary Survey (continued)

APA Survey Psychologist Salary Positions	Median Salary
Doctorate, 5–9 years of experience, counseling	$55,000
Doctorate in private research organization	$54,500
Doctorate, clinical psychologist in public psychiatric hospital	$51,000
Doctorate in school psychology	$59,000
Master's degree, counseling psychology	$38,000
Master's degree, clinical psychology	$43,000
Master's degree, research position	$41,500
Master's degree, school psychology	$60,000
Master's degree, I/O psychology	$55,000

Note. From *Occupational Outlook Handbook*, January 15, 1998, Psychologists, [online], retrieved September 20, 1998, at http://www.bls.gov/oco/ocos.056.htm.

Of interest is the difference between the bachelor's degree ($19,500) and the bachelor's degree with a superior academic record ($24,200). What does it mean to get good grades, be active and involved as an undergraduate, participate in the activities of the department, serve as a research or teaching assistant, etc.? It looks like it is worth about $4,700 in starting salary! With a 5% raise per year, it would take almost five years to match the bachelor's with a superior academic record compared to the starting salary of the bachelor's degree. Even economically, it makes sense to make the most of your undergraduate education!

HOW TO APPLY TO GRADUATE SCHOOL

The message is clear about the benefits of receiving a master's degree or a doctorate. These advanced degrees prepare you for a career as a professional—they afford you greater job opportunities and flexibility, and the salary benefits are clear. So you want to earn your master's or doctorate in psychology—how do you get started? The remainder of this chapter is dedicated to providing an overview of the details of the graduate school application process. You'll need to have some clear ideas about your short-term and long-term goals before you can start the graduate school search process in any meaningful manner.

Before we jump into the details of the process, an overview is in order. These suggestions are taken primarily from APA (1997b), APA (1998a), and Hayes and Hayes (1989). APA (1997b) suggests that the three keys of getting into graduate school are (a) preparation, (b) application know-how, and (c) patience. For instance:

- Decide the areas of psychology that you are interested in.
- Determine the type of degree you wish to pursue: master's or doctoral, and if doctoral, Ph.D. or Psy.D.
- Submit an application to take the Graduate Record Examination (GRE); plan to take the exam during the fall semester prior to your expected admission to a graduate program.
- When you have narrowed your program list and have taken your GRE, you are ready to apply.

Earlier portions of this chapter covered the distinctions between degrees, such as the master's and the doctoral degrees. Later parts of this chapter address the GRE and the entire process. How do you narrow your program list and select the right program?

Narrowing Your Program List. An excellent guide to finding information about graduate programs in psychology in the United States is the *Graduate Study in Psychology* (APA, 1998a). This book contains the following suggestions (p. x):

- Apply to a range of programs, with most offering you a reasonable chance at acceptance. It takes too much time, effort, and money to apply to programs that you have no reasonable chance of acceptance at.
- When possible, apply to programs that offer the degree that you ultimately want to obtain. That is, do not earn a *terminal* master's degree knowing that you want to obtain your doctorate right away and will have to go to another school.
- Apply to programs that offer the specialty in which you would like to eventually gain employment. It is difficult to change your major emphasis or area "midstream" in your graduate education.
- Apply to programs that match your interests and your experience. Know who the faculty are, do your homework, and apply to programs where you believe you will be a good "fit."
- Be informed about the issues related to career opportunities of your chosen area of psychology. Although your graduate program is responsible for your educational opportunities, *you* are responsible for your employment opportunities.

Understanding the Application Process. The second area of expertise that you'll have to develop in this endeavor is a good working knowledge of the whole application process (APA, 1997b). Some concerns and activities in this area include the following:

- Contact programs to request an application, departmental information, and financial aid information (if necessary).
- Prepare the materials required by most applications (in addition to the application fee):
  - ➢ Letter of intent/autobiographical statement/personal statement
  - ➢ Letters of recommendation and transcripts/grades
  - ➢ GRE scores forwarded directly from the Educational Testing Service (ETS)
  - ➢ Curriculum vita or resume (see more below), and a cover letter
  - ➢ Personal interview (in some cases for some programs)

Thinking about the sub-bullet "Curriculum vita or resume," what is the difference? A curriculum vita is an academic document that chronicles your accomplishments and achievements related to the discipline. A resume is more of a work history and advertisement of your skills and abilities. In general, a resume needs to be short, one to two pages, whereas a long vita means a long list of accomplishments. More on these two documents is presented later in this chapter. A guide to vita preparation and sample vitae of undergraduate students are presented in Appendix B.

Diehl and Sullivan (1998) also offer additional suggestions to make this process result in a desired outcome. Several of their suggestions cover a timetable of activities for an ideal process; we'll present a slightly different version of the timetable in a moment. They suggest that when you are applying, send more than what is asked for. Send more than the required number of letters of recommendation. If the application materials do not request a vita, send one anyway (unless you believe your vita hurts your application). Send copies of your written work, such as an impressive term paper from an upper division psychology course, or a copy of some work from a senior thesis, internship, independent study, or directed research project. After you've sent off your packet of application materials, make sure that the department received *everything*. It is *your* responsibility to make sure that letters of recommendation and transcripts are received. Appropriately timed telephone calls can save an application. An incomplete application package is an easy excuse for a graduate admissions committee to *not* review your materials. Also, when filling out applications, type everything. Be sure to fill out all forms completely, including those forms that you must give to the people who write your letter of recommendation. You usually have to sign a waiver of your rights to inspect your documents—be sure to fill out all the information; your faculty member can't fill this out for you, and often the document is sent directly from the faculty member to the graduate institution. Watch for more tips about the application process through this chapter.

Patience. The third component in this overview of the process is patience. Sometimes patience is the hardest part.

- You will usually be notified of your acceptance or rejection before April 15; sometimes earlier, and sometimes later (if you are on a wait list); however, you should receive some feedback by April 15.
- Accept or reject an offer, in writing, by or on April 15; if you decide to attend, it's good to have that decision over with; if you decide not to attend, the school can go to the next person on the wait list and make that person an offer; although you may need some time to make your decision, it is not appropriate to delay this decision after April 15.

In the remainder of this chapter, we'll look at the details of navigating through this process, finish up with some of the keys to being a successful applicant and a successful graduate student, and present some graduate school admissions statistics. Much of the work in this field came from *The Complete Guide to Graduate School Admission: Psychology and Related Fields* by Keith-Spiegel (1991). Reading this book and following the advice will probably improve your performance in the entire admissions process.

For instance, Table 3.5 gives a modified version of the ideal timetable for undergraduates from Keith-Spiegel (1991). It is the *ideal* version, and perhaps not very realistic for most students—however, it can give you some insight into the level of planning necessary to achieve the goal of successful entrance into graduate school.

Table 3.5: The Ideal Timetable for Undergraduates	
Check √	**Freshman Year Through First Term/Semester of Sophomore Year**
	Concentrate on fulfilling your university's general education requirements. Do not avoid taking math and science courses.
	Take any lower-division required psychology courses, such as general/introductory psychology and statistics. Avoid taking lower-division psychology elective courses.
	From the beginning, work hard to obtain good grades. It is difficult to recover after a poor start. The reality is that every "C" grade hurts your chances for graduate school admission.
	Meet with an academic and/or career advisor to tentatively map out a course for your navigation through the major. Update as needed. Pay particular attention to course sequencing and prerequisites—mistakes here could add extra semesters to your anticipated graduation date.
	Learn about and use the resources around you: learn to use PsycINFO in the library as well as your library's computerized systems; make yourself aware of the career counseling and other services available on campus.
	Start to create a regular habit of attending events sponsored by your psychology department. Go hear guest speakers—attend department colloquia. You may not feel like an insider, and you may not know other people there—but go anyway. These are part of the professional activities of psychologists!
Check √	**Sophomore Year Second Term/Semester**
	If possible, take a required upper-division psychology course or two. Try to finish up any general education courses.
	Find out about Psi Chi and other psychology-related clubs. Plan to join as soon as you meet the requirements.
	Begin to learn as much as your can about the psychology faculty. What are their research areas? What courses do they teach? Get to know one or two highly successful junior- or senior-level students, and learn what you can from them about the department and the faculty.
	Start a filing system where you put notes of activities or accomplishments that you might use on your resume or vita, items about graduate school, teaching or research assistantships, etc., that you come across. Keep the file open and active. Start saving term papers, and be sure to keep the syllabus and course materials for psychology classes. Whenever possible, keep your textbooks—they will come in handy in later classes and can be a good source of review for the GRE psychology test. If you start now with this organizational plan, you'll be thankful you did!
	Learn about any professional meetings that your psychology faculty attend. Are they student-friendly? Do the faculty sometimes take students with them? If a meeting is held locally, be sure to go. Whenever you have the chance to present some of your own work at such a meeting, be sure to take advantage of the opportunity.
Check √	**Summer Between Sophomore and Junior Year**
	If you haven't finished your general education classes, do so.
	If you need to work over the summer, try to find a psychology-related job if possible. This job may be a good contact for later and a potential letter of recommendation source. If you can do research-related work, do it.
	If possible, buy textbooks for first semester junior year, and start reading early.
	If you plan a career in a human service related field, consider a volunteer placement a few hours each week in a nonprofit community agency.

Table 3.5: The Ideal Timetable for Undergraduates (continued)	
Check √	**Junior Year First Semester**
	Begin taking required upper-division psychology courses. Do not "save" hard courses for your senior year.
	Start to get to know one or more of your psychology professors.
	Look for opportunities for research experience starting later this semester, or next semester at the latest.
	Start to become familiar with the graduate admissions process and requirements—if you are reading this book, you are well on your way!
Check √	**Junior Year Second Semester**
	Continue to complete required upper-division psychology classes.
	Begin to try to focus your interests in a particular program area (e.g., clinical, counseling, social, developmental, experimental, etc.).
	Continue to get to know psychology professors, thinking in terms of who would be a good source of letters of recommendation. If possible, try to take a second course from those professors you are intending to ask for letters.
	Join Psi Chi (if you qualify) if you haven't already. Volunteer to get involved with club activities. Become a student affiliate of APA and/or other appropriate organizations.
	Look for an opportunity to get research experience this semester and into next year. Think about working with more than one faculty member. Try to become involved in a project that could lead to authorship credit on a conference presentation or publication— talk to the faculty researcher about this up front.
	Keep checking on financial aid opportunities for graduate students, set up a file in your career planning and placement office, check with advising that you are on course to graduate on time.
	Create the first draft of your resume or vita; use your previous organizational file to aid in its preparation.
Check √	**Summer Between Junior and Senior Year**
	If possible, try not to work a full-time job so that you can devote some time to the tasks below.
	Visit any campuses with graduate programs of interest to you, if possible. The best timing would be just before the fall semester starts, to catch the most faculty and students on campus.
	Study consistently and diligently for the GRE's by using the study guides available, including the software packages.
	Research your graduate programs in depth. Write letters to acquire program materials (descriptions, applications, faculty profiles, financial aid forms, etc.). Wait to mail these letters until the semester starts (late August/early September).
	Sign up for the GRE. Try to arrange taking the verbal, quantitative, and analytical portions of the exam on a different day from the psychology advanced test.
	Start thinking about the types of questions you will be asked in preparing "letters of intent" or "biographical statements." (See information later in this chapter for how to do this.)
	Line up the financial resources needed to *apply* to graduate schools.
	Keep up with your resume or vita.

Table 3.5: The Ideal Timetable for Undergraduates (continued)	
Check √	**Senior Year First Semester**
	If possible, take a slightly lighter load than usual if the bulk of your graduate school applications will need to be filed by late December; be sure to take at least two more required courses in the major. In general, think of the graduate application/GRE studying experience as a three-credit course; adjust your course load appropriately.
	Complete the tasks from the summer list if necessary.
	Take advantage of any workshops offered by the department or career planning and placement office about applying to graduate schools, preparing a vita, writing an autobiographical statement, etc.
	Try to obtain the most recent issue of *Graduate Study in Psychology* (published annually by the APA). Check the most recent information about your graduate schools of interest.
	Continue studying for and take your GRE exams around October; you need to take them early enough so that the scores can be submitted to your graduate programs before the application deadline.
	Start to create the materials that you will need to give to each of your references. Provide mailing addresses, due dates, special forms, special envelopes, etc.
	Negotiate for three *strong* letters of recommendation from faculty, internship supervisors, anyone who can speak to your professional abilities and competencies.
	Make final decisions about where to apply.
	Order transcripts at least six (6) weeks before each application deadline. Get an unofficial copy for yourself to submit with your application, but have official copies sent to your graduate programs directly from the registrar as required.
	Order GRE test score reports at least six (6) weeks before each application deadline.
	If possible, visit any campuses that you have not seen prior to your application.
	Compose your essay statements. Let professors and other students whose opinions you value proofread your statements for you. Edit and revise.
	Complete filling out application materials.
	Mail out applications two to four weeks prior to the deadline if possible, but the materials must be *received*, not sent, by the deadline date.
	Gently remind your referees (letter writers) about impending deadlines, and ask if they need any additional materials or clarification.
Check √	**Senior Year Second Semester**
	Fill out any remaining applications or "late-adds" to your application process.
	Be sure to finish graduation requirements; can take some courses of interest as elective credits—any courses you told your graduate schools you were going to take, take.
	Double-check to make sure that your referees sent their letters before the deadline dates.
	Follow up with each graduate department to make sure that all components of your application arrived intact—your materials, letters, scores, transcripts, etc.
	Depending on the timing, you may have to start the process of applying for student loans at some point during this semester.
	Plan to send transcripts of spring semester classes as requested by graduate programs.
	If you receive an acceptance or acceptances, be sure to reply by the date indicated by the graduate program no later than April 15 (unless instructed otherwise).
	If you are rejected at your schools, fall back and reevaluate; you have options available to you to strengthen future applications.

Note. From *The Complete Guide to Graduate School Admission: Psychology and Related Fields*, by P. Keith-Speigel, 1991, Hillsdale, NJ: Erlbaum.

Please remember that this is an ideal timeline, not a realistic one! If you add psychology late in your academic career or change majors, you won't be able to complete the tasks in the semesters listed, but you'll still have to complete most of them. If you transfer in from another school, your timeline will be different as well. These are the tasks—the timelines vary, but some of the deadlines are absolute.

As you can see from close examination of Table 3.5, getting ready for, and applying to, graduate school is an arduous process, and not for the lighthearted. It is a lot of work to gain admission to graduate school. You need to think seriously about this career avenue before going down this path.

What can you do to make your application more competitive? What do graduate admissions committees look for? How do they make these decisions about whom to admit into their program or reject? The primary selection criteria are your GPA, your GRE scores, and your letters of recommendation (Keith-Spiegel, 1991)—sometimes called the "big three." Later research by Landrum, Jeglum, and Cashin (1994) examined the decision-making processes of graduate admissions committee members and found that in addition to the big three, two more factors have bubbled up to the surface—research experience and the autobiographical statement/letter of intent. The importance of these latter two factors is also seen in Table 3.6, which presents Keith-Spiegel's (1991) secondary selection criteria. Based on Landrum et al.'s (1994) work, the big three might be expanded into the big five or top five—these factors are certainly important in the selection process. Interestingly, work by Cashin and Landrum (1991) found that undergraduates understand the importance of factors such as GPA but tend to *underestimate* the importance of GRE scores and letters of recommendation, and they *overestimate* the importance of extracurricular activities.

These conclusions are further supported by Keith-Spiegel's (1991) secondary selection criteria. Imagine this scenario—a top graduate program attracts many qualified applicants, who meet the standards set with respect to GRE scores and GPA, and all applicants have excellent letters of recommendation. How does the committee distinguish among applicants in this group—that is, after qualifying on the primary selection criteria (GRE, GPA, letters of recommendation), what information does the committee now use to make its decisions (in essence, what are the tie-breakers among a group of well-qualified students where not enough graduate student slots exist to admit all applicants who qualify on the primary selection criteria)? Keith-Spiegel (1991) presented a detailed list of these factors, empirically based, presented by rank of importance (ranked in Table 3.6 from highest to lowest).

Table 3.6: Secondary Selection Criteria in Rank Order of Importance
Items Rated as "Very Important"
• Research experience, resulting in a publication credit in a scholarly journal
• Degree to which applicant's skills and interests match those of the program
• Research experience, resulting in a paper presented at a professional meeting
• Degree of interest expressed by one or more of the members of the selection committee in working with particular applicants
• Clarity and focus of applicant's statement of purpose

Table 3.6: Secondary Selection Criteria in Rank Order of Importance (continued)
Items Rated as "Generally Important"

- Research assistant experience
- Writing skills as revealed in the applicant's statement of purpose
- Status and reputation of applicant's referees
- Strong, supportive mentor actively involved in advocating applicant's candidacy
- Degree to which applicant possesses a knowledge of and interest in the program
- Underrepresented ethnic minority membership of applicant
- Number of statistics/research methodology courses taken as an undergraduate
- Number of hard science courses taken as an undergraduate
- Prestige and status of psychology faculty in applicant's undergraduate department
- Prestige of applicant's undergraduate institution
- Potential for success as judged by preselection interviews or some other form of personal contact
- Honors or merit scholarships awarded to applicant by undergraduate institution

Items Rated as "Somewhat Important"

- Area of undergraduate major
- Relevant field/volunteer experience in placement relevant to your program
- Social/personality style as revealed through preselection interview or some other form of personal contact
- Relevant paid work experience related to program
- Neatness and "professional look" of the application materials
- Teaching assistant experience
- Level of applicant's active participation in department activities

Items Rated as "Minimally Important" or "Not Important"

- Student affiliate status in a relevant professional organization
- Gender balance in the program applied to
- Psi Chi membership
- Multilingual capabilities
- Contribution to geographical diversity

Note. From *The Complete Guide to Graduate School Admission: Psychology and Related Fields*, by P. Keith-Speigel, 1991, Hillsdale, NJ: Erlbaum.

If you're not careful, it is easy to misunderstand some of the items in this table. For example, the information about Psi Chi membership does not mean that participation in Psi Chi is not important—it means that Psi Chi membership is an unlikely factor to make or break an application—it is not a tie-breaker. However, the contacts that you make in Psi Chi, the opportunities to go to conferences, gain leadership ability, work with faculty members one on one (that may lead to the very important letters of recommendation) are all good things that come out of Psi Chi participation. Membership itself may not be an application tie-breaker, but that does not mean that the activity is unimportant.

Your graduate school application package is bound to be a very complex series of documents. Unfortunately, there is no uniform method of applying to graduate schools, and each school wants each bit of information in its own format—as an applicant, you have very little power in this situation, so you need to play the game exactly by the rules set by the school. This is not the place to ad lib and do it your own way—that strategy almost always backfires. What might be in your application package? Keith-Spiegel (1991) generated a fairly comprehensive list:

- Curriculum vita or resume
- Biographical statement (sometimes called personal statement, autobiographical statement, letter of intent), including a statement of your interests and career goals
- Overall grade point average (GPA) and perhaps your GPA in psychology, verified by an official copy of your transcripts
- List of relevant courses you have completed in the major, and a timetable for those courses not yet completed but planned for the future
- GRE scores
- Letters of recommendation, sent by you or directly to the school by the referees as directed in the application materials
- Application fee (if applicable)
- Cover letter, if necessary

In this section, we'll address some of the key components of this application process, by examining (a) grades, (b) the GRE, (c) the curriculum vita, (d) letters of recommendation, (e) the personal statement, (f) your research experience, and (g) the match or fit between you and the graduate programs you are applying to.

Grades. Your grades in college serve as one of the big three admissions factors. Although programs vary, as a general rule most graduate programs are going to have a minimum GPA cutoff of 3.0; many programs have higher minimum requirements. The best sources of information about these requirements comes from the APA's *Graduate Study in Psychology* (1998a) published annually, and from materials received directly from your institutions of interest. Although exceptions are occasionally made about the minimum cutoff, they must be accompanied by an explanation about why an exception to the rule is warranted. Given that more students want to attend graduate school than graduate school slots are available for students, universities can be (and must be) selective in choosing those students who have the best potential to be successful graduates of their program. A low GPA, without any accompanying information, is taken as a predictor of your future performance. C or average work is not acceptable in most graduate programs. If you are striving for admission into a graduate program, and a 3.0 is probably the minimum requirement, think about this—*every C that you earn as an undergraduate hurts your chances for admission to graduate school* because every C (and of course, lower grades) drags that GPA down.

If you are serious about graduate school and have modest grades (a GPA of 2.7 to 3.2 on a 4-point scale), you may want to consider the following additional strategies as suggested by Keith-Spiegel (1991):

1. **Delay graduation**. Take extra time to get better grades in the classes that you have left to take. If you do this, however, make sure that you earn mostly A's in these remaining classes—low grades at a slower pace won't look good at all in your quest for graduate school.

2. **Take selected courses over again**. Check the policies at your school—does the last grade replace the first, or are the grades averaged together? What happens if the second grade is lower? Repeat courses not to hide a problem grade, but to prove that you can do better work.

3. **Become a post-baccalaureate student at your undergraduate school**. Go ahead and graduate, but stay at your school another semester or year, taking selected classes, working with faculty on research and other projects, etc., doing all the things you can to strengthen your application.

4. **Perform exceptionally well on the GRE**. Very high GRE test scores may be able to compensate somewhat for a modest GPA. Some selection committees allow a strong GRE score to make up for a weak GPA; the reverse is rarely true.

5. **Take classes at your desired graduate institution**. You can probably enroll as an unclassified graduate student (like having an undeclared major as an undergraduate), and, space permitting and as long as you meet the prerequisites and requirements, you may be able to take some of the classes with the first-year (admitted) graduate students. This approach can be a high-risk tactic because there is no guarantee of eventual admittance into the program; you've got to get into the classes and do *well*; you may have to relocate to take these classes, etc. If you take this route, however, volunteer to work in a professor's lab, without pay if necessary. The goal is to make your services so valuable to that professor that when you do apply for graduate admission, you have an advocate on the faculty who will attempt to champion your acceptance.

6. **Settle for programs with lower academic requirements**. With modest grades, you may not be able to gain admission to your top-tier or dream schools. You may have to go to a lesser known school in a part of the country you don't know much about. Some schools may admit you provisionally, a type of probationary status that gives you a chance to demonstrate your competency.

7. **Earn a master's degree before applying to a doctoral program**. Your grades may not get you into a doctoral program, but they might get you into a master's degree program. This program becomes your proving ground, and when you apply for doctoral programs, more emphasis is placed on your graduate work and less emphasis is placed on your undergraduate work. Be sure to choose a master's program that is rigorous—getting your master's degree from a poorly regarded school will do you more harm than good in the doctoral long run. Again, you must make an effort to do more than just classroom work. *Great* grades are important, but the bottom line is research, research, research!

8. **Earn the master's degree instead of the doctoral degree**. As you've seen in earlier sections of this chapter, there are a number of excellent opportunities for employment with a master's degree, and the employment projections for opportunities are actually predicted to be better for master's students than doctoral students in the next ten years. You may be able to have a satisfying career without the Ph.D. or Psy.D.

Graduate Record Examination. Another significant component of the big three is the GRE, a series of tests administered nationally by the Educational Testing Service. There are two versions of the GRE test available, paper-based testing and computer-based testing (ETS,

1998a). The paper-based testing is what most faculty are familiar with, where the general test is given on a series of national testing dates. The computer-based test is the newer option, where you take the GRE in authorized test centers located throughout the nation (and literally the world). As an example, the paper-based tests during the 1998–99 academic year were given November 7, 1998, and April 10, 1999 (the psychology subject test was given exclusively on December 12, 1998). The computer-based test is administered continuously October through January, from February to September you can take the test the first three weeks of each month. You schedule the computer-based test at your convenience; another benefit is that you know your unofficial test scores prior to leaving the test center. It is unclear at this time just how much longer the paper-and-pencil version of the GRE General Test will be around—eventually, only the computerized version may be available.

What does the GRE test measure? According to ETS (1998b), "the general test measures verbal, quantitative, and analytical developed abilities that have been acquired over a long period of time. The verbal measure tests the ability to analyze and evaluate written material and synthesize information obtained from it, to analyze relationships among component parts of sentences, and to recognize relations between words and concepts. The quantitative measure tests basic mathematical skills and understanding of elementary mathematical concepts, as well as the ability to reason quantitatively and to solve problems in a quantitative setting. The analytical measure tests the ability to understand structured sets of relationships, deduce new information from sets of relationships, analyze and evaluate arguments, identify central issues and hypotheses, draw sound inferences, and identify plausible causal explanations" (p. 5). In addition, a subject test is available in psychology, and psychology subject test scores may be required by some graduate schools.

The range of each of the general test measures (verbal, quantitative, and analytical) is from 200 points to 800 points. Each graduate school you are interested in may have different preferences in your scores. Some may want at least a 450 in both verbal and quantitative but not care about analytical. Some schools may just look at your total score (all three added together), or perhaps V+Q (your verbal score + your quantitative score). Hence, the minimum cutoff may be a V+Q of 1,200, meaning any combination of V+Q to reach 1,200 points, not necessarily 600 verbal and 600 quantitative. The psychology subject test has a range of 200 to 990 (ETS, 1998b). It should be noted that many disciplines require potential graduate students to take the GRE general test, not just psychology; other disciplines also have specialized subject area tests.

When examining all GRE general test takers from October 1994 to September 1997 (a total of approximately 1.14 million examinees), the average verbal ability score was 474, the average quantitative score was 558, and the average analytical score was 547 (ETS, 1998b). When looking at just psychology students taking the general test during that same time frame (over 55,000 students), the average verbal score was 472, the average quantitative score was 514, and the average analytical score was 550. One new wrinkle to report—ETS has announced that beginning October 1999, a GRE Writing Assessment will be available for graduate schools to potentially require of their applicants. Examinees are asked to complete a 45-minute "Present Your Perspective on an Issue" task and a 30-minute "Analyze an Argument" task. According to ETS (1998c), the writing assessment "serves as a reliable index of candidates' ability to articulate their own ideas about complex issues and arguments rather than to select among answers presented to them" (p. 2). Of particular interest, will graduate psychology departments require the writing assessment, and what will be the relative weight of this new information, compared to the weight given to scores such as the verbal or quantitative scores from the GRE general test?

Curriculum Vita. Another component of this arduous graduate school application process involves the preparation of a *curriculum vita*, which literally means "academic life." Although related to the resume, the vita chronicles your accomplishments, whereas the resume is a brief introduction to your skills, abilities, and employment history. A goal in resume writing is keeping the resume short, such as one or two pages. Because a long vita is an indicator that you have accomplished much in your field, the ultimate goal is length. Many of the preparation tips that were offered in Chapter 2 also apply to the curriculum vita (sometimes called a CV); Plous (1998b) offers some additional tips for creating your CV:

- Your vita should be a clear and concise summary of your professional qualifications. Take care in every word used.
- Try to obtain copies of vitae from people who are at your stage or slightly ahead of you; although a faculty member's vita might give you some organizational ideas, some sections will be inappropriate due to your entry-level status in the discipline.
- Create an inviting and elegant format. Take the time to add some style, and include white space (but, don't overdo it).
- Make absolutely sure that there are *no* errors in your vita. Have more than one person proofread it for you—show it to your professors to review. It must be completely error-free.
- Avoid padding your vita because you feel you don't have much to list. Do not list high school accomplishments or excessive details about activities you have completed en route to your bachelor's degree.
- Do not list irrelevant personal information, such as height, weight, or general health. List hobbies only if you think they make you look like a more well rounded individual.
- Try not to list categories of your vita if you have only one accomplishment in that category (like the outlining rule, you need a B. for every A.). The exception to this rule would be if you have only one publication—it is so worthy of note, the category will draw the attention to this accomplishment. Remember, publication credit is the number one secondary selection criterion for graduate admissions committees (see Table 3.6).
- When using category headings and subheadings, don't get too ambitious. This is where copying the format of a faculty member may be a bad idea; don't have a "Grants and Contracts" section if you have no grants or contracts.

Plous (1998c) also offers an example of a sample vita, providing some organizational tips. Some of the categories you might want to think about in your vita include the following:

- Personal information (address, phone number, perhaps birthdate)
- Education (degrees earned, when and where)
- Honors and awards (list each, who awarded, and date awarded)
- Association memberships (relevant clubs and societies, student affiliate status)
- Professional experience (beginning with college, list jobs relevant to the major)
- Research interests (if applicable and appropriate)

- Current research and teaching experience (if applicable and appropriate)
- Professional presentations (titles, organizations, in APA format if possible)
- Publications (use APA format, be careful with "in press," "under review")
- References (list names, titles, and addresses of three to four people whom you have asked)

For more tips on preparing a vita, see Appendix B.

Letters of Recommendation. Your letters of recommendation serve as the third component of the big three primary selection criteria. Letters of recommendation are interesting and somewhat different from the GPA or your GRE scores. Although others certainly have some degree of influence over GRE and GPA, your professors have direct influence over the letters of recommendations given. You are going to need to choose people who know your professional development, skills, and abilities and know them *well*. For a faculty member to get to know you this well, you are going to have to get involved outside of the classroom. It takes more than being a good book student to get superb letters of recommendation. In fact, Table 3.7 presents a listing of items that your letter writers might be asked write about you. By inspecting this list carefully, you'll realize that you have to *interact personally* with faculty members for them to recognize your talents to the degree that it benefits you in a letter of recommendation.

Table 3.7: Possible Characteristics to Be Described in Letters of Recommendation

• Academic achievement	• Flexibility, adaptiveness
• Research ability, experience, or potential	• Ability to work independently
• Teaching potential or experience	• Knowledge of the field
• Verbal skills, public speaking ability	• General knowledge base
• Writing skills, level of writing proficiency	• Desire to achieve, seriousness of purpose, initiative
• Industriousness, motivation, perseverance, energy level, drive	• Professionalism, maturity
• Quantitative abilities	• Social awareness, level of concern for others
• Creativity, originality, imagination	• Physical grooming, personal appearance
• Analytical ability	• Character, honesty, integrity, ethical and moral standards
• Leadership skills, level of respect accorded by others	• Ability to work with others, teamwork potential, cooperativeness
• Sociability, social skills, ability to get along with peers	• Dependability, level of responsibility
• Emotional stability, level of emotional adjustment	• Potential as a teacher
• Judgment, ability to make sound decisions, ability to reason	• Potential as a practitioner

Note. From *The Complete Guide to Graduate School Admission: Psychology and Related Fields*, by P. Keith-Speigel, 1991, Hillsdale, NJ: Erlbaum.

This is quite a list! If you are a student in one class with a faculty member, do the bare minimum work, never speak up in class, and never have a conversation with the faculty member outside of class, then that faculty member will have a difficult time with almost all of the ideas presented in Table 3.7. Whom should you ask? Keith-Spiegel (1991) found that the best sources for letters are from (a) a mentor with whom the applicant has done considerable work, (b) an applicant's professor who is also well-known and highly respected, (c) an employer on a job related to the applicant's professional goals, and (d) the department chair.

In her survey of writers of letters of recommendation, Keith-Spiegel (1991) asked faculty to rate particular behaviors or attitudes that letter writers want to write about most. Examine this list carefully (see Table 3.8), and think about what your letter writer is going to write about you. The left column presents the best options, whereas the right column presents the worst options.

Table 3.8: What Letter Writers Want and Do Not Want to Write About	
Student Behavior in the Classroom	
BEST	WORST
Seems very interested in the course	Cheats on an exam
Usually has good answer to questions in class	Plagiarizes a written assignment
Very attentive during lecture	Sleeps during lectures
Disagrees with opinions but in a respectful way	Talks to neighbors during lectures
Asks lots of questions in class	Sneers/rolls eyes during your lecture
Student Behavior Outside of Class	
BEST	WORST
Drops by office occasionally to comment on topic that has sparked some interest	Is openly hostile toward you
	Is very complementary but manipulative
Comes to office during office hours for assistance	Is flirtatious and seductive
Always smiles and says hi in the hallways	Is openly critical of you
Personal Characteristics	
BEST	WORST
Highly motivated to achieve	Arrogant
Responsible and dependable	Always depressed
Professional and mature manner and attitude	Silly
Very likable	Requires considerable, structured direction
Miscellaneous Behaviors and Characteristics	
BEST	WORST
Top student in the class	Caught cheating on one exam, appeared genuinely contrite and promised to change
Puts extra effort into term paper, class assignment	
Top 5% (GPA) in graduating class	Dresses and grooms very unconventionally
Shows up frequently to departmental colloquia	

Note. From *The Complete Guide to Graduate School Admission: Psychology and Related Fields*, by P. Keith-Speigel, 1991, Hillsdale, NJ: Erlbaum.

The Personal Statement. Although the letters of recommendation communicate the faculty members' perspectives about you, you also have the opportunity to present yourself. Most graduate programs require applicants to submit something called a personal statement (or statement of intent, or autobiographical statement, or letter of intent). This activity is becoming more and more important in the admissions process (Landrum et al., 1994). It allows you to provide valuable background information about yourself, and it also provides the graduate admissions committee with a writing sample. The requirements for completing this task are about as varied as most graduate programs—there is not a uniform method or procedure to follow. Hence, you need to make sure that you completely satisfy the requirements of each school when you are preparing your personal statement.

Keith-Spiegel (1991) found that in the personal statement instructions that she examined, 13 themes emerged. One point to be stressed—*do not write a single one-size-fits-all letter for all schools*. Do your homework, and give the committee the answers it wants, not a generic statement that vaguely addresses the school's information needs. To help personalize your responses, you may wish to closely examine the 13 themes listed below. Also, addressing these issues should help you focus on why you want to go to graduate school, what you want to accomplish with your degree, and how best to get from here to there.

1. **Career plans** (Tell us about your plans, What do you see yourself doing five to ten years from now?)
2. **General interest areas** (What are your academic interests?)
3. **Research experiences** (Have you had any research experiences? What types of work did you do as a research assistant?)
4. **Academic objectives** (Why are you interested in graduate study? What can our graduate program do for you?)
5. **Clinical or other field experience/practicum/internship** (Tell us about any of these experiences that you may have had.)
6. **Academic background and achievements** (What should we know about your academic work? Are your GRE scores and GPA representative of your ability?)
7. **What do you see in us** (Why did you choose us? What can you do for our graduate program?)
8. **Motivation** (Why did you choose this area of graduate study? What events shaped your current career aspirations?)
9. **Personal material** (Tell us about yourself. What do you think we should know about you?)
10. **Autobiography** (Provide a brief biographical sketch. Tell us a bit about your background.)
11. **Specific graduate faculty of interest** (Cite two faculty members who most closely represent your own interests in psychology. Whom would you like to work with in our graduate program?)
12. **Anything else we should know?**
13. **Special skills** (Languages known, mathematics or computer skills)

One final note on this topic—be sure to answer the questions exactly. Graduate admissions committee members will actually read your personal statement, so make sure that you answer the questions that you are asked. Answer completely and concisely.

Research Experience. As alluded to earlier, research experience is becoming a growing influence on the admissions process. It is at the top of the secondary selection criteria, and by serving as a research assistant you will gain valuable knowledge, skills, and abilities (see Chapter 4), and you will likely have enough meaningful interactions with a faculty member through the research process that he or she will be able to write you a strong letter of recommendation. Plus, psychology is an empirical science—we investigate and test our theories and hypotheses about the nature of human behavior—research skills lay at the core of this discipline.

Match or Fit With the Program. Finally, you need to carefully consider your own personal goals (answering the 13 themes above will help you) with respect to the goals and orientation of the graduate schools to which you are applying. The "match" or "fit" between you and the school is not to be underestimated. In a study by Landrum et al. (1994), graduate admissions committee members were asked to describe the exact procedures and decision-making rules they followed in the selection process. Content analysis of these decision protocols indicated that the most frequent strategy used in selection was the match between the applicant and the school and faculty. On another level, although the prospects of gaining admission may be daunting at this point, you don't want to go to any school just for the sake of going to graduate school. You might be admitted, but if the program is not a good match or good fit, you may be miserable and drop out (this chapter ends with some of the acceptance and persistence rates in graduate school). A disastrous first experience may impact everything you attempt to do later in psychology. We would encourage you not to underestimate the importance of the match or fit between you and the schools you are applying to.

On the other hand, it is more positive to visualize your acceptance into graduate school and the opportunity to materialize your goals. According to Appleby (1990), there may be two general types of students in graduate school: students who find the experience unpleasant, to be endured, survived, and eventually forgotten, and students who thrive in the system, are respected by the faculty, and end up with the best employment prospects. If you would rather be in the latter group, here are some of the characteristics (Bloom & Bell, 1979) of those individuals who became graduate school superstars:

- Visibility—highly motivated, seem to always be in the department at all hours
- Willingness to work hard—seen by faculty as hard-working, persevering
- Reflection of program values—seen by faculty as having professional values that lead to research and scholarly success
- True interest in research—engaged in research projects in addition to the master's thesis and dissertation; curious enough about a problem and wanted to see data on it
- Development of a relationship with a mentor—listen, learn, grow, and are productive through a close working relationship with one or two faculty members

As Appleby (1990) alluded to, none of these characteristics mention intellect, GPA, or writing ability. Perhaps those are constants that are expected in all graduate school students. The above list constitutes qualities *over and above* those needed for entrance into the graduate program.

We have presented a fairly extensive overview of the opportunities that are available with a master's degree or doctorate, the outlook for the job market, and a review of the process needed to gain admission to a graduate program. Now for the statistics. Of course, your chances for admission into graduate school depend on all of the factors we presented in this chapter. Your chances also depend on the number of openings available, your competition for those openings (remember you have regional, national, and perhaps international competition for those slots), etc. Table 3.9 presents the acceptances and enrollments for various programs at both the master's and doctoral levels.

Table 3.9: Acceptance and Enrollment Percentages for Doctoral and Master's Program by Specialty Area in Psychology

Doctoral Program	Percent of Students Who Apply and Are Accepted	Percent of Students Who Are Accepted and Enroll
Clinical	6%	71%
Counseling	9%	85%
School	27%	75%
Cognitive	22%	50%
Developmental	17%	70%
Educational	50%	75%
Experimental	12%	76%
General/social/personality	11%	50%
Industrial/organizational	14%	61%
Physiological, neurosciences, biological or comparative	18%	60%
Psychometrics/quantitative	33%	60%
Other programs	18%	75%
All programs	13%	70%
Master's Program	**Percent of Students Who Apply and Are Accepted**	**Percent of Students Who Are Accepted and Enroll**
Clinical	41%	61%
Counseling	59%	77%
School	43%	78%
Cognitive	N/A	N/A
Developmental	50%	56%
Educational	54%	84%
Experimental	53%	66%
General/social/personality	41%	71%
Industrial/organizational	41%	64%
Physiological, neurosciences, biological or comparative	N/A	N/A
Psychometrics/quantitative	N/A	N/A
Other programs	51%	68%
All programs	45%	68%

Note. From "Acceptance and Enrollment Rates in the Fall of 1996 in U.S. Graduate Departments of Psychology by Degree Level and Program Area," American Psychological Association, 1998, [online], retrieved November 28, 1998, at http://research.apa.org./inserttable4.html. N/A means not available.

Of the total number of students starting a doctoral program in 1990, by 1996, 10% had formally left the program without earning the degree (APA, 1998k). For master's students in the same time frame, 9% left the program without the degree. Very few doctoral and master's students (10% and 9%, respectively) drop out of graduate programs without gaining the degree they intended to earn. It is quite a process, but that is what it takes to become a psychologist. If it were easy, many people would do it, and the value of the skills and abilities learned would be lessened.

Chapter 4
UNDERGRADUATE OPPORTUNITIES

If you've carefully read the first three chapters of this book, one of the main themes is that you should get involved outside the classroom to obtain the full range of skills and abilities you need to be successful in psychology. These experiences are invaluable to you whether you are going to graduate school or not. This chapter directly addresses such opportunities as research and teaching assistantships, field experiences and internships, and getting involved in organizations such as Psi Chi and your local psychology club.

These extracurricular activities give you an opportunity to increase your skills in applying the psychological principles you are learning in the classroom. Also, reading about research results and being involved in collecting data and actually doing research are two very different things. Furthermore, by being involved, you give your psychology faculty more opportunities to get to know you and become familiar with your professional abilities and potential. Moreover, these faculty-student collaborations can often lead to strong letters of recommendation. If you are a student in my class, I have a relatively limited exposure to your skills and abilities. If you are a student in my class and also did research with me for a year, did an off-campus internship, and served as a teaching assistant for another professor, I'll be able to write a stronger letter because you are a more well rounded student (and because you worked with more than one faculty member, you'll have additional sources of letters of recommendation). Whether you're looking for a job with your bachelor's degree or looking for admission into graduate school, you need to make yourself a competitive applicant. If you can take advantage of some of the opportunities presented in this chapter, you'll be well on your way to achieving a competitive edge.

RESEARCH AND TEACHING ASSISTANTSHIPS

In an article by Clay (1998), Eugene Zechmeister, the director of the undergraduate program at Loyola University (in Illinois), said, "I know this will sound sacrilegious, but skills are actually more important than course content" (p. 2). He's right. Courses lay the foundation for information and knowledge about psychology, but that information and knowledge will do little good without the skills needed to utilize that knowledge. Since its inception in 1879, psychology has been an empirical, research-based discipline. Teaching and research focus on the heart of the matter—we expand our knowledge about psychology through research, and it is this research that gives us the subject matter that we teach. In this context, it seems perfectly appropriate that as an undergraduate, you need to have some active, hands-on exposure to the research and teaching aspects of psychology.

What is a **research assistantship**? It is an opportunity for undergraduate students to assist a faculty member (or members) in a program of research. When you serve as a research assistant (RA), you'll actually be involved in *doing* the research rather than reading about it in your textbook or journal article. As alluded to earlier, there are a number of advantages to serving as a research assistant:

- Acquisition of skills and knowledge not easily gained in the classroom
- Opportunity to work one on one with a faculty member
- Opportunity to contribute to the advancements of the science of psychology
- Exposure to general research techniques helpful for pursuing later graduate work
- Opportunity to practice written and oral communication skills by preparing for and attending professional conferences and preparing and submitting manuscripts for publication
- Cultivation of a mentoring relationship with a faculty member that will be helpful for acquiring letters of recommendation

Depending on the type of research a faculty member is doing, and what area of psychology he or she is studying, there may be additional advantages for you to get involved in research. What do you do as a research assistant? This is best answered by asking the faculty member directly. Although the answer will vary from research topic to research topic, the following list describes some of the general tasks and duties that you may be asked to perform:

- Administer research sessions with student participants (this procedure is called data collection, or "running subjects")
- Score and/or code the collected data, and enter them into a spreadsheet or statistical analysis program (such as SPSS)
- Conduct literature searches using resources like *PsycINFO* and Social Sciences Citation Index; search your local library database for books and periodicals; make copies of articles available; order unavailable resources through interlibrary loan; general library research (for more on this topic, see Chapter 5)
- Work with the faculty member to develop new research ideas; often these ideas are developed from research just completed, the need that arises from a particular situation, or reviews of the existing literature
- Attend lab meetings with other undergraduate research assistants, discuss research ideas, collaborate on projects
- Use word processing, spreadsheet, scheduling, and statistical analysis programs to complete the research project
- Work on project outcomes so they can be submitted for presentations at local or regional conferences, prepare abstracts; if accepted, work on poster or oral presentations of the research materials for presentation at professional conferences (see Tables 4.1 and 4.2 later in this chapter)
- Collaborate with faculty member to submit work to an appropriate journal to share the results with the broad scientific community

Your commitment to serve as a research assistant is a weighty one—you will be given some responsibility to see that several aspects of the research process get done. It is a serious commitment that should not be taken lightly. The faculty member you are working with will be counting on you to get things done, and done right; here is the place you want to shine. By watching you complete tasks and by observing you take on more and more responsibility, your faculty mentor will have plenty of good things to write about in those letters of recommendation. However, the reverse is true. If you don't take the commitment seriously, if you make repeated mistakes on important tasks, then the recommendations the faculty member can make will be weakened. If you choose to take on this commitment, know what you are getting into. At many schools, research assistants can also earn course credit—it may have a title such as directed research, independent study, or supervised research—and these credits are often senior-level upper-division psychology credits. Take advantage of this opportunity; these credits make a positive impression on your transcripts.

Getting Involved. How do you get involved as a research assistant? Here are some suggested methods:

1. Review the listing of the faculty in your psychology department and their research interests. You might find this information available in a pamphlet in the department, as part of advising materials, or perhaps on the department's Web site. If there is no such list available, encourage your Psi Chi chapter or local psychology club to create one.
2. Then, make appointments with faculty members, preferably during their posted office hours, to discuss research possibilities.
3. When you meet with the faculty members, be yourself. Let them know that you are willing to work hard on their program of research. Ask them about the specific requirements that they expect from their research assistants. You'll want to know about the duration of the project, what your responsibilities will be, grading practices, weekly time commitment, etc. Also, what length of commitment is the faculty member looking for? Some may want RA help only for a semester, some will ask for a one-year commitment, and some may want longer. Here is another reason to try to keep to the timelines suggested in Chapter 3 in mind—you want to have enough coursework completed early enough so you can have enough time to do some meaningful research with a faculty member (who might be expecting a one-year commitment).
4. If you come to an agreement with a faculty member to serve as an RA, there may be additional forms that you have to fill out to register for credit. The faculty member should be able to assist you in getting these forms and getting them filled out and turned in correctly.

While there are many benefits for psychology majors to be involved in research, there are also benefits for the students who participate in research. In a study conducted by Landrum and Chastain (1995), participants in research at a large western university significantly agreed with statements such as "I was treated fairly and with respect during my research session," "The research experience is a good way to add variety to introductory psychology," and "I think that participating in this project helped me understand research better." The primary justification for requiring students to participate in research (always with alternative options, however) is that it provides a learning experience for the student. Studies such as the one by Landrum and Chastain

(1995) are important to verify that students themselves feel that the experience is valuable. For more on this topic and related research topics, see Chastain and Landrum (1999).

Paper and Poster Presentations. By becoming involved in research, you'll give yourself a number of additional opportunities as well. For instance, if the results of your research turn out favorably, you may be able to make a presentation at a local or regional professional conference. Even if the results don't turn out as you would have liked, you may be able to present at a more student-centered session at that local or regional conference, such as the Psi Chi session at a regional conference. Two types of "presentations" are typically made at conferences—papers and posters. A paper presentation is usually a 12- to 15-minute talk given to an audience about your research project. You may have handouts for your audience, or use audiovisual aids (such as overhead transparencies, slides, or a PowerPoint presentation), or do both. Table 4.1 offers suggestions for oral paper presentations.

Table 4.1: Paper Presentation Suggestions

- Decide on a limited number of significant ideas that you want your audience to comprehend and remember.
- Minimize the nitty-gritty details (like procedure, data analysis strategies, etc.) and highlight the main points.
- State clearly, without jargon, the point of your research, what you found, and what it means—try to tell a good story.
- Write out your presentation as a mini-lecture, with a clear outline. You may use these as cues while you make your presentation.
- Practice your presentation out loud, making sure it fits into the time restraints, and have a small audience listen to you to give you constructive feedback.
- Do not read your paper. Talk to your audience about what you did to complete the work. At a professional conference, it is very irritating to be read to—everyone there can already read.
- Try to speak loudly and clearly enough to hold the attention of your audience. There will be distractions—people coming in, others getting up and leaving. Don't be offended. Try to be enthusiastic enough to sustain interest over these distractions.
- State your final conclusions and end on time. Be prepared to answer audience questions if time permits.
- Bring copies of your paper to the conference, or provide a sign-up sheet for persons who may want copies to be sent to them.

Note. From "Tips for Paper/Poster Presentation," 1998, *Eye on Psi Chi, 2,* pp. 35, 42.

A poster presentation is substantially different from a paper presentation. In the paper presentation, you present your findings to a large audience in a relatively short time period. The method is somewhat impersonal, but it is an efficient method to present the materials to a large number of people. In a poster presentation, you present your research work in a poster format for a longer period of time (1½–2 hours). You are available to speak personally with "audience members" who are interested in your work. In the poster session, you will probably reach fewer people, but you'll have more personal conversations with people who are genuinely interested in your work. Your poster is displayed on a freestanding bulletin board in a session with other posters, in a room large enough to hold the posters, the presenters, and the people who wander through the session. The audience picks and chooses what presentations to attend to; they can acquire more detailed information from the poster authors in this one-on-one conversation format. Table 4.2 presents tips for preparing for and making poster presentations.

Table 4.2: Poster Presentation Suggestions

- Construct the poster to include the title, authors, affiliations, and a description of the research.
- Minimize the detail that is presented, and try to use jargon-free statements.
- Pictures, tables, and figures are especially useful and helpful in poster presentations.
- If possible, use color in your poster panels.
- Make sure the lettering is neatly done and large enough to be read from a distance—poster session attendees will quickly scan the content before stopping to inquire further—use fonts not smaller than 18 point; try to use 24 point or larger if possible.
- Don't overwhelm the viewer with excessive amounts of information; try to construct a poster display that encourages and enhances conversation.
- Be ready to pin up and take down your poster at the specified times (you may want to bring your own thumbtacks or pushpins); often poster sessions are scheduled back to back, so you want to be on time so the next session can also be on time.

Note. From "Tips for Paper/Poster Presentation," 1998, *Eye on Psi Chi, 2,* pp. 35, 42.

Carmody (1998) surveyed graduates of psychology programs who were Psi Chi members as undergraduates about their views and perceptions of value about undergraduate presentations. One of the questions addressed who inspired the student to become a research assistant. Carmody found that the motivators to get involved were (a) course instructors (56%), (b) self-motivation (55%), (c) mentors (33%), and (d) fellow students (14%). Why did students choose to do research? Students mentioned personal challenge (89%), for graduate school purposes (76%), encouragement from a professor (59%), and for career aspirations (34%). "All groups strongly agreed that presentations helped to advance one's career and increase one's skills. Presenters agreed more strongly than nonpresenters that going beyond coursework was fun and promoted personal growth" (Carmody, 1998, p. 13).

If you have the opportunity, try to get involved as a research assistant. If you do not have the opportunity, try to create it. When you work with a faculty member on a research project, it is a mutually beneficial relationship. What does the faculty member get out of this relationship? He or she gets a hard-working, eager student to do some of the labor-intensive portions of any research project. Many faculty, especially those at institutions that do not have a graduate program in psychology, depend on undergraduate students to help further their own research agenda. If this research culture does not exist at your school, try to develop it. Find that student-friendly faculty member who realizes how important the research opportunity is to you, and chances are you'll find a way to collaborate on some sort of research project. Many faculty members have ideas for studies that they would like to do but don't have the time nor the assistance. A talented undergraduate student assisting that faculty member can make that project happen. Davis (1995) clearly articulated the advantages faculty members receive from conducting collaborative research with undergraduate students:

1. Witnessing student professional growth and development—perhaps the best reward
2. Facilitating reviews of the current literature in a particular research area, keeping current
3. Keeping analytic skills fine-tuned and active through the design and the completion of research
4. Generating useful and meaningful empirical data
5. Maintaining and expanding professional networks through attending conventions, especially for students
6. Enhancing effectiveness as a teacher through active involvement in research

What about being a **teaching assistant**? Serving as a teaching assistant is usually much less involved and time-consuming than being a research assistant. Usually, a teaching assistant helps a faculty member for one semester (or term) in the administration of a specific course, such as Introduction to Psychology or Statistical Methods. You might have a number of different responsibilities as a teaching assistant, depending on the instructor, the course, the history of the institution in utilizing teaching assistants, etc. Below is a list of some of the tasks you might be asked to do:

- Attend class and take notes so that students have a resource available to get notes when they miss class

- Hold office hours where you may conduct tutoring sessions, review notes with students, review class assignments before they are due, and answer class-related questions

- Help to proctor exams, help to grade exams and/or term papers, and help to enter these scores in the instructor's gradebook

- Hold general review sessions prior to tests where groups of students can receive supplemental instruction over course-related topics

- Help the instructor in the general administration and completion of the course to provide the best experience possible for enrolled students

The teaching assistantship is an excellent way to build a mentoring relationship with a faculty member. Almost certainly during the course of the semester, a situation will occur where you can step in and provide some real assistance to a faculty member teaching a course. These are the types of events that faculty members will be thankful for and may write about in a letter of recommendation. Also, many of our students tell us that sitting in on the general psychology course is a great study strategy when they prepare for the GRE Advanced Test in Psychology. There are significant benefits for those who serve as a teaching assistant. If you are faced with a choice of serving as a research assistant or as a teaching assistant, try to do both. You'll be busy, but you'll gain valuable skills, abilities, and knowledge for your future.

FIELD EXPERIENCES AND INTERNSHIPS

Field experiences and internships are opportunities to learn about and apply psychological principles out of the classroom and in the field. These placements are in agencies that relate to some aspect of human behavior—hence, you can imagine that many places are possible internship sites. They also differ from teaching and research assistantships in that a nonfaculty member at the placement site typically supervises field experiences. A faculty member usually serves as the campus coordinator of the field experience or internship program.

If you do an internship in your community, what might you do? You might be an intern at a social service agency, assisting in intake interviews, psychological testing, report writing, and behavior modification. You might be an intern in a human resources department, where you learn to administer structured interviews, write performance appraisals, and coordinate special projects and programs. The opportunities are endless. In some instances, if an internship opportunity is not available to meet your needs, you may be able to arrange your own specialized internship.

What are the benefits of participating in an internship? The following list was compiled from Jessen (1988), Mount Saint Vincent University (1998), and the University of Michigan at Dearborn (1998):

- Practical, on-the-job experience
- Development of professional and personal confidence, responsibility, and maturity
- Understanding of the realities of the work world and acquire human relations skills
- Opportunity to examine a career choice closely and make professional contacts
- Opportunity to test the ideas learned in the classroom out in the field
- Opportunity to make contacts with potential employers
- Enhancement of classroom experiences
- Learning what careers *not* to pursue
- Development of skills that are difficult to learn and practice in the classroom
- College credit
- Possible earnings to help offset college expenses

How do you find out about field experiences and internships? There is probably a key faculty member in your department who makes sure that internships sites are suitable, establishes the policies and procedures for working with agencies, ensures that grades are submitted on time, handles inquiries from internship supervisors, etc. Find that person. Most departments have some well-established connections with agencies in and around your community; if you want to do something where the relationship is not established, you may have to do more of the groundwork yourself. This latter approach gives you the chance to show some initiative and really demonstrate to your internship site your willingness to work hard and persevere at the task.

What will you do as an intern? Ideally, you'll get a realistic glimpse of the types of tasks necessary for success in a particular office or agency. Where appropriate, you will have the opportunity to acquire new skills and hone those that you already have. Internships are not designed to provide agencies with extra office staff or gophers, although you may occasionally be asked to help pitch in when agencies are under time and budget constraints. Although you might not be running a group therapy session, you might sit in on such a session and help facilitate that session under the supervision of appropriately trained and licensed personnel. In addition to these tasks, there may be group supervisory sessions if your site has multiple interns, and your on-campus faculty internship coordinator will probably require that you keep a weekly journal of your intern experiences (Jessen, 1988).

The internship opportunity is a valuable opportunity to have a realistic job tryout. It will tell you about the type of environment you would work in and the type of economic support you might receive in doing your job, give you an example of the clientele that you might work with under particular conditions, etc.   Although most students have an invigorating internship experience, we have known some students who come back from an internship with the conclusion "I definitely do *not* want to do that for my entire career." This decision is a very valuable outcome of the internship process. Although it is unfortunate that the student didn't enjoy the internship process, it is better to have an unsatisfying 16-week internship experience than to go to a graduate program to get a degree to enter a job that leads to a lifetime of misery.

Related to these field experiences and internships are some other options to gain practical, hands-on experiences. You might not have all these opportunities available on your campus, or they might exist under different names, so look carefully. These other methods of getting involved include service learning, peer advising, and paraprofessional programs. Service learning (in some cases, called the fourth credit option) involves adding one credit to a three-credit class and involves providing volunteer services to the community. Supervised by the course instructor, students receive an additional one credit for completing the volunteer service. Some psychology departments have a peer-advising program that provides academic advising services to undergraduate majors. This program is an opportunity for undergraduates to become involved in interviewing and conversational skills, and gain professional and personal confidence in dealing with the issues related to undergraduate education. Additionally, some psychology departments that have a counseling center affiliated with them also have a paraprofessional program.   In a paraprofessional program, undergraduates are trained in some therapeutic approaches and, under the supervision of counseling faculty, practice these skills by providing workshops to other students. Check with your department to see if any of these types of outside-of-class opportunities are available for you. As an example, see the description of the Paraprofessional Program at Boise State University presented in Table 4.3. The details of such a program might differ at your university, or you may have the same program but under a different name.

Table 4.3: Sample Characteristics of a Paraprofessional Program
Who Are the Paraprofessionals?
The "paraprofessionals" are undergraduate and graduate students who receive training in the areas of test anxiety, career planning, and stress management. Paraprofessionals come from a variety of fields including communication, education, sociology, psychology, social work, nursing, and business.
What Do They Do?
The paraprofessionals co-lead workshops at the Counseling Center and for student groups on campus. Paraprofessionals receive extensive training and supervision in the relevant areas and in the interactive skills needed to successfully lead workshops.
Why Are They Here?
First, the Paraprofessional Program expands the kinds of services the Counseling Center is able to offer by training students to work with frequently occurring issues that can be approached in a structured fashion. Second, interacting with a peer is sometimes more helpful than meeting with a professional counselor or psychologist. As students, the paraprofessionals have a special understanding of the social and academic pressures students face.
How Much Time Does It Take to Be a Paraprofessional?
Usually a minimum of 7 hours per week or 90 hours per semester. This includes a 1 ½-hour weekly class held on Wednesdays from 3:00-4:30 PM, ½ hour of weekly supervision, and 2 hours co-leading a workshop. Also 2-3 hours studying workshop material plus weekly sessions of 1-2 hours planning with another paraprofessional co-leader are necessary. A mandatory two-day training session is held the week prior to the first week of classes.

Table 4.3: Sample Characteristics of a Paraprofessional Program (continued)
What Happens When Paraprofessionals Conduct Workshops?
Paraprofessionals present information, lead exercises, and help the students explore their concerns and establish plans for action. Paraprofessionals often make referrals to appropriate campus resources.
What Are the Benefits of Being a Paraprofessional?
The training and experience provide firsthand experience that may better qualify you for future jobs—especially in the human services field. The class is a pass/fail internship that gives 2 hours of upper-division credit.
What Kinds of People Is the Program Looking For?
We are looking for full-time (8 hours or more) degree-seeking graduate or undergraduate students of at least junior standing with a minimum GPA of 2.5 who are interested in helping other people. We are also looking for individuals who are interested in staying with the program for more than one semester.
Note. From "BSU Counseling and Testing Center Paraprofessional Program," Boise State University Department of Counseling, 1998, [Online.] Retrieved January 7, 1999, at http://www.boisestate.edu/counsel/workshop/parapro.htm.

ORGANIZATIONAL INVOLVEMENT

The opportunities discussed in this chapter (research assistant, teaching assistant, field experience, and internship) all focus on skill and ability development. Organizational involvement also provides the chance to enhance knowledge about the discipline and to find opportunities to network within it. On a regional or national level you can become involved in organizations designed for students, and/or join organizations (as a student affiliate) designed for psychology professionals. In addition, you may have some opportunities on your own campus to get involved and gain valuable information and skills.

The best-known organization explicitly designed for students is Psi Chi, the National Honor Society in Psychology (www.psichi.org). Psi Chi was founded in 1929 for the purpose of encouraging, stimulating, and maintaining excellence in scholarship, and for the advancement of psychology. Psi Chi membership is conferred on students who have met minimum qualifications at institutions where there is a chapter (there is an application process, and not all students can be members). If you are a student at a community or junior college (and if there is a chapter), you can become a member of Psi Beta (www.ivc.cc.ca.us/psibeta), Psi Chi's sister honor society.

Psi Chi has grown into an impressive organization benefiting students on many levels. Involvement in your local chapter can lead to opportunities to develop leadership skills, and Psi Chi members are often the most involved and well connected psychology students around. On the regional and national levels, Psi Chi has various offerings. At major regional and national conferences held each year, Psi Chi has an important presence in promoting the scholarly achievements of undergraduate psychology students. Psi Chi has a long tradition of providing student-friendly programming at these conferences. The quarterly magazine *Eye on Psi Chi* is packed with practical advice and useful information about pursuing a career in psychology—in every issue you will be able to find at least one article directly related to your interests. Psi Chi also publishes the *Psi Chi Journal of Undergraduate Research*, a national, peer-reviewed, scholarly journal dedicated to undergraduate student research. (Dr. Stephen Davis, one of the authors of this book, is currently the editor of this journal.) All three of your authors were Psi

Chi members as undergraduate psychology students! If your school does not have a Psi Chi chapter, consult with a faculty member about starting a chapter. You can find more information about this process on the Psi Chi Web site (www.psichi.org).

Even if your institution does not have a Psi Chi chapter, there may be a psychology club on campus. Usually, these clubs are open to anyone with an interest in psychology, and members do not have to be psychology majors. Often, students who are unable to join Psi Chi (perhaps due to GPA problems) can be active and involved as members of the local psychology club. On campuses where both groups exist, they often coordinate activities and opportunities for the benefit of all students interested in psychology.

In addition, you can gain more information and knowledge about the discipline through learning about the two major national organizations for psychologists, the American Psychological Association (www.apa.org) and the American Psychological Society (www.psychologicalscience.org). Much of the up-to-date career information in Chapters 2 and 3 of this book was gathered and published by the American Psychological Association. Also, APA offers a student affiliate status for undergraduates where you can join the association for a reduced fee, and receive discounts on books and journals with membership. Both organizations can provide valuable advice for entering the profession and help keep members informed about the critical issues in society that have an impact on the practice and science of psychology.

One last recommendation is that you get involved in activities in your own department! Often during the academic year your department may sponsor guest speakers, or faculty members may participate in some sort of colloquium series (sometimes held over the lunchtime, these are called "brown bags"). As a student, you want your faculty to be supportive of your efforts—you also need to be supportive of the faculty. Attending such presentations also gives you a chance to hear about faculty research, which might interest you and lead to an opportunity to serve as a research assistant. Perhaps hearing about research being conducted at a homeless shelter in your community might inspire you to think about an internship. Attending these departmental events shows your commitment to psychology and your general interest in the happenings of the department. Taking advantage of the opportunities highlighted in this chapter should lead to a more well rounded education and give you the skills, abilities, and knowledge to make you more marketable with your bachelor's degree or better qualified as a candidate for graduate school. It's up to you to seize the opportunity!

MISTER BOFFO

© Tribune Media Services, Inc. All rights reserved. Reprinted with permission.

Chapter 5
LOCATING PRIOR RESEARCH

Beginning with this chapter and continuing throughout the rest of this book, we will focus on the skills and abilities needed to navigate the psychology major and be a successful college student. In this chapter, we focus on how to find research that has already been conducted; in the next chapter we address how to write about it and your own research ideas. Before we cover how to find research that is already completed, you'll need to know what you are looking for. Sometimes, this task might be a paper or project idea that your instructor assigns, but you may also be asked to generate your own ideas for research projects (such as in an independent study, senior thesis, or perhaps even in a research methods/experimental design course).

GENERATING RESEARCH IDEAS

When they are asked about their own ideas for research, students are frequently stumped. How do you get these ideas? How do experimental psychologists get ideas for doing research? The following guidelines, based in part on Martin (1991), should give you some starting points in thinking about topics to study:

1. **Observation**. Just look at the world around you and feel free to tap into your own interests. If you enjoy being a people-watcher, go watch some people and be willing to wonder about their behavior and why people behave the way they do. Remember that the better questions to be asked in a research-type format are (a) repeatable, (b) observable, and (c) testable.
2. **Vicarious observation**. Vicarious observation is a sophisticated way of saying observe through the observations of others. Simply put, read about research that has already been done and then think about follow-up studies that are needed. Find a psychological journal in the library with articles in your favorite subject area, and look for ideas and issues to explore.
3. **Expand on your own previous ideas**. Perhaps in other courses you have written a paper, done a project, studied a topic, or heard a lecture that you found especially interesting. Why not pursue that avenue of interest through a research project?
4. **Focus on a practical problem**. Many students select topics that are of practical, everyday concern as opposed to theoretical, basic research. Select a facet of real life that interests you, and study it systematically as your research project.

When you work with a faculty member on a research project, you may not be able to select what you want to study. In fact, that faculty member might want you to generate research ideas specific to his or her research domain. In that case, much of the work is already focused for you—what will be important here is that you have a firm understanding of the literature. In any research project, it is critical to have an understanding of the work that has come before you. Hence, the literature review is a critical component of the research project.

THE LITERATURE REVIEW

Each manuscript published in a scholarly journal reviews (to some extent) prior, relevant studies and develops a background to the problem of interest. This introductory portion of the journal article is called the literature review. By reviewing previous research, you set the theoretical foundation for your topic. The author also discusses why the present study is valuable and states the hypotheses that will be tested. This section organizes the articles you have identified as important.

Sometimes new researchers are so excited about the prospects of doing their own original research that they minimize or overlook the importance of the literature search. If you try to skip this step, it could be very costly in terms of your investment of time and energy to complete a research project. Also, if you have long-term goals of presenting the outcomes of your research at a professional conference and/or submitting a manuscript for publication, it will be absolutely necessary for you to have "done your homework," that is, review the literature and place your current work in the context of your particular area in psychology. There are a number of benefits that accrue from reviewing the literature:

- Maybe someone has already done something very similar to your idea. Why reinvent the wheel? Although there are a number of areas in psychology that are not well understood (hence ripe for new research efforts), other areas in the field are fairly well understood. You won't know which is which unless you review the literature.
- Other investigators might have already identified some of the key challenges to doing research in a particular area. Learn from their efforts and avoid their mistakes. Many publications end with a discussion of where future research should go—you might get an idea for your own research project just by reading and understanding what has already been done.
- New ideas in psychology (actually, in any science) must fit within the framework of existing ideas and theories. New theories can put forward new information, but those theories also must explain why former theories were wrong, inaccurate, or inappropriate. To be able to do the latter, you must be familiar with those former theories—hence the importance of the literature review.

THE SPECIAL ROLE OF REFERENCES

The references listed at the conclusion of a research report make the cited literature accessible to the reader. This documentation enables other scientists to locate and explore firsthand the prior research or theoretical sources that constitute the framework for the current research. The reference section is critically important because it is a demonstration of the scholarly nature of your work. The scientist and the critical thinker examine and use evidence to support ideas and contentions; you provide your evidence in the reference section (as well as in the results section). Be sure that, when you cite a source, you are familiar with the article. It can be a dangerous practice to cite references that you have never seen or actually read. This type of citation is called a reference from a secondary source and there are specific ways to list such references. Be careful: Your instructor or professionals just might be familiar with that reference. You should note that reference lists are *not* bibliographies. Bibliographies refer the interested reader to additional sources for further reading that were not necessarily cited in the manuscript through paraphrasing or direct quotation, and are not used in APA-style manuscripts. Remember that the reference section contains *only* the articles directly cited in the text of the paper.

LIBRARY RESEARCH STRATEGIES

At some level you have to choose or select a research topic. Again, the faculty member whom you are working with may dictate this choice, or it could be an assigned class project. Nevertheless, you will probably have some range of topics to select from within your specific areas of interest. The list in Table 5.1 should help in your choice of a topic. Inevitably, this choice also involves the next step, which is finding the background information.

Table 5.1: Tips for Selecting a Research Topic	
Check √	*Considerations/Recommendations*
	Try not to choose a topic that is too broad.
	Choose a topic that is of interest to you—choose an additional backup topic.
	Choose a topic that will enable you to read and understand the literature.
	Choose a topic that has resources available.
	Make sure that the resources are available in time for you to meet your deadlines.
	Read through the background information.
	If there is not enough information available, you may want to go to your backup topic.
	State your topic idea as a question—this will help you outline and frame your paper.
	Start making a list of key words to use in later searches.

Note. From "Choosing a Topic," University of California-Santa Cruz, 1998, [online], retrieved October 27, 1998, at http://bob.ucsc.edu/library/ref/instruction/research/topic/htm; "How to Select a Research Topic," Vanderbilt University, 1996, [online], retrieved October 27, 1998, at http://www.library.vanderbilt.edu/education.topic.html.

There are numerous library research strategies that you can use to find useful information. In the remainder of this section we'll cover how to (a) make the best use of books, (b) find journal articles, (c) use the Web, and (d) use other strategies that savvy researchers are familiar with. Perhaps one of the best tips we can offer is to be sure to utilize the reference librarians who are available to you. Not only can they help you determine the library's holdings, but they can also offer additional, specific search strategies for your particular library.

Books. With respect to *books*, there are at least two avenues to pursue. First, there are general reference books that can lead you to other sources, and then there are specific books in psychology that may be written about your topic. To find books in the latter category, you can use the search methods discussed in how to find journal articles. Here we summarize some of the reference-type books that might have some valuable information on your topic; these books can lead you to other resources of value (see Table 5.2).

Table 5.2: Using Books to Find Information

Subject Encyclopedias

Corsini, R. J. (Ed.). (1994). *Encyclopedia of psychology* (4 vol.). New York: Wiley.

Eysenck, H. J., Arnold, W., & Meili, R. (Eds.). (1972). *Encyclopedia of psychology* (3 vols.). New York: Herder and Herder.

Ramachandran, V. S. (Ed.). (1994). *Encyclopedia of human behavior* (4 vols.). San Diego: Academic Press.

Dictionaries

Goldenson, R. M. (Ed.). (1984). *Longman dictionary of psychology and psychiatry*. New York: Longman.

Popplestone, J. A., & McPherson, M. W. (1988). *Dictionary of concepts in general psychology*. New York: Greenwood Press.

Reber, A. S. (1985). *The Penguin dictionary of psychology*. London: Viking Press.

Research Guides and Bibliographies

Baxter, P. M. (1993). *Psychology: A guide to reference and information sources*. Englewood, CO: Libraries Unlimited.

McInnis, R. G. (1982). *Research guide for psychology*. Westport, CT: Greenwood Press.

Books

American Psychological Association. (1998). *PsycBOOKS: Books & chapters in psychology*. Arlington, VA: Author. (Published annually)

Impara, J. C., & Plake, B. S. (Eds.). (1998). *The thirteenth mental measurements yearbook*. Lincoln, NE: University of Nebraska Press. (Published biennially)

Murphy, L. L., Conoley, J. C., & Impara, J. C. (Eds.). (1994). *Tests in print IV*. Lincoln, NE: University of Nebraska Press.

Spence, J. T., Darley, J. M., & Foss, D. J. (Eds.). (1998). *Annual review of psychology*. Palo Alto, CA: Annual Reviews. (Published annually)

Yaremko, R. M. (Ed.). (1982). *Reference handbook of research and statistical methods in psychology*. New York: Harper & Row.

Note. From "Library Research Guides--Psychology," Brandeis University, 1998, [online], retrieved October 27, 1998, at http://www.library.brandeis.edu/resguides/subject/psycguide.html.

In addition to these resources, your university library has an electronic card catalog that contains the inventory of the library. Terminals for access to this database are probably located in the library and around campus, and may be available through an Internet/Web connection. In courses where research is time-dependent, you may want to get a jump-start on your library literature search because some of the books and journal articles that you need will probably not be available in your library. You can usually obtain these materials through *interlibrary loan*, but depending upon where this information has to come from, your request will probably take between two to six weeks to fill. Also, do not overlook other libraries in your community, such as the public library, other college and university libraries in your region, or perhaps even a hospital library if your topic is physically or medically related. Most college and university libraries are organized using the Library of Congress Cataloging System. Table 5.3 presents some of the more psychology-related categories for finding books in this system.

Table 5.3: Library of Congress Classification Schedules Related to Psychology	
Code	Area
BF 1-940	Psychology
BF 173-175	Psychoanalysis
BF 180-210	Experimental psychology
BF 231-299	Sensation
BF 309-499	Cognition, Perception
BF 501-504.3	Motivation
BF 511-593	Emotion
BF 608-635	Will, Choice
BF 636-637	Applied psychology
BF 660-685	Comparative psychology
BF 698-698.9	Personality
BF 699-711	Genetic psychology
BF 712-724.85	Developmental psychology
BF 721-723	Child psychology
BF 795-839.5	Temperament, Character
BF 840-861	Physiognomy
BF 866-885	Phrenology
BF 889-905	Graphology
BF 908-940	The Hand, Palmistry
BF 1001-1389	Parapsychology
BF 1404-1999	Occult sciences
HM 251-291	Social psychology
LB 5-3640	Theory and practice of education
LB 51-885	Systems of individual educators and writers
LB 1025-1050.7	Teaching, principles and practices
LB 1050.9-1091	Educational psychology
LB 1101-1139	Child study
LB 1131-1134	Psychical development
LB 1140-1140.5	Preschool education
LB 1141-1489	Kindergarten
LB 1501-1547	Primary education
LB 1555-1602	Elementary or public school education
LB 1603-1695	Secondary education, high schools
LB 1705-2286	Education and training of teachers
LB 2300-2430	Higher education
LB 2801-3095	School administration and organization
LB 3201-3325	School architecture and equipment
LB 3401-3499	School hygiene
LB 3525-3640	Special days, school life, student manners and customs

Note. From *LC Classification Outline*, Library of Congress, 1990, Washington, DC: Author.

Journal Articles. Although books are an important resource for information and leads to additional information, perhaps the most important communication mode of the results of psychological research comes in the form of journal articles. Journals have a more timely publication frequency, can reach large numbers of people, have a rigorous acceptance and publication process, and are a well-established means of information distribution. There are hundreds of journals in psychology that publish 4, 6, or 12 issues per year (i.e., per volume).

As a psychology major, if you haven't started reading psychology journal articles on a regular basis yet, you will soon. Upon reading a journal article for the first time, you immediately notice some important differences in relation to regular magazine articles; it may seem as if a journal article follows a quirky set of rules. The rules that dictate how articles are to be written in psychology are found in the *Publication Manual of the American Psychological Association* (APA, 1994). Knowledge of the APA format rules aids you in reading psychological research and is essential for success in writing your own paper.

How is a journal article different from a magazine article? Perhaps the fundamental difference between a magazine and a journal is how the article is published. Journals in psychology operate under a *peer review system* where several professionals review article submissions before an acceptance decision is made. Let's say that you wanted to publish the results of your research in a psychology journal. After selecting a journal to send your manuscript to (not always an easy task), you would send multiple copies to the journal editor. You may submit a manuscript to only one journal at a time. The editor sends copies of your manuscript out for review. Here is where the process begins. Your peers in the field (other psychologists) are asked to review your manuscript and decide if it is suitable for publication. The peers who are asked to make this decision are also called referees, and sometimes you hear the phrase "refereed journal" (which means the journal follows this peer review process).

How does an individual reviewer evaluate a manuscript? (To be clear about terminology, authors submit a manuscript in hopes that it will be accepted; this accepted manuscript becomes a journal article.) The answer to this question varies across journals and individuals, but in general, scholarship is the key. For the manuscript to be considered scholarly, there should be a thorough review of the literature, a keen grasp of the subject matter, concise writing, adequate research skills, demonstrated importance of the work to psychology, and an understanding of the journal readership (the journal subscribers). Often reviewers are individuals with prior success in publishing their own manuscripts. Once the editor has received the reviews, a decision must be made whether to accept the paper, suggest that the author make some revisions and resubmit, or reject the paper. Journals go through this long, tedious, and expensive process to select the articles to be published (by the way, reviewers do not get paid for this service, and reviews are often done anonymously). This procedure is used in an effort to be as fair and objective as possible. Also, in an effort to keep the process fair, the author of the manuscript typically does not know the identity of the reviewers (i.e., a blind review).

This process also differs from a magazine in that magazines pay people to write articles; authors of journal articles are not paid and are sometimes even asked to help defray the cost of journal publishing. Whereas magazine articles may be checked for accuracy, they do not undergo the same scrutiny, examination, and review as journal articles. The majority of journal articles are well documented with supporting references noted as to when an idea has been adopted from another source. A magazine article is rarely as extensive in documenting the academic and scholarly work of the author. Another difference between the two is that journals are typically not available for purchase at newsstands but must be subscribed to, whereas magazines are typically available at a newsstand. However, magazines can be a great resource if you are trying to *get* some ideas about research topics.

Now that you are familiar with what a journal article is, where do you find it? The best place to begin your search is the library. Academic journals are expensive (and foreign journals are *extremely* expensive), and your library likely subscribes to selected journals of interest to faculty and students. Care and respect should be given to these resources: Never tear or cut any page out of a journal, and take the journal out of the library only if permissible and if necessary. When you photocopy an article, always copy the entire reference section. Sometimes students try to cut corners by not copying the references, and often regret it later; those references are valuable sources of information on your topic.

The key component of the database for searching the psychological literature is a product called *Psychological Abstracts* (Psych Abstracts, or PA). PA is an APA product, where journal articles published in psychology are indexed into a database that is made available to the public in various forms. Most journals that publish empirical research of a psychological nature are abstracted or indexed in PA. Technically speaking, *Psychological Abstracts* is the paper version of this index. Each month new indexing information becomes available in hard copy, or in paper/booklet form. Because other indexing products have become much more popular and user-friendly since the inception of PA, your library may not still subscribe to PA. Regardless of the format used, a key to success in using this resource is to have the appropriate key words or search terms (more on this later).

An electronic version of PA (*PsycLIT*, SilverPlatter Information Services, 1998) is now available at many college and university libraries. Under the auspices of APA, SilverPlatter publishes on a regular basis the entire *Psychological Abstracts* database from 1967 to the current date (new releases incorporating this most recent information are released about twice a year). *PsycLIT* provides the advantage of a computerized database search engine and interface. When using the computer program, you indicate what terms to search for in the titles and abstracts of articles indexed in PA since 1967, and the search yields a listing of those articles with all of the key bibliographic information needed to retrieve the information; this listing can usually be printed in the library or saved to disk and printed later. Speed of use and power of the search are two key advantages of *PsycLIT* over PA. Searching for the same topic over a 30-year span can be achieved in minutes during a *PsycLIT* search; the same search could easily take hours using *Psychological Abstracts* (because the volumes are cataloged by year, to search that same 30-year span you would have to search in 30 separate, individual volumes). You should use the *Thesaurus of Psychological Index Terms* published by APA to help you find the correct search words. Often, the search for a seemingly obvious topic results in fewer hits because the wrong search word is being used. Because the search terms in the *Thesaurus* are taken directly from PA, this resource can help streamline your search and make you more efficient in finding the information you need.

The newest incarnation of PA is an APA service called *PsycINFO*. *PsycINFO* is an Internet/Web interface where users can do multiple, unlimited searches of the PA database. Although this service provides a great deal of convenience for the user, one additional benefit is that the journal database has been expanded to an index of psychological articles published since 1889—that's right, 1889. In *PsycINFO* you can print out the bibliographic citation as well as the abstract, and you can use many if not all of the search operators (e.g., "and," "or," "not") that are available in *PsycLIT*. As a service, *PsycLIT* would normally be free for you to use in your university's library—*PsycINFO* is a service that individual users must pay for. Also, some APA journals also have full-text versions available over the Internet. For more information about the variety of costs and services available to psychology students, check the APA Web site at www.apa.org. In addition, the APA publishes a monthly journal called *Contemporary Psychology: A Journal of Reviews,* which contains reviews of books and other information relevant to psychology. Sometimes book information is more difficult to search for, so this makes *Contemporary Psychology* an important resource.

The resources that are available from *PsycLIT* and *PsycINFO* are staggering—as of this writing 1,409 journals are covered in this indexed database. Table 5.4 contains a listing of some of the journals published by the APA—these are some of the most prestigious journals published in the field.

Table 5.4: Journals Published by the American Psychological Association

American Psychologist	*Journal of Family Psychology*
Behavioral Neuroscience	*Journal of Occupational Health Psychology*[a]
Clinician's Research Digest	*Journal of Personality and Social Psychology*
Consulting Psychology Journal: Practice and Research[a]	*Neuropsychology*
Contemporary Psychology	*Neuropsychology Abstracts (previously PsycSCAN: Neuropsychology)*
Cultural Diversity and Mental Health[a]	
Developmental Psychology	*Prevention & Treatment*
European Psychologist[b]	*Professional Psychology: Research and Practice*
Experimental and Clinical Psychopharmacology	*Psychoanalytic Psychology*[a]
Group Dynamics: Theory, Research, and Practice[a]	*Psychological Assessment*
Health Psychology	*Psychological Bulletin*
History of Psychology[a]	*Psychological Methods*
Journal of Abnormal Psychology	*Psychological Review*
Journal of Applied Psychology	*Psychology and Aging*
Journal of Comparative Psychology	*Psychology of Addictive Behaviors*[a]
Journal of Consulting and Clinical Psychology	*Psychology, Public Policy, and Law*
Journal of Counseling Psychology	*Psychological Abstracts*
Journal of Educational Psychology	*PsycSCAN: Applied Psychology*
Journal of Experimental Psychology: Animal Behavior Processes	*PsycSCAN: Behavior Analysis & Therapy*
	PsycSCAN: Clinical Psychology
Journal of Experimental Psychology: Applied	*PsycSCAN: Developmental Psychology*
Journal of Experimental Psychology: General	*PsycSCAN: Learning Disabilities and Mental*
Journal of Experimental Psychology: Human Perception and Performance	*PsycSCAN: Psychoanalytic Abstracts*
	Retardation
Journal of Experimental Psychology: Learning, Memory, and Cognition	*Rehabilitation Psychology*[a]
	Review of General Psychology[a]

[a] Published by the Educational Publishing Foundation   [b] Distributed by the Educational Publishing Foundation

Note. From "Library Instruction for Psychology Majors: Minimum Training Guidelines," by J. Merriam, R. T. LaBaugh, and N. E. Butterfield, 1992, *Teaching of Psychology, 19*, pp. 34-36.

Using the Web. In the past five years, the Internet via the World Wide Web has become an important source of information about psychology and life in general. The Internet is still in its infancy, and caution should be used in interpreting information taken from the Web. In particular, look for the signs of scholarship that you would expect to find from a scholarly research article or from a legitimate scientific entity: accuracy, authority, objectivity and reliability, and currency (Brandeis University, 1998). Look for information from reliable sources such as professional organizations (e.g., APA, APS, Psi Chi) or from colleges and universities. Although you should evaluate any type of information critically, Web materials necessitate additional scrutiny. It is easy for anyone to post a Web page to the Internet and make it universally accessible—it is not nearly so easy to start your own peer-reviewed scholarly research journal and publish it yourself. Below is a brief list of reputable places to start on the Web (Brandeis University, 1998):

- American Psychological Association: www.apa.org
- PsychWeb by Russ Dewey: www.psywww.com
- American Psychological Society: www.psychologicalscience.org
- Links to psychological journals: www.cpa.ca/jours.htm
- Electronic journals, periodicals in psychology: psych.hanover.edu/Krantz/journal.html

These sites contain links to many other psychology Web sites—the combinations and avenues that you can travel are virtually endless.

Additional Literature-Search Strategies. Before we conclude this chapter with some of the library skills that a psychology major should have (and one instrument to measure some of those skills), there are a handful of other strategies that you can use in your search for prior research. "Treeing" is a technique that can be used forward and backward. To tree backward through your references, try to find a great, current article that is right on target with your research idea—then look at that article's reference section (you can begin to see the special role of references and why it's important to copy every page of the article). You may find some good references in the reference section of articles you already have. Also, don't forget about your textbooks—they have reference sections that you can use to tree backward.

Treeing forward through the references involves the use of another bibliographic resource, the Social Sciences Citation Index (SSCI) (Institute for Scientific Information, 1998). To tree forward, find a classic article that is commonly referenced in your field of study—perhaps a major article that shaped the direction of research since it was published. By using the SSCI, you can look at all the authors of articles who have cited that classic article since it was published. That is, you can find the more current information related to your area of interest by looking for other researchers who cited that classic article, and then obtain the papers published by these researchers. SSCI is a valuable resource; however, it uses incredibly small print and may be difficult to use initially. Ask your instructor or the reference librarian for help if you have difficulty.

If your library does not carry a journal that you need for a particular author (and you have some time), why not write the author directly? Some authors have reprints (copies) made of each one of their publications. As a professional courtesy, most researchers will send you a free reprint upon request. If you know the author's name and affiliation, you should be able to determine a phone number, mailing address, or e-mail address that you can use for contact. Search engines on the Internet can help, and both the APA and APS publish membership directories that may be available in your library (or from a faculty member in your department if they belong to either organization). If you have the good fortune to attend a professional conference, you might have the chance to meet the researcher in person and make your request at that time. Similarly, at a conference you can often obtain a preprint, which is a manuscript that is either submitted for publication, or has been accepted for publication but is not yet in print.

Finally, be sure to evaluate all sources of information for your research. Although you want to be especially cautious of Internet information, you should critically evaluate *all* of your sources. The University of California–Santa Cruz (1998) library makes these recommendations when evaluating sources:

- Look for articles published in scholarly journals or sources that require certain standards or criteria to be met prior to publication.
- Use the bibliographies or reference lists cited from scholarly journal articles or books.
- Compare several opinions by scholars in your topic area as another method of evaluating your sources.
- Consult with an instructor or the faculty member who is supervising the research project.

Using these methods does not guarantee that you will have a perfect or complete literature search. The more you do literature reviews and the more familiar you become with the ideas and terminology in psychology, the better you will become as a consumer and evaluator of psychological knowledge.

LIBRARY SKILLS PSYCHOLOGY MAJORS SHOULD HAVE

Merriam, LaBaugh, and Butterfield (1992) proposed minimum training guidelines for library instruction of psychology majors. They suggested that students should become familiar with (a) locating known sources, (b) conducting a literature search, (c) making effective use of those resources that are found, and (d) developing an increased awareness of the places that one can find information in psychology. To meet each of these goals, they suggested the training guidelines listed in Table 5.5.

Table 5.5: Minimum Library Training Guidelines for Psychology Majors

1. To locate known sources, the student should be able to
- detect whether known books, journals, or other materials are available in their institutional library, the format available (print, microfiche, microfilm), and where it is located (e.g., be able to work from a reference list to retrieve resources)
- follow procedures for obtaining materials not available in the institutional library (e.g., interlibrary loan, other local/regional libraries)

Table 5.5: Minimum Library Training Guidelines for Psychology Majors (continued)
2. To conduct a literature search, the student should be able to • define the research topic • determine whether the problem has been addressed previously, and if so, by whom (using literature search strategies such as those presented in this chapter with resources such as *PsycLIT* and *PsycINFO*) • understand the importance of key terms in searching the literature (e.g., using resources such as the *Thesaurus of Psychological Index Terms* and *the Library of Congress List of Subject Headings*) • understand the classification system of books and materials in your institutional library, and understand the benefits and costs of browsing as a search strategy • use bibliographic references (treeing backward) as a source of search material • understand the concept of citation indexing (or treeing forward using SSCI) • search computerized databases and be able to manipulate search parameters to focus on a particular topic • identify ways of keeping current on a topic • interact effectively with reference librarians, instructors, and research supervisors about the methods used to retrieve information
3. To make effective use of resources once they are found, the student should be able to • identify ways of evaluating materials • distinguish between scholarly and popular treatments of topics in the literature, recognizing the publication's intended audience and purpose • demonstrate ethical behavior in using library resources
4. To develop an increased awareness of information resources available in psychology, the student should be able to • use indexes and abstracting services relevant to the student's area of concentration • use other types of standard reference materials (e.g., encyclopedias, handbooks, dictionaries, membership directories, book reviews, reviews of tests and measures) • find current electronic retrieval options for information through computerized databases • identify professional associations and the provision of services relating to literature searches and information retrieval (e.g., APA, APS)
Note. From "Library Instruction for Psychology Majors: Minimum Training Guidelines," by J. Merriam, R. T. LaBaugh, and N. E. Butterfield, 1992, *Teaching of Psychology, 19*, pp. 34-36.

This chapter has focused on the importance of the formulation of research ideas, and the pursuit of information related to those ideas. The strategies used in the literature review are critical to the success of this component of the research endeavor. Landrum and Muench (1994) found four types of strategies that influence a student's success in the library:

• Person-specific: the self-confidence and skill level in using the library
• Library-specific: your knowledge of your local library, knowing what resources are available
• Paper-specific: the details about how to write the paper and how to use the resources in the library to help write the paper

- Reference-specific: how to use journal articles and books in the library

We close this chapter with the complete Library Research Strategies Questionnaire (Landrum & Muench, 1994) (Table 5.6). We have not provided the answers, but by reading the questions you might think about your own library research strategy. Think about your answers to these items before your next trip to the library.

Table 5.6: The Library Research Strategies Questionnaire
Item
What is your class level?
The required length of my paper will determine whether or not I use the library.
Are you familiar with using keywords as a research source in the library?
Using the electronic card catalog (ECC) has made library research easier.
When researching in the library, I find most of my information from encyclopedias.
I would rate my library skills as
Are you familiar with using abstracts as a research source in the library?
Are you familiar with using a thesaurus as a research source in the library?
When writing my paper, I tend to rely on journal articles as my primary sources.
Given a paper assignment with five required sources, about how many sources would you look at overall?
When writing my paper, I tend to rely on books as my primary sources.
When I come to the library to work on a paper, I know where to start.
I use the reference section from one article to find information about other related articles.
How many times do you use the library in a semester?
When I need information on current events, I look at indexes.
When researching in the library, I find most of my information from journals.
When I need information on current events, I look at the ECC.
I think I spend too much time researching.
I try to locate more information than what I really need when researching in the library.
When I need information on current events, I look at abstracts.
Are you familiar with using indexes as a research source in the library?
Before going to the library to do research, I know what reference materials I am going to use.
I would rate my use of the library as
When writing my paper, I tend to rely on popular magazines as my primary sources.
When writing my paper, I tend to rely on encyclopedias as my primary sources.
Have you ever used interlibrary loan?
I feel confident I know how to use the library well.
When I need information on current events, I look at the CD-ROM indexes.
About how many hours do you spend researching a paper in the library?
I find using the library confusing.
About how many hours total do you spend on a paper?
When working on a research paper I know what steps I will follow.
Using CD-ROM indexes has made library researching easier.
Note. From "Assessing Students' Library Skills and Knowledge: The Library Research Strategies Questionnaire," by R. E. Landrum and D. M. Muench, 1994, *Psychological Reports, 75,* pp. 1619-1628.

Reviewing the items above may help you to focus on the strategies that will allow you to be successful in locating prior research. In Chapter 6, we'll look at how to put this information and more into creating an APA-format paper.

Chapter 6
PUBLICATION MANUAL PRIMER:
TIPS FOR APA FORMAT

As you begin to read more and more journal articles in psychology, you may wonder, "Why APA format?" For years the APA has published the *Publication Manual of the American Psychological Association;* the 1994 version is the fourth edition. Psychologists all over the world follow these steps and guidelines in the preparation of manuscripts. In fact, a number of scientific disciplines have adopted basic APA format as the *de facto* standard of manuscript preparation.

The first formal presentation of manuscript instructions appeared in the *Psychological Bulletin* (an APA journal) in 1929. A six-member panel attending a Conference of Editors and Business Managers of Anthropological and Psychological Periodicals issued a report on manuscript guidelines called "Instructions in Regard to Preparation of Manuscript." This document was offered as general guidance for authors preparing manuscripts for publication. Although many of the details of page layout and preparation have changed and evolved into the current edition, some of the advice given in 1929 still holds true today. Consider this comment on the general form of the manuscript: "A safe and useful prescription is to be as brief as possible without sacrificing clarity or pertinent facts. Pressure upon space in the scientific journals and the present heavy demands upon the informed reader both reinforce this prescription. Careless writing is usually diffuse, incoherent, and repetitious. Careful reading by a competent critic will usually suggest means for reduction" ("Instructions," 1929, p. 57).

Why the specific format? One of the basic tenets of science and scientific knowledge is communicability (the other basic tenet of scientific knowledge is replication). APA format facilitates this communication of scientific, psychological knowledge by the reporting of results in a consistent, reliable format. Any paper written by a psychologist in APA format has the following order: an abstract, an introduction, a method section, a results section, a discussion section, and a reference section. Knowing the parts of the manuscript and where they are located gives an advantage to the reader; you may not understand the jargon used, but you know there is a description of how the study was conducted in the Method section, and the statistical findings of the study are recorded in the Results section.

This common format facilitates the communication of ideas in the scientific community. Some students are initially confused by APA format because they have already been taught a paper-writing format such as Turabian (Turabian, 1982), *Chicago Manual of Style* (1993), or

MLA (Gibaldi & Achtert, 1988). APA format is not necessarily superior to any other of these formats; in fact, APA format can be confusing and tedious at times. However, it is the standard of communication in psychology for all authors. Whether you are submitting your work to a journal for publication or writing a paper in a psychology course, you should follow the established standards and use APA format

WRITING PSYCHOLOGY PAPERS

Although the APA *Publication Manual* (APA, 1994) is 368 pages long, the basic rules for writing in APA format are relatively straightforward and are presented in this chapter. Much of the APA manual is dedicated to contingencies and events that do not occur very often. For example, in using APA format in the reference section of your paper, the *Publication Manual* lists 77 different methods of referencing; whereas the two basic references are journal articles and books.

Assume that you are eventually going to write a journal–style paper. Perhaps you are writing about your own experiment, a group project, or an experiment proposal. How do you get your notes organized to write the paper? An often-used method is called the notecard method. The notecard method is a technique of conducting library-type research in such a way that it facilitates later writing of the introduction and discussion sections of a manuscript by increasing the synthesis of a paper. By integrating multiple sources from your library research into the paper, it reads better, it flows better, and is one sign of scholarly writing. The notecard method is an organized procedure for collecting research notes when preparing a major term paper. Students are challenged in such papers to not only analyze information from various sources, but also to synthesize the views and reports of these sources. The difference between a good paper and an excellent paper is often the level of synthesis. By using the notecard method, students organize their thoughts and ideas beforehand, rather than at the moment of paper creation/typing/completion.

Step 1. Select a paper topic. Try to generate a topic that interests you. Be sure, however, to keep within the confines of the instructor's assignment. The challenge is to select as specific a topic as possible for which there are library materials readily available (if interlibrary loan is used, plan ahead; it can take at least two to three weeks to receive materials not found in the library). Try to decide on a paper topic after a trip to the library. This allows you to make sure that there are adequate resources available before you are totally committed to a topic. See Chapter 5 for some tips about coming up with research ideas and ways to find information about those ideas.

Step 2. Create an outline. Sketch an outline of the major points you want to make in your paper. Again, this step should be done after taking a quick look at the available library materials. You may already know what kinds of points you want to make, but the library quick search may give you more ideas. Try to be as concrete and specific as possible in your outline.

Step 3. Make reference notecards. On 3" x 5" notecards, create your reference list/bibliography. Place only *one* reference on each notecard, and in the upper left corner give each reference a code (A, B, C, etc.). Write each reference in APA style. APA has a very specific format for writing references, and references from books are written differently from those taken from a journal; be sure to note the differences (see the examples in this chapter or at the end of the book). Writing the reference notecard in APA format saves you time later when you type the reference section of your paper; putting one reference per card makes it easy to alphabetize your references.

Step 4. Make idea notecards (take notes on sources). On 4" x 6" notecards, take your notes on each source/reference you have selected. Write down ideas that you may think you might use in your paper. Write only *one* idea on each card. So for Reference A, you may have four separate ideas you might incorporate into your paper, labeled A1, A2, A3, and A4. If you think you might like to use the idea in a direct quote, be sure to note the page number on the idea notecard. It is important to have only one idea on each card so that organizing your paper later is facilitated.

Step 5. Plan the paper. Before you actually begin writing the paper, plan the course of the paper. With your revised outline and your idea notecards, organize your paper by selecting ideas (notecards) and grouping them together. Try to integrate the paper as much as possible (i.e., don't talk about all the ideas from your A reference, then your B reference, etc.). The whole point of this system is to help you synthesize similar ideas from different contexts. In this step, you lay out the course of the paper by physically placing your 4" x 6" idea notecards in the order you are going to use them. How do you know what order? Your outline (Step 2) is your general roadmap for writing your paper.

Step 6. Write the rough draft. Now it's time to actually start writing "the paper." Of course, you've already done much of the writing, which has helped you to become very familiar with your reference materials and the points you want to make. Following your paper plan, write the text by following the notecards you've already organized. You need to make the text smooth and readable, providing the necessary transition between ideas. Be sure to include a title with your rough draft. Remember that this is a rough draft, not the finished product. See if your instructor will review your rough draft without assigning a grade. This option may not be available in larger classes; if it is not, try to get one of your classmates to read your paper. If you're not sure about something, try it; the worst that can happen in the draft stage is that you receive some free advice. With the rough draft, your reference list is typically not required (it normally appears at the end of the paper), although you should cite your sources in the text of the paper in APA format. If you see a lot of red ink on your returned draft, just think of it as free advice; remember, the rough draft is not the final version, and the comments are designed to improve your paper. At some point we all need outside consultants to help us improve and sharpen our skills.

Step 7. Write the final draft. Consider the comments from the instructor and your classmates. Improve the paper where indicated; these changes may include correcting typographical errors, rewriting paragraphs, or reorganizing the flow of ideas. It's to your benefit to be a careful editor and proofreader of your work. It is strongly recommended that you have a fellow classmate read your paper before handing it in—someone else may catch a mistake that you have overlooked. Simple, repetitive mistakes can be extremely irritating to an instructor. Be sure to follow the APA format rules when preparing the final draft of the paper. There are many rules, so be careful.

THE PARTS: INTRODUCTION, METHOD, RESULTS, AND DISCUSSION

The parts listed above are actually not the only parts to an APA-formatted paper, but they are the major portions of the text. There are various details that must be attended to in preparing a manuscript in APA format, and a discussion of each of these sections follows. First, Table 6.1 provides a quick overview of these sections.

Table 6.1: Sections of the Manuscript

Title page **(Take credit)**
    Author's name
    Author's affiliation
    Other information as your professor requests
    Running head information
Abstract **(Quick summary)**
    No more than 100 words
    Some assignments will not require an abstract
Introduction **(What you are studying)**
    Introduce the problem
    Develop the background
    State the purpose and rationale for the present study
Method **(What you did)**
    Participants
    Apparatus or materials
    Procedure
    Should be in enough detail to replicate if desired
Results **(What happened)**
    Presentation of statistical outcomes
    Tables and/or figures if necessary
    Presentation, not interpretation
Discussion **(What it means)**
    Was there support for the research idea?
    Did the study help resolve the original problem?
    What conclusions can be drawn?
    Suggest improvements, avenues for further/new research
Reference page **(Give credit where credit is due)**
    Starts on its own page
    Authors listed alphabetically by last name
    No first names used, only initials
    Be sure all citations in the text are referenced
    Shows your scholarly ability and how you did your homework

The Introduction and Literature Review. This section is especially frustrating to persons who are unfamiliar to writing in APA format. The *Publication Manual* (APA, 1994) suggests that authors should try to accomplish three goals in this opening portion of the paper. First, introduce the problem. The body of the paper opens with an introduction that presents the specific problem under study and describes the research strategy. Before writing the introduction, consider the following: What is the point of the study? How do the hypotheses and the experimental design relate to the problem? What are the theoretical implications of the study? How does the study relate to previous work in the area? A good introduction answers these questions in a paragraph or two and, by summarizing the relevant arguments and the data, gives the reader a firm sense of what was done and why.

Second, develop the background. Discuss the literature, but do not include an exhaustive historical review. Assume that the reader has knowledge in the field for which you are writing and does not require a complete listing. Although you should acknowledge the contributions of others to the study of the problem, cite only research that is pertinent to the specific issue and avoid references with only general significance. Refer the reader to general surveys or reviews of the topic if they are available. A real challenge for writers is to demonstrate the logical continuity between previous research and the present work (your project). Develop the problem with enough breadth and clarity to make it generally understood by as wide a professional audience as possible. Do not let the goal of brevity mislead you into writing a statement understandable only to the specialist. As you can see in the sample paper (at the end of this chapter), the author takes about five double-spaced pages to develop the idea. You may want to use subheadings (as in the sample paper) to better organize your thoughts.

Third, state the purpose and rationale. After you have introduced the problem and developed the background material, you are in a position to tell what you did. Make this statement in the closing paragraphs of the introduction. At this point, a definition of the variables and a formal statement of your hypotheses give clarity to the paper. Often you will see the sentence containing the hypothesis clearly beginning "It is hypothesized that . . . ." Clearly develop the rationale for each hypothesis. End the introduction with a brief overview of your own study. This overview provides a smooth transition into the Method section, which immediately follows. In the sample paper, see the last two paragraphs on page 7. They provide the transition for the reader. Bordens and Abbott (1988) provide a checklist for the introduction and literature review found in Table 6.2.

Table 6.2: Introduction and Literature Review Checklist	
Check √	Item
	Introduction to the topic under study
	Brief review of the research findings and theories related to the topic
	Statement of the problem to be addressed by the research (identifying an area in which knowledge is incomplete)
	Statement of purpose of the present research
	Brief description of the method intended to establish the relationship between the question being addressed and the method being used to address it
	Description of any predictions about the outcome and of the hypotheses used to generate those predictions
Note. From *Research Design and Methods: A Process Approach*, by K. S. Bordens and B. B. Abbott, 1988, Mountain View, CA: Mayfield Publishing Co.	

The Method Section. The goal of this section is to describe your participants, apparatus, and procedures so clearly that another person in your field could replicate or repeat your research. You are inviting others to repeat what you have done. This section is conventionally divided under three headings: participants, apparatus or materials, and procedure (a design heading is sometimes included).

Participants. Describe the major demographic characteristics of the participants, such as age, sex, type of institution they were drawn from, and geographic location. Describe the procedures by which the participants were available for participation, such as student volunteers or students fulfilling course requirements. See page 8 of the sample paper for an example. Include any criteria that were used in determining who could be a participant. Describe the procedures by which participants were assigned to groups. If certain participants were dropped from the study, explain why in this section.

Apparatus or Materials. If specialized equipment is an integral part of your research, describe this equipment and how it was used. If the equipment is standard, cite the manufacturer and any relevant identifying labels or numbers. If standardized test materials were used, briefly describe them under a heading of materials. If the materials were specially designed for your study, describe them in enough detail so that someone experienced in your field could reproduce them for replication or further research purposes.

Procedure. Describe the research chronologically, step by step. In descriptive research, describe the conditions under which participants were observed or tested as well as specific instructions or tasks presented to them. In experimental research, indicate how the participants in each group were exposed to the independent variable, and describe any control procedures used in the design. Instructions to the participants should be included verbatim if they were a key part of the study. Provide clear details on the measurement of participants' behavior.

The Results Section. Verify that all conditions stipulated in the Method section were accomplished. If any variations occurred, describe them here; then briefly describe the procedures used for data collection and analysis. How were your observations converted into analyzable data? What type of statistical analysis was selected, and how was it conducted? It is now time to present the findings. Briefly describe your results in writing. After doing so, repeat the results in numerical form. When reporting the results of statistical tests, include the following: the name of the test (such as t or F), the degrees of freedom, the results of the specific computation, and the alpha level (usually $p < .05$). Now, you may elaborate or qualify the overall conclusion if necessary in writing. Be sure to end each section of the results with a summary of where things stand. APA format requires that when you report the mean, you also report the standard deviation. For particular analyses, you'll need to report the effect size along with the inferential statistic. In the sample paper, you'll see a combined results and discussion section—this is common in single-experiment ("one shot") papers. The results part presents the statistics (as presented above), whereas the discussion part interprets the statistical results. The sample paper is organized to look at several themes of interest to the researcher—presenting the results and discussion together under each theme.

Figures and Tables. Unless a set of findings can be stated in one or two numbers, a table or figure should accompany results that are sufficiently important to be stressed. The basic rule of presentation is that a reader should be able to grasp your major findings either by reading the text or by looking at the tables and figures. Be careful in preparing figures and tables: There are very specific APA rules governing their construction, they are time-consuming, and they are often difficult and expensive for journals to publish.

The Discussion Section. Begin the discussion by telling the reader what you have learned from the study. Open with a clear statement on the support or nonsupport of the hypotheses or the answers to the questions you first raised in the introduction. Do not simply reformulate and repeat points already summarized in the Results section. Each new statement should contribute something new to the reader's understanding of the problem. What inferences can be drawn from the data? What are the theoretical, practical, or even political implications of the results? Next, compare your results with those reported by other investigators and discuss possible shortcomings of your study—that is, conditions that might limit the extent of legitimate generalizations. Do not dwell compulsively on flaws in your study. Typically there is a section included that considers questions which remain unanswered or have been raised by the study itself, along with suggestions for the kinds of research that would help to answer them.

References. You list the scholarly works that you used (cited) in your paper in the reference section. List only works that you actually used; the reference section is *not* a bibliography (in a bibliography, you would list all the research that you gathered, regardless of whether or not that information was used in the paper). Also, note that references have their own rules of capitalization, and these rules are counterintuitive to students at first. For example, most students think that every word of a book title or journal article is always capitalized—in APA format in the reference section, that is not true.

There are many, many different types of reference materials that you can use in an APA format paper. Unfortunately, each type has a slightly different APA format. For the listing of examples on how to format references, see the *Publication Manual* (APA, 1994, pp. 194–221). In Table 6.3, we have left the references with the underlining that you would use in your paper. In manuscripts that are submitted for publication to journals, underlining is an instruction to the printer to use italics. You should use underlining (and *not* italics or bold) unless your instructor tells you otherwise.

Table 6.3: Examples of APA Reference Styles

Periodicals/Journal Articles

Davis, S. F., & Ludvigson, H. W. (1995). Additional data on academic dishonesty and a proposal for remediation. Teaching of Psychology, 22, 119-122.

Landrum, R. E., & Chastain, G. (1998). Demonstrating tutoring effectiveness within a one-semester course. Journal of College Student Development, 39, 502-506.

Plager, H., & Landrum, R. E. (1997). Individual and family characteristics of juvenile sexual offenders. Psi Chi Journal of Undergraduate Research, 2, 54-57.

Meliska, C. J., Landrum, R. E., & Landrum, T. A. (1990). Tolerance and sensitization to oral caffeine: Effects on wheelrunning in rats. Pharmacology Biochemistry and Behavior, 35, 477-479.

Table 6.3: Examples of APA Reference Styles (continued)

Books
Davis, S. F., & Palladino, J. J. (1997). <u>Psychology</u> (2nd ed.). Upper Saddle River, NJ: Prentice Hall.
Horvat, J. J., & Davis, S. F. (1998). <u>Doing psychological research</u>. Upper Saddle River, NJ: Prentice Hall.
Landrum, R. E. (1998). <u>A guide to teaching introductory psychology</u>. Fort Worth, TX: Harcourt Brace.
Landrum, R. E. (1997). <u>Introduction to psychology: A general guidebook</u> (2nd ed.). Dubuque, IA: Kendall/Hunt.
Smith, R. A., & Davis, S. F. (1997). <u>The psychologist as detective: An introduction to conducting research in psychology</u>. Upper Saddle River, NJ: Prentice Hall.

Edited Book
Chastain, G., & Landrum, R. E. (Eds.). (1999). <u>Protecting human subjects: Departmental subject pools and institutional review boards</u>. Washington, DC: APA Books.

Book Chapters
Davis, S. F. (1994). You take the high road, I'll take the low road: A satisfying career at a small state university. In P. A. Keller (Ed.), <u>Academic paths: Career decisions and experiences of psychologists.</u> Hillsdale, NJ: Erlbaum.
Landrum, R. E., & Chastain, G. (1999). Subject pool policies in undergraduate-only departments: Results from a nationwide survey. In G. Chastain & R. E. Landrum (Eds.), <u>Protecting human subjects: Departmental subject pools and institutional review boards</u> (pp. 24-36). Washington, DC: APA Books.

Internet Materials
American Psychological Association. (1997). A guide to getting in to graduate school. [Online]. Retrieved November 28, 1998, from http://www.apa.org/ed/getin.html.
Lloyd, M. A. (1997, August 28). Exploring career-related abilities, interests, skills, and values. [Online]. Retrieved March 30, 1998, from http://www.psych-web.com/careers/explore.htm.

Note. From *Publication Manual of the American Psychological Association* (4th ed.), 1994, Washington, DC: American Psychological Association.

APA format concerning citing information from the Internet is still a bit unclear. Although APA has made some recommendations available (www.apa.org/journals/webref.html), these guidelines are being interpreted differently by different people. As with all reference materials, the ultimate goal is to provide enough information in the reference so that other researchers are able to follow your path to the same information. Inevitably, the fifth edition of the *Publication Manual* will be better suited to deal with electronic information.

Title and Abstract. The title and abstract of your article permit potential readers to get a quick overview of your study and decide if they wish to read the article itself. Titles and abstracts are also indexed and compiled in reference works (*Psychological Abstracts*) and computerized databases (*PsycINFO* and *PsycLIT*) (see Chapter 5 for more information about these resources). For this reason they should accurately reflect the content of the article; write the abstract after you have completed the article and have a firm view of its structure and content. The recommended length for a title is 10 to 12 words. The title should be fully explanatory when standing alone and identify the theoretical issue(s) or the variable(s) under investigation. A good title is hard to write; plan to spend some time on it. The abstract should not exceed 960 characters and spaces (approximately 120 words). It should state the problem under investigation, in one sentence if possible, the participants (specifying pertinent characteristics), the experimental method (including apparatus, data-gathering materials, test names), the findings (including statistical significance levels), and the conclusion with the implications or applications. Be warned: a good abstract is often the most difficult portion of the paper to write.

The Appendix. The appendix contains materials important to the research that are too lengthy or detailed for inclusion in the Method section. These items may include technical materials, listing of a computer program, word lists used as stimuli, or an original survey/questionnaire. Try to minimize the use of appendices.

APA Format Typing Instructions. There are a number of specific details that are followed when preparing a manuscript in APA format. Some of the more basic guidelines are presented here. As always, heed your instructor's modifications to this list.

- Do not use italics, only underlining.
- Double-space everything!
- Use a one-inch margin on *all* sides.
- Do not justify lines if using a word processing program (i.e., you should have a ragged right margin).
- Use a 10- or 12-point font, preferably Times New Roman or equivalent—always make sure the font is absolutely readable.
- Number every page, including the title page (except figures)—upper right-hand corner, inside the one-inch margin.
- Indent the first line of every paragraph using the tab key (usually set at one-half inch indention), or use five to seven spaces to indent.
- Center the title page information on a page; it should contain the paper's title, the author's name, and the author's affiliation.
- Place the abstract on a page by itself (page 2 of the paper). The word "Abstract" should be centered at the top of the page. The abstract should be about 120 words in length and must be typed as one blocked (not indented) paragraph.

Spacing and Punctuation. APA format requires only *one* space after punctuation in the body of the paper and Reference section. Check with your instructor on his or her preference. Some instructors may want you to follow APA format exactly; others will want two spaces because they believe it improves readability; and others won't care. Also leave a space after the period used in the initials of people's names listed in your reference section. The Reference section starts on its own page.

Table 6.4: Where to Go for More Help in the APA *Publication Manual*

Topic	Section	Topic	Section
Abbreviations	3.20–3.29	Parentheses	3.07
Brackets	3.08	Personal communication	3.102
Capitalization	3.12–3.19	Quotation marks	3.06
Colon	3.04	Reporting statistics	3.53–3.61
Dash	3.05	Semicolon	3.03
Figures	3.75–3.86	Slash	3.09
Hyphenation	3.11	Tables	3.62–3.74
Numbers	3.42–3.49		

Note. From *Publication Manual of the American Psychological Association* (4th ed.), 1994, Washington, DC: American Psychological Association.

GRAMMAR AND VOCABULARY

You can imagine that with all of these sections, the flow of a research paper might be choppy and the text difficult to read. The skilled writer uses transitions between sections and paragraphs to improve the flow and readability. Table 6.5 contains suggestions on the use of transitions.

Table 6.5: Examples of Transitions

Type of Transition	*Transition Examples*
Time links	then, next, after, while, since
Cause-effect links	therefore, consequently, as a result
Addition links	in addition, moreover, furthermore, similarly
Contrast links	but, conversely, nevertheless, however, although, whereas

Note. From *Publication Manual of the American Psychological Association* (4th ed.), 19 Washington, DC: American Psychological Association.

One of the most confusing aspects to the writer new to the use of APA format regards the use of verbs. The verb tense that is used depends upon the section of the paper (see Table 6.6). As a general note, the *Manual* does a good job at providing the basics of formatting, and does have helpful examples. You should remember to always consult your instructor to determine his or her particular preferences in the application of APA format rules. At times, instructors may want you to vary from the rules to improve readability or to fulfill a departmental or institutional requirement.

Table 6.6: Verb Use in Particular Sections of the Paper

Introduction (Literature review)
      Past tense ("Davis concluded")
      Present perfect tense ("Researchers have concluded")

Table 6.6: Verb Use in Particular Sections of the Paper (continued)
Method
Past tense ("Participants completed the task in 5 min")
Present perfect tense ("The task was completed by the participants in 5 min)
Results
Past tense ("Scores declined after the intervention")
Discussion (discuss results and present conclusions)
Present tense ("Participants take the computer task seriously")

Table 6.7 lists the different types of verb tense and an example of each.

Table 6.7: Examples of Verb Tense
When appropriate, use the active voice. Try to increase the frequency of active voice construction.
• Davis designed the study.
The passive voice is acceptable when you focus on the outcome of the action, rather than who made the action happen.
• The survey was administered by the students.
Use past tense to discuss something that happened at a specific, definite time in the past (e.g., writing about another researcher's work or when reporting your results).
• Landrum (1998) found that 63% of students reporting average work expected a grade of B or a grade of A.
Use the present perfect tense to discuss a past action that did *not* occur at a specific, definite time in the past.
• Since the completion of the study, we have found further evidence to support our conclusions.

Using Direct Quotes vs. Paraphrasing. Use a direct quote only if the author has stated the idea so perfectly that any paraphrasing of the original would not do it justice. In general, you should paraphrase information you take from other sources. To paraphrase means that you read and comprehend the material, but then you write it in your own words, not the author's words (as a direct quote would do). *You still need to give the writer credit for his or her work*, even though you have put it in your own words. If you do not, that is plagiarism (for more on this topic, see Chapter 8).

In general (and this is *our* suggestion, not APA format), use direct quotations sparingly. No more than one or two per paper, and do not use block quotes (quotes longer than 40 words). When instructors see a string of quotations or a bunch of block quotes, they are drawn to the conclusion that the student thought that stringing quotes together would look good and satisfy the requirement. A scholarly paper is *not* a string of direct quotations.

Examples of paraphrasing include some sentences that have phrases like those below:

- Landrum (1998) found that . . .
- . . . as reported in a previous study (Landrum, 1998).
- In 1998, Landrum concluded that . . .

Sample Paper

We conclude this chapter with a mock-up of a sample paper. In actual APA format, each page is contained on one piece of paper, and pages are printed on one side of the page. Writing an APA format paper early in your academic career can be a daunting and frustrating task—try not to be discouraged. It is a skill and it takes time to acquire skills. As with most other things, practice helps; the more papers you write, the better you will become at writing in this style. The conventions used in APA format will become familiar over time, and you will eventually appreciate the organizational structure and logical sequence of thought that a well-prepared APA paper provides.

Running head: MEASURING ATTITUDES ABOUT DIVERSITY

Assessing Collegiate Climate: The Campus Diversity Questionnaire

R. Eric Landrum

Boise State University

Abstract

A new measure called the "Campus Diversity Questionnaire" (CDQ) was developed to assess the campus climate on diversity issues. Students at a large, western metropolitan university ($\underline{N}$ = 577) were given the CDQ—validity and reliability of the instrument were analyzed, and CDQ outcomes were examined in the context of age, gender, and racial differences. Validity analyses indicated three distinct types of diversity—institutional, interpersonal, and instructional. Reliability analyses indicated that more work needs to be done on the subscales, with more diverse populations at multiple universities. This instrument was particularly robust in detecting differences amongst majority group and minority group students. The benefits to quantifying the campus diversity climate are discussed.

Assessing Institutional Climate: The Campus Diversity Questionnaire

How do students feel about cultural diversity on college campuses today? Among campus administrators, community leaders, and many in the general public, appreciating and achieving diversity is a sought after goal. If students are highly aware of and value diversity, they may be active participants and agents of change. In this scenario, the campus diversity 'climate' may be warm and open to change. It also seems clear that students may be too engaged in their undergraduate education to put much thought or effort into achieving diversity. Part of this may be due to apathy among some students on any campus. Alternatively, as the number of non-traditional students increases at many campuses, these students orient more toward school as work—they commute, are very focused, take little time for extracurricular activities (McAdams, Hood, & Landrum, 1996). Students operating under this model may have little time for campus activism concerning social issues such as diversity; education is more job-like. In looking at the institutional climate concerning diversity, students may have very different attitudes even among racial groups.

In examining the literature concerning how students live and function in their environment, most of this work addresses efforts to understand diversity, and to change attitudes about diversity. Although seemingly equally important, there is little work on the measurement of attitudes concerning diversity. If it is important to understand the impact of diversity, then there needs to be some mechanism to measure attitudes about diversity, and the degree of change instigated by intervention programs aimed at raising student awareness about diversity. An additional goal of this study was to develop a valid and reliable measurement instrument that can quantify the campus climate concerning diversity. In examining the published work on diversity on college campuses, this work tends to fall into three general categories: understanding the role

---

of diversity, attempts to change attitudes about diversity, and some work measuring attitudes about diversity. Each of these areas is reviewed below.

Understanding Attitudes About Diversity

A substantial amount of work done in this area has involved educational concerns. For instance, Steward, Gimenez, and Jackson (1995) stressed the importance of multicultural counselor training. An important issue in their study was the consideration of high within-group diversity (e.g., the differences between individual minority group members) as well as the more traditional, between-group expression of diversity (e.g., different minority groups). McCargar (1993) found that individuals from various cultures do not share similar expectations about teacher roles and student roles—an important concept to understand in our training of future teachers. In a similar vein, Talbot (1996) expressed concern for the lack of diversity of master's students in a student affairs program, suggesting that this pool of graduate students does not represent a diverse population, and has limited exposure to diverse populations.

Institutions have also been a focal point in studying the attitudes underlying diversity. Wilcox and Ebbs (1992), for example, describe a 'values audit' for raising issues related to institutional sensitivity to diversity awareness. Globetti, Globetti, Brown, and Smith (1993) actually examined the awareness and sensitivity toward minority students on a college campus. This study closely examined (a) social boundaries, (b) differences between majority/minority-status students, and (c) students' perceptions of parental attitudes toward diversity. Through this endeavor, Globetti et al. (1993) developed a 5-question social interaction index. They found that although majority and minority groups (in the deep South) expressed similar degrees of diversity awareness, they also found minority students expressing much more multicultural sensitivity than majority students. That is, majority and minority students had a good understanding of problems that a person might have in "fitting in" to a campus subculture (awareness), but that groups often lacked appreciation (sensitivity) for other groups.

In understanding how entrenched some of these issues are, Barr and Strong (1988) spoke in plain but powerful language about what a commitment to multiculturalism means. In speaking about the risks, they wrote: "the structure of higher education is a well-oiled, rationalized, inherently racist system providing many privileges to the dominant group. Why would anyone who benefits from this system want to change it? For multiculturalism to exist, those with privilege will have to share their access to resources with less privileged groups. Why should we expect leaders and executives to make this commitment? They won't make it unless doing so will maintain their personal or institutional interests" (p. 87). Perhaps the ability to measure the impact of diversity would be one step in a positive direction.

Changing Attitudes About Diversity

Raising awareness and sensitivity about multicultural issues is clearly a goal of many educators today. However, some strategies have been implemented by others to actively change opinions about diversity. These interventions are typically aimed at goals such as raising awareness or improving sensitivity. For example, DeVoe, McMillan, Zimmerman, and McGrew (1996) found that in the coaching education field, one course was not sufficient to change attitudes about diversity or have students overcome prejudice. They did report, however, that diversity-oriented programs were not as intrusive as expected by some. Bruschke, Gartner, and Seiter (1993) used a simulation game called BAFA BAFA to educate college students about culture shock and ethnocentrism. Interestingly, and ironically, they report that the simulation led students to be more favorable and motivated toward multicultural instruction, yet it also lead to increases in ethnocentrism! Kleeman (1994) developed a model of how campuses adapt to the

growing role of diversity. Stage 1 of this model is reactive, where the institution works to reduce barriers for minority students to receive an education. Stage 2 involves helping students change in their opinions about diversity. Stage 3 addresses improvement in learning by changing (i.e., growing) the university's positive approach to diversity issues. Kleeman (1994) concludes that there are five key factors to success in this regard: (a) a belief in self and the realization for a need for change; (b) financial support from the institution; (c) academic skills and support for student; (d) social support, and (e) family and community support.

Measuring Attitudes About Diversity

In thinking about trying to achieve attitude change concerning diversity, it would seem inherent to the process that some sort of measurement device or outcome variable would be available to document and quantify any changes in attitudes about diversity. In the present review of the literature, there does not seem to be a plethora of measures. Globetti et al. (1993) spoke of creating a social interaction index, Bruschke et al. (1993) developed some sort of measure to assess levels of ethnocentrism, and DeVoe et al. (1996) mention the Cultural Diversity Awareness Inventory. The closest approximation to the measurement of attitudes about diversity in the published literature comes from McClelland, Cogdal, Lease, and Londoño McConnell (1996). They developed the 'multicultural assessment of campus programming' questionnaire, asking students about (a) how they feel about the university's commitment to diversity, (b) how they perceive majority and minority student relations on campus, and (c) how campus programming efforts increase the awareness and understanding of diversity. In this study, McClelland et al. (1996) found that faculty and staff seemed to perceive the institution as more culturally sensitive than students. Also, they concluded that "cultivating an environment

that values diversity can only be accomplished through innovative assessment and successful implementation of substantiated results" (p. 95).

Simply put, if we want to study the impact of diversity on the way students live and interact with each other in the environment, we need a way to measure that impact. The goal of this project is to develop a psychologically sound measurement instrument to gauge the 'diversity climate' of a college campus. Knowledge of faculty, staff, and students' current levels of awareness is critical in designing interventions and awareness programs. We already know from McClellan et al. (1996) that those groups (faculty, students, staff) can differ in their attitudes about diversity on the same campus. Additionally, such a measure can provide a benchmark or baseline that can be used to evaluate a program's effectiveness in raising diversity awareness, for example. We already know from Bruschke et al. (1993) that sometimes awareness programs can have the opposite of the intended effect.

The goal of this study was to create a measurement instrument to assess an institutions' 'diversity climate.' That is, at what level of awareness about diversity does the university currently possess? How sensitive are we to the differences between majority and minority students? Can we measure this 'climate' to get a reading as to where we stand? Further, if a national sample of institutions were tested, would significant differences emerge between institutions regarding diversity? If some institutions emerge more favorably than others regarding their diversity climate (which inevitably would happen), could we then look to these institutions for intervention strategies and "best practices" for other institutions wishing to improve their diversity climate?

Method

Participants. Students enrolled in a General Psychology course ($\underline{N}$ = 577) at a large, metropolitan non-residential university participated for course credit. Students had multiple options to complete the research experience component of the course, and those students participating in this study were debriefed following its conclusion.

The average age of the participants was 22.9 years old ($\underline{SD}$ = 7.14; $\underline{Min}$ = 17, $\underline{Max}$ = 62). Considering sex, 307 (53.5%) were female, 267 (46.5%) were male, and 3 chose not to disclose sex. Regarding race, there were 10 American Indian/Alaska Natives (1.8%), 5 Black/African Americans (0.9%), 40 Hispanics (7.1%), 491 White/Caucasians (87.5%), and 15 Asian American/Pacific Islanders (2.7%). Although this distribution does not reflect much diversity, the distribution is remarkably accurate with respect to the population from which it was drawn.

Materials. The "Campus Diversity Questionnaire" (CDQ) is an original instrument created by the author. This was done in accordance to standard test construction methods (see Anastasi, 1997; Cohen, Swerdlik, & Smith, 1994 for details). A thorough review of the literature was included to ensure that items were selected and retained following the principles of content validity. The complete CDQ is presented in Table 1.

Procedure. Students were recruited to participate by use of a human subject pool procedure administered by the Psychology Department. Participants were tested in groups, and were given the two-page questionnaire to complete. Although students could use all 50 min of the testing session, most students completed the CDQ in 20 min or less.

Results and Discussion

Initial use of the CDQ appears promising. Preliminary indicators on psychometric properties such as validity and reliability are in a positive direction, but more work with a more diverse population is needed to verify these properties. However, the CDQ is useful in detecting differences and relationships among the 16 questions with regard to gender, race, and age. A description of those outcomes follows. For means and standard deviations on the 16 key questions, see Table 2.

Validity and Reliability. Establishing the construct validity of a new measurement instrument is similar to a lawyer building a case—evidence must be accumulated to build a persuasive case, and on the basis of the evidence and rules of evidence that exist, a conclusion is drawn. This study provides initial evidence that the CDQ has some of the properties exhibited by an instrument with construct validity. Additional work needs to be completed to accumulate more evidence to support the conclusion of reliability.

In this study, the CDQ responses of 577 participants were subjected to factor analysis using a varimax rotation and minimum eigenvalue of 1.0. Using factor loading scores > .50, four factors emerged, explaining 50.3% of the variance. The first three factors are discussed throughout the remainder of this article. The fourth factor was not retained due to only 2 items loading on that factor, and that the factor exhibited unacceptably low reliability.

The first factor that emerged was labeled "Institutional Diversity," and this factor explained 19.6% of the variance, and the inter-item reliability (as calculated by Cronbach's α) = 0.8046. The items that load significantly on this factor (all positively) include questions 8, 9, 7, 12, 3, and 10 (see Table 1 for these questions). These questions address institutional concerns

about diversity, including questions about a diversity plan, training of faculty and staff, the curriculum, and recruitment of minority students as an institutional priority.

The second factor that emerged was labeled "Interpersonal Diversity," and this factor explained 13.4% of the variance, and the inter-item reliability (as calculated by Cronbach's α) = 0.6311. This low level of reliability indicates that more work needs to be done with this factor. The items that load significantly on this factor (all positively except for Item 11) include questions 1, 11 (negatively), 4, 6, and 2 (see Table 1). These questions tend to address more personal feelings about diversity on campus, as reflected in questions about personal conflict, discrimination, comfort, and friendships and relationships.

The third factor that emerged was labeled "Instructional Diversity," and this factor explained 10.4% of the variance, and the inter-item reliability (as calculated by Cronbach's α) = 0.4947. This level of reliability is also low, and more work is indicated. The questions that load on this factor (all positively) include questions 16, 5, and 13 (see Table 1). These questions address the practices that take place in the classroom/instructional setting, such as the materials that professors present, that students, faculty and staff are exposed to the history and culture of minority groups, and the adequacy of student orientation addressing multicultural diversity issues.

Gender Differences. Only one question emerged with a significant difference between males and females, Question 8, "This university should have a diversity plan." The response for males averaged 3.54 (SD = .99) on the 1-5 Likert scale, and females averaged 3.37 (SD = .97), and this difference was statistically significant, $t(570)$ = -2.05, p < .05. While both gender averages hover in the uncertain area, males tended to agree more with this question than females.

Race Differences. Remarkably, even with relatively low n's for some of the minority groups, significant differences among racial groups were found for 11 of the 16 questions. Even with these outcomes, it seems questionable to compare groups of 490 students with groups of 5 students—hence, the results of these by-group analyses are not reported here. More work with a larger sample with more racial diversity needs to be conducted before these by-group differences attain any statistically appropriate meaning.

When the separate minority groups (in this sample) are combined into one larger minority group, majority-minority groups differences emerge on 13 of the 16 questions. These majority-minority group differences are presented in Table 3. In this sample, the White/Caucasian group constituted the vast majority (87.5%) of the respondents. As indicated by higher means, this group of majority students agreed more that: (a) the campus is free from racial conflict, (b) minorities feel comfortable at this university, (c) the relationship between majority-minority students is a friendly one, (d) hiring practices at this university indicate that racial barriers are eroding, and (e) professors address multicultural issues in the classroom. For each of these questions, majority students (White/Caucasian) reported significantly higher agreement scores than minority students (American Indian/Alaska Native, Black/African American, Hispanic, and Asian American/Pacific Islander students combined). Whether or not the perception is accurate, White/Caucasian students tend to have the outlook that there are minimal race problems on campus, and that the general trend is that relations are improving.

Interestingly, that does not appear to be the perceptions of students in the minority. As indicated by higher means, this group of minority students agreed more that: (a) this university should be doing more the promote diversity, (b) this university should train faculty and staff in multicultural sensitivity, (c) this university should have a diversity plan, (d) this university needs

classes that emphasize multicultural diversity, (e) recruitment of minority students is an institutional priority, (f) I have encountered racial discrimination on this campus, (g) I think that the course curriculum should require courses on multicultural diversity, and (h) participation in most campus activities is racially segregated. This pattern of results paints a much different picture of the same campus.

In reality, both sets of perceptions are probably accurate. To majority students (87.5% in this sample), they are probably unaware of the struggles of students outside of their own racial group. Also, they have the optimistic perception that conditions are improving and that relations are friendly. From their perspective, they probably are. To minority students (12.5% in this sample), the university needs to be doing more with respect to promoting diversity, training faculty and staff, planning, curriculum, and campus activities. From their perspective, these students clearly have a better understanding of what it is like to be a minority student on campus. Both of these sets of beliefs are not incongruous. The campus climate, as characterized by diversity in the form of institutional, interpersonal and instructional perspectives, is probably improving and getting better (as majority students believe) but there are still certain conditions of campus life that could be improved (as minority students believe).

Relationship to Age. Age was significantly, positively correlated with the following questions: (a) this university should be doing more to promote diversity, $r(575)$ = 0.131, p < .005, (b) this university should train faculty and staff in multicultural sensitivity, $r(575)$ = 0.169, p < .001, (c) this university should have a diversity plan, $r(574)$ = 0.212, p < .001, (d) this university needs classes that emphasize multicultural diversity, $r(574)$ = 0.105, p < .05, and (e) the core curriculum should require courses in multicultural diversity, $r(574)$ = 0.145, p < .005. Age was significantly negatively correlated with the question 'as far as I know, minorities feel comfortable at this university.' $r(575) = -0.135$, $p < .005$. Older students tend to see the need for more planning, training, and teaching of diversity in the curriculum, while younger students have the perception that minorities presently feel comfortable. This may be due to the younger age cohorts of students at universities, or those older students have a different perspective on the campus diversity climate than younger students.

Conclusions. The Campus Diversity Questionnaire makes a significant contribution to the campus diversity literature. This new measurement instrument has shown some initial useful qualities, and in this study the CDQ was sensitive to group differences. This new instrument shows good evidence for validity, but some of the reliability issues with certain subscales need to be improved or resolved.

The idea of diversity, whether it be considered on the college campus or not, does not appear to be a unitary concept. In this study, three distinct types of diversity emerged. It is fair to note, however, that these results are based on the conclusions from one state university without much diversity in the student population. Regardless, the results of the current study were interesting. Institutional diversity is reflected in the planning, training, policies and procedures that govern a university. Interpersonal diversity speaks to a student's individual experience on a campus, his or her interactions with other students, and how friendships and relationships are made and maintained. Instructional diversity addresses those events that occur in the classroom or related settings—how professors treat diversity issues in the classroom, how multicultural diversity is integrated into orientation activities, etc. Colleges and universities might find the CDQ useful in ascertaining current attitudes on campus about these three types of diversity.

Furthermore, with a longitudinal study and repeated use of the CDQ, an institution may be able to track changes in one type of diversity independent of changes in other types. For example, a Student Affairs division might institute a new program to attract and maintain minority students. Those students might rate that university's institutional diversity as more positive because of the efforts of Student Affairs. However, that might not change the status of instructional diversity at that institution. As the CDQ develops and evidence accumulates to support its validity and reliability, it may be a sensitive enough instrument to detect changes to one type of diversity while others are held constant. This type of instrument would be especially helpful in quantifying the effectiveness of diversity programs and initiatives on college campuses. Also, it would be helpful to have a national database available based on the administration of the CDQ so that colleges and universities would be able to interpret relative standings as an aid in putting institutional data in a context and also identify 'best practices' and successful diversity programming. The efforts to confirm and improve the validity and reliability of the CDQ as well as to begin the formation of a national database are currently underway.

References

Anastasi, A. (1997). Psychological testing (7th ed.). Upper Saddle River, NJ: Prentice Hall.

Barr, D. J., & Strong, L. J. (1988). Embracing multiculturalism: The existing contradictions. NASPA Journal, 26, 85-90.

Bruschke, J. C., Gartner, C., & Seiter, J. S. (1993). Student ethnocentrism, dogmatism, and motivation: A study of BAFA BAFA. Simulation & Gaming, 24, 9-20.

Cohen, R. J., Swerdlik, M. E., & Phillips, S. M. (1995). Psychological testing and assessment: An introduction to tests and measures (3rd ed.). Pacific Grove, CA: Mayfield.

DeVoe, D., McMillan, B., Zimmerman, A., & McGrew, J. (1996). Infusing a multicultural component into coaching education. Journal of Instructional Psychology, 23, 14-20.

Globetti, E. C., Globetti, G., Brown, C. L., & Smith, R. E. (1993). Social interaction and multiculturalism. NASPA Journal, 30, 209-218.

Kleeman, G. L. (1994). Achieving academic success with ethnically diverse students: Implications for student affairs. NASPA Journal, 31, 137-149.

McAdams, J., Hood, J., & Landrum, R. E. (1996, May). Non-traditional and traditional students attitudes toward learning in the classroom. Midwestern Psychological Association, Chicago.

McCargar, D. F. (1993). Teacher and student role expectations: Cross-cultural differences and implications. The Modern Language Journal, 77, 192-207.

McClellan, S. A., Cogdal, P. A., Lease, S. H., & Londoño-McConnell, A. (1996). Development of the Multicultural Assessment of Campus Programming (MAC-P) questionnaire. Measurement and Evaluation in Counseling and Development, 29, 86-99.

Steward, R. J., Gimenez, M. M., & Jackson, J. D. (1995). A study of personal preferences of successful university students as related to race/ethnicity, and sex: Implications and recommendations for training, practice, and future research. Journal of College Student Development, 36, 123-131.

Talbot, D. M. (1996). Master's students' perspectives on their graduate education regarding issues of diversity. NASPA Journal, 33, 163-178.

Wilcox, J. R., & Ebbs, S. L. (1992). Promoting an ethical campus culture: The values audit. NASPA Journal, 29, 253-260.

Author Notes

The author wishes to acknowledge the thoughtful contributions and support of Gaylord Walls, Minority Assistance Coordinator at Boise State University, and to acknowledge the financial support from a National Association of Student Personnel Administrators (NASPA) grant.

Correspondence, including requests for reprints, should be directed to Eric Landrum, Department of Psychology, Boise State University, 1910 University Drive, Boise, ID 83725 or by Email: elandru@boisestate.edu.

TABLE 1. Campus Diversity Questionnaire

Strongly Disagree	Disagree	Uncertain	Agree	Strongly Agree
1	2	3	4	5

Question

1. The campus environment is free from racial conflict.
2. Friendships are more likely to be determined by common interests rather than by race.
3. This university should be doing more to promote diversity.
4. As far as I know, minorities feel comfortable at this university.
5. Students, faculty and staff at this university are exposed to the history and culture of minority groups.
6. In general, the relationship between minority and majority students is a friendly one.
7. This university should train the faculty and staff in multicultural sensitivity.
8. This university should have a diversity plan.
9. This university needs classes that emphasize multicultural diversity.
10. Recruitment of minority students is an institutional priority.
11. I have encountered racial discrimination on this campus.
12. I think that the core curriculum should require courses in multicultural diversity.
13. This university provides a new student orientation that adequately addresses multicultural diversity.
14. Participation in most campus activities is racially segregated.
15. Hiring practices at this university indicate that racial/ethnic barriers are gradually eroding.
16. Professors address multicultural issues in the classroom.
17. What are the benefits or advantages (if any) to diversity?
18. What are the drawbacks or disadvantages (if any) to diversity?
19. Age _____
20. Gender (circle one)   Male   Female
21. Race (circle all that apply)   American Indian/Alaska Native   Black/African American
    Hispanic   White/Caucasian   Asian American/Pacific Islander
22. University status (circle one)   Student   Faculty   Classified Staff   Professional Staff

---

TABLE 2. Campus Diversity Questionnaire Means and Standard Deviations

Question	Mean	Standard Deviation
1. The campus environment is free from racial conflict.	3.08	0.93
2. Friendships are more likely to be determined by common interests rather than by race.	3.99	0.92
3. This institution should be doing more to promote diversity.	3.36	0.96
4. As far as I know, minorities feel comfortable at this institution.	3.53	0.77
5. Students, faculty and staff at this institution are exposed to the history and culture of minority groups.	3.00	0.87
6. In general, the relationship between minority and majority students is a friendly one.	3.71	0.72
7. This institution should train the faculty and staff in multicultural sensitivity.	3.51	1.00
8. This institution should have a diversity plan.	3.45	0.98
9. This institution needs classes that emphasize multicultural diversity.	3.40	1.07
10. Recruitment of minority students is an institutional priority.	2.70	1.01
11. I have encountered racial discrimination on this campus.	1.97	1.16
12. I think that the core curriculum should require courses in multicultural diversity.	2.75	1.23
13. This institution provides a new student orientation that adequately addresses multicultural diversity.	2.91	0.73
14. Participation in most campus activities is racially segregated.	2.40	0.97
15. Hiring practices at this institution indicate that racial/ethnic barriers are gradually eroding.	3.16	0.67
16. Professors address multicultural issues in the classroom.	3.05	1.10

Note: Responses were made on a 5-point Likert scale: 1 = Strongly Disagree, 2 = Disagree, 3 = Uncertain, 4 = Agree, 5 = Strongly Agree.

TABLE 3. Majority-Minority (Race) Differences on the Campus Diversity Questionnaire

Question	Item Mean, Majority	Item Mean, Minority	t Test
1. The campus environment is free from racial conflict.	3.12	2.89	t(573) = 2.66, p < .05
2. Friendships are more likely to be determined by common interests rather than by race.	4.00	3.94	t(574) = 0.52, n.s.
3. This institution should be doing more to promote diversity.	3.32	3.58	t(574) = 2.34, p < .05
4. As far as I know, minorities feel comfortable at this institution.	3.58	3.25	t(574) = 3.54, p < .001
5. Students, faculty and staff at BSU are exposed to the history and culture of minority groups.	3.02	2.85	t(574) = 1.63, n.s.
6. In general, the relationship between minority and majority students is a friendly one.	3.75	3.51	t(574) = 2.76, p < .01
7. This institution should train the faculty and staff in multicultural sensitivity.	3.47	3.74	t(574) = 2.29, p < .05
8. This institution should have a diversity plan.	3.40	3.72	t(573) = 2.73, p < .01
9. This institution needs classes that emphasize multicultural diversity.	3.35	3.73	t(573) = 3.06, p < .01
10. Recruitment of minority students is an institutional priority.	2.65	3.02	t(572) = 3.09, p < .01
11. I have encountered racial discrimination on this campus.	1.89	2.45	t(573) = 4.99, p < .001
12. I think that the core curriculum should require courses in multicultural diversity.	2.68	3.19	t(572) = 3.51, p < .001
13. This institution provides a new student orientation that adequately addresses multicultural diversity.	2.91	2.94	t(571) = 0.30, n.s.
14. Participation in most campus activities is racially segregated.	2.34	2.75	t(573) = 3.53, p < .001
15. Hiring practices at this institution indicate that racial/ethnic barriers are gradually eroding.	3.20	2.92	t(572) = 3.51, p < .001
16. Professors address multicultural issues in the classroom.	3.11	2.68	t(572) = 3.66, p < .001

Note: Responses were made on a 5-point Likert scale: 1 = Strongly Disagree, 2 = Disagree, 3 = Uncertain, 4 = Agree, 5 = Strongly Agree. Minority group members include American Indian/Alaska Native, Black/African American, Hispanic, and Asian American/Pacific Islander. Bold lines indicate statistically significant differences between the majority and minority groups.

Used with permission of Psi Chi, the National Honor Society in Psychology.

There simply is no substitute for consistent, high-quality work!

Chapter 7
TIPS FOR DOING WELL IN PSYCHOLOGY COURSES

In preparing this chapter, you can't help but notice that most of our tips to help you do well in *psychology* courses are tips that will help you do well *in college*, whatever your major. Especially in psychology, our grounding in the scientific method necessitates the use of scientific procedures. Another feature that you might notice in this chapter is redundancy. When giving study tips, it is difficult to separate out time management from test preparation from study distractions—they all seem to relate to one another.

Hopper (1998a) offers these ten tips for surviving college. They serve as a good overview for the materials that follow.

- **Try not to schedule back-to-back classes.** You'll wear yourself out, and you'll miss some of the best times to study—right before and right after class.
- **Be a student starting with the first day of class.** Don't take the first two weeks of the semester off—even if your classes are off to a slow start. If possible, try to get ahead on reading so you'll be able to keep up later in the semester.
- **Establish a routine time to study for each class.** Studying means more than just doing your homework. Studying involves general organizational and planning strategies (finishing assignments early, organizing notes), task preparation strategies (literature reviews in library, rereading textbooks), environmental restructuring (finding the right place to study, minimizing distractions), processing/recall ability (remembering), and typical study strategies (taking notes, studying notes) (Garavalia & Gredler, 1998). Prepare for each class as if there will be a pop quiz.
- **Establish a place to study.** Make your study place a place with minimal distractions. Table 7.1 will help you to determine the best place to study.
- **Do as much of your studying in the daytime as you can.** Nighttime brings more distractions for adults.
- **Schedule breaks.** Take a brief break after every block of study time. Try to avoid long blocks of studying unless you are sure that is your optimum method of studying. Don't be *unrealistic* in how long you can study—that is, don't schedule an eight-hour study session for Saturday afternoon and evening if that is something that you just won't do when the time comes.
- **Make use of study resources on campus.** Find out about the opportunities for tutoring, study sessions, test review in class, etc. Ask questions in class of your professors.

- **Find at least one or two students in each class whom you can study with.** A fellow student might be able to explain a concept in terms that you can understand better than your professor might. Also, you might feel more comfortable asking questions of another student, and you'll have an opportunity to observe another person's study habits. Try to study with students who are academically equal to, or better than, you; they will stimulate and challenge your abilities.
- **Study the hardest subject first.** Work on the hardest subjects when you are fresh. Putting those subjects off until you're tired compounds their difficulty.
- **Be good to yourself.** Take care of your other needs—physical, emotional, social, financial, etc. If you can minimize other problems in your life, you can use your efforts to study and understand the subject matter.

In using Table 7.1 think of the three most common places that you study, and give each an arbitrary label (Place A, Place B, Place C). Answer the true-false questions for each of the locations. *The location that has the most "false" responses may be the least distracting place to study.* Try to plan your day so that the bulk of your studying is done in the most favorable place (University of Wyoming, 1998).

Table 7.1: Study Distractions Analysis						
Place A		Place B		Place C		Questions
True	False	True	False	True	False	
						1. Other people often interrupt me when I study here.
						2. Much of what I can see here reminds me of things that don't have anything to do with studying.
						3. I can often hear radio or TV when I study here.
						4. I can often hear the phone ringing when I study here.
						5. I think I take too many breaks when I study here.
						6. I seem to be especially bothered by distractions here.
						7. I usually don't study here at regular times each week.
						8. My breaks tend to be too long when I study here.
						9. I tend to start conversations with people when I study here.
						10. I spend time on the phone here that I should be using for study.
						11. There are many things here that don't have anything to do with study or school work.
						12. Temperature conditions here are not very good for studying.
						13. The chair, table, and lighting arrangements here are not very helpful for studying.
						14. When I study here I am often distracted by certain individuals.
						15. I don't enjoy studying here.

Note. From "Ten Tips You Need to Survive College," by C. Hopper, 1998, [online], retrieved September 28, 1998, at http://www.mtsu.edu/~studskl/10tips.html.

GENERAL STUDY TIPS

Many students enter college unprepared or underprepared for the academic challenges ahead. The strategies that worked for you previously may not be effective now. In fact, you may find that different college classes, even different psychology classes, may require different study strategies. The following information is designed to give you some tips on how to improve your study habits, improve your reading, get more out of lectures, and improve your test-taking skills.

Students Are Different. Techniques and strategies that work for one student may not work for another. Some students claim that they do not study at all! You need to concentrate on what you know, and you need to discover what works and does not work for you. The studying process involves a complicated sequence of behaviors. One instrument used to assess this complex behavioral pattern is the Learning and Study Strategies Inventory (LASSI) (Weinstein, Palmer, & Schulte, 1987). The list below summarizes the areas of learning and studying that the LASSI measures:

- Attitude and interest
- Motivation, diligence, self-discipline, and willingness to work hard
- Use of time management principles for academic tasks
- Anxiety and worry about school performance
- Concentration and attention to academic tasks
- Information processing, acquiring knowledge, and reasoning
- Selecting main ideas and recognizing important information
- Use of support techniques and materials
- Self-testing, reviewing, and preparing for classes
- Test strategies and preparing for tests

If you have an interest in taking the LASSI, ask a psychology instructor about it, or better yet visit your campus Counseling and Testing Center to see if they can administer this inventory to you. If that opportunity is not available to you, Table 7.2 presents a Study Skill Checklist by McConnell (1998) that can give you some insight into several of the same areas covered by the LASSI.

Table 7.2: Study Skills Checklist		
Yes	**No**	**Items**
		1. I spend too much time studying for what I am learning.
		2. I usually spend hours cramming the night before the exam.
		3. If I spend as much time on my social activities as I want to, I don't have enough time left to study, or when I study enough, I don't have time for a social life.
		4. I usually try to study with the radio or TV turned on.
		5. I can't sit and study for long periods of time without becoming tired or distracted.
		6. I go to class, but I usually doodle, daydream, or fall asleep.
		7. My class notes are sometimes difficult to understand later.

Table 7.2: Study Skills Checklist (continued)

Yes	No	Items
		8. I usually seem to get the wrong material into my class notes.
		9. I don't review my class notes periodically throughout the semester in preparation for tests.
		10. When I get to the end of a chapter, I can't remember what I've just read.
		11. I don't know how to pick out what is important in the text.
		12. I can't keep up with my reading assignments, and then I have to cram the night before a test.
		13. I lose a lot of points on essay tests even when I know the material well.
		14. I study enough for my test, but when I get there my mind goes blank.
		15. I often study in a haphazard, disorganized way under the threat of the next test.
		16. I often find myself getting lost in the details of reading and have trouble identifying the main ideas.
		17. I rarely change my reading speed in response to the difficulty level of the selection or my familiarity with the content.
		18. I often wish I could read faster.
		19. When my teachers assign papers, I feel so overwhelmed that I can't get started.
		20. I usually write my papers the night before they are due.
		21. I can't seem to organize my thoughts into a paper that makes sense.

Note. From "Study Skill Checklist," by K. McConnell, 1998, [online], retrieved September 28, 1998, at http://wwwmc.nhmccd.edu/elc/reading_writing_area/studycl.html.

How to score the results—look at the categories below that correspond to the questions in Table 7.2. If you answered yes to two or more questions in any category, you might want to concentrate on those areas.

- Items 1, 2, 3—time scheduling
- Items 4, 5, 6—concentration
- Items 7, 8, 9—listening and note-taking
- Items 10, 11, 12—reading
- Items 13, 14, 15—exams
- Items 16, 17, 18—reading
- Items 19, 20, 21—writing papers

DEVELOPING EFFECTIVE STUDY HABITS

There is no doubt about it—studying isn't one of your most enjoyable tasks. Studying is hard work. It can be made easier, however, by being efficient, organized, and consistent. Here are some tips.

Create a Regular Schedule for Studying. You probably have more obligations now than before college; hence, finding time to study may be difficult. Set aside times during the week that are specifically used for studying (*and studying only*). Choose times when you are at your mental peak—wide awake and alert. Some people are "morning" people, some are "night" people; choose your time to study accordingly. When scheduling study time, write it down. Many students use appointment books to keep track of classes, assignments, commitments, etc. Get an appointment book that breaks the day into individual hours, and carry the book with you. You can then schedule certain hours for specific activities. Be realistic; don't plan to study for six hours if you know that you can't really do that.

Writing your schedule down helps to make it concrete and allows for time management. *Time management* is even more important if you have many other responsibilities (like working, family, sports). Here are some tips for time management:

- Set aside times and places for work.
- Set priorities; then do things in priority order.
- Break large tasks into smaller ones.
- Plan to do a reasonable number of tasks for the day.
- Work on one important task at a time.
- Define all tasks specifically (e.g., not "write paper").
- Check your progress often.

Once you develop your basic schedule, add school events (exams, papers, presentations). Sticking to a schedule can help you to avoid cramming and procrastination. Cramming isn't a good study idea, because it strains your memory processes, drains you of energy, and exacerbates test anxiety. When people are faced with a number of tasks, most of us do the easy things first, saving the harder tasks for later. Unfortunately, by the time you get to the harder ones, you're tired and not at your best. To avoid this, break difficult tasks into smaller tasks. To emphasize this aspect even further, Hopper (1998b) offers these ten principles of scheduling:

1. Make use of daylight hours.
2. Study before a class that requires discussion or frequently has pop quizzes.
3. Study immediately after lecture classes (this is why it is best not to schedule back-to-back classes).
4. Study at the same time everyday to establish a study habit.
5. Plan enough time to study.
6. Space your study periods.
7. List your study activities according to priorities, and tackle the most difficult task first.
8. Study during your own prime time, paying attention to your own daily cycles and levels of alertness.
9. Leave unscheduled time for flexibility—if you don't do this, you probably won't get much use out of your schedule.
10. Analyze your use of time—keep a log every once in a while to see how you are using your time and where you might make improvements.

Find a Regular Place to Study Where You Can Concentrate With Minimal Distractions. Avoid TV or listening to conversations (as often happens in the library). Find your special nook somewhere on campus or elsewhere that is *your* study place.

Reward Your Studying. Try to reward your *successful* study sessions with something you like (watching TV, a healthy snack, or calling a friend). Many of the traditional rewards of studying take time (good grades, a college degree), so give yourself some immediate rewards. Take breaks and be realistic about what you can accomplish in one study session.

IMPROVING YOUR READING

Much of your study time is spent reading. To be successful, you need to actively think about what you are reading. Highlighting the boldfaced terms isn't enough. A very popular reading system developed by Robinson (1970) is SQ3R, which divides the reading task into these steps: Survey, Question, Read, Recite, and Review.

1. **Survey**. Before reading the chapter word for word, glance over the topic headings and try to get an overview for the chapter. You will know where the chapter is going.
2. **Question**. Look at the chapter headings. Turn the headings into questions, questions you want to be able to answer when finished reading. If the heading is "Auditory System," ask yourself, "How does the auditory system work?" If the heading is "Multiple-Personality Disorder," ask, "What are the characteristics of multiple-personality disorder?"
3. **Read**. Now you're ready to read the chapter. Your purpose is to answer the questions you just asked. If you finish reading and haven't answered your questions, go back and reread.
4. **Recite**. Once you know the answers to your key questions, recite them out loud to yourself *in your own words*. Personalizing these concepts will help you later when you are tested. Once you've said them, write them down.
5. **Review**. When you are finished with the entire chapter, test your memory by asking yourself the key questions. Try not to look at the written answers.

Practice the SQ3R system and you will find you have developed a method for successful studying. SQ3R works because the reading assignment is divided into more manageable portions.

GETTING MORE OUT OF LECTURES

Lectures can occasionally be boring and tedious; however, poor class attendance is associated with poor grades. Even if the instructor is disorganized, going to class helps you understand how the instructor thinks, which may help you to anticipate exam questions or assignment expectations. Most lectures are coherent and understandable, and accurate note taking is related to better test performance. Here are some tips on improving your note-taking skills:

- You need to listen actively to extract what is important. Focus all attention on the speaker, and try to anticipate meanings and what is coming up.
- If the lecture material is particularly difficult, review the material ahead of time in the text.
- Don't try to be a human tape recorder. Try to write down the lecturer's thoughts *in your own words* (as much as you can). Be organized even if the lecture isn't. Practice determining what is important and what is not (sometimes instructors give verbal or nonverbal cues).

- Ask questions during lecture. You can clarify points you missed and catch up in your notes. Most lecturers welcome questions and often wish students weren't so bashful.
- If the lecture is fast-paced (or if you are a slow note-taker), try to review your notes right after class if possible. Consult with a fellow classmate to make sure you didn't miss anything important. You may want to form a study group to regularly review lecture materials and/or textbook readings.

IMPROVING TEST-TAKING STRATEGIES

Your strategy should depend on the type of test you're taking. Most students study differently for a multiple-choice test compared with an essay exam. One myth about multiple-choice tests is that you should go with your first answer and not go back and change answers. Research indicates that this idea is *wrong*, and that 58% of the time students changed wrong answers to right; 20% of the time students changed right answers to wrong; and 22% of the time students changed a wrong answer to another wrong answer (Benjamin, Cavell, & Shallenberger, 1984). Here are some general tips for test-taking situations:

- Pace yourself. Make sure that when half the time is up, you're halfway through the test.
- Don't waste lots of time by pondering difficult questions. If you have no idea, guess (don't leave a question blank). If you think you can answer a question but need more time, skip it and come back later.
- Don't make the test more difficult than it is. Often simple questions are just that—simple.
- Ask a question if you need clarification.
- If you finish all the questions and still have time, review your test. Check for careless mistakes.

Here are some tips for **multiple-choice exams**:

- As you read the question, anticipate the answer without looking. You may recall it on your own.
- Even if you anticipated the answer, read all the options. A choice further down may incorporate your answer. Read each question completely.
- Eliminate implausible options. Often questions have a right answer, a close answer, and two fillers. Eliminating filler items makes for an easier choice.
- Often tests give away relevant information for one question in another question.
- There are exceptions, but alternatives that are detailed tend to be correct. Pay extra attention to options that are extra long.
- Options that create sweeping generalizations tend to be incorrect. Watch out for words such as *always*, *never*, *necessarily*, *only*, *must*, *completely*, and *totally*.
- Items with carefully qualified statements are often correct. Well-qualified statements tend to include words such as *often*, *sometimes*, *perhaps*, *may*, and *generally*.

Here are some tips for **essay exams**:

- Time is usually a critical factor in essay exams. When reviewing questions, consider what you know, the time you think it will take to answer, and the point value. Answer questions that you know first, but don't neglect questions with high point values.
- Organize your thoughts so you can write them down coherently. Take one or two minutes and plan your essay (make an outline). Then make your answer easier to read by numbering your points.
- The challenge with essays is to be both complete and concise. Avoid the "kitchen-sink" method (you don't know the exact answer, so you write all you know hoping the answer is in there somewhere).
- You've probably learned a great deal of jargon and terminology in the course, so demonstrate what you've learned in your essay.

Here are some tips for making the most from **returned tests** (University of California-Berkeley, 1998):

- If you receive your test back to keep, rework your errors trying to reason out why the correct answer was correct and yours was not.
- If you do not receive your test back, visit your instructor's office to take a look at your answer sheet and the questions you missed.
- Look for the origin of each question—textbook, class notes, labs, supplementary readings, Web information, etc.
- Identify the reason you missed a question. Did you read it incorrectly? Was it something that you were not prepared for? Did you run out of time?
- Check the level of detail and skill of the test. Were most of the questions over precise details and facts, or over main ideas and principles (the big picture)? Did questions come straight from the text, from lecture and class discussion, or from both?
- Did you have any problems with anxiety or blocking during the test?

Study skills, reading, understanding lectures, and test-taking skills are all important to achieving academic success. You cannot develop these skills overnight; however, they will emerge with practice. The rewards can be worth the effort—knowledge gained, a feeling of accomplishment, improved grades, and progress toward your degree.

MATH ANXIETY

According to Conners, Mccown, and Roskos-Ewoldsen (1998), "Math anxiety is an emotional state of dread of future math-related activities. It interferes with statistics learning by making students so nervous they cannot concentrate and by lowering motivation, which, in turn, lowers effort and achievement" (p. 40). Throughout this book we have tried to emphasize the skills and abilities that are necessary to be successful in psychology. Math skills (especially statistics) are going to be an important part of your undergraduate career, and also your career in psychology. Math anxiety is not insurmountable, and to be successful in your undergraduate and graduate careers, you have to tackle and confront it.

Dealing with this type of anxiety is not something that you can waive your hand at and make go away, and it's not the type of thing where you wake up one morning and your math anxiety is gone. One method of dealing with this anxiety is to shape your behavior using successive approximations. Success in a math course also helps. If you have a problem in this area, try to schedule your math classes during a semester where you can give math you best level of attention. Don't wait until the end of your career to take all of your required math classes! You'll do better in statistics and research methods, and be a more useful research assistant (and, as this sequence progresses, get better letters of recommendation, score better on the quantitative GRE section, etc.) if you take the math and statistics courses early. If you are serious about graduate school, try to take an advanced statistics course if one is available. Don't be afraid to look outside your department—sociology, political science, economics, and math departments might also offer useful upper-division advanced-level statistics courses.

Next, we present a list of some professor's pet peeves, with the final tip for success to avoid these behaviors in and out of the classroom.

BEHAVIORS TO AVOID

This chapter has focused on providing tips for better performance as a psychology major. We end this chapter with a modified list (Table 7.3) of behaviors that tend to irritate professors—their pet peeves about students. This somewhat humorous, somewhat serious list might give you some ideas about how to avoid getting on the bad side of your professors—these are valuable tips for success in any course.

Table 7.3: Student Behaviors to Avoid In and Out of the Classroom (Or, What Professors Don't Want to Hear From Their Students)

- Are we doing anything important in class today?
- Can I be excused from class this week? I have a friend coming to visit.
- I don't understand why I got such a low grade. I really enjoyed the class and thought that you liked me.
- I don't understand why I got such a low grade. I came to class everyday.
- I've been trying to reach you all week. You are never in your office.
- If I had more time, I could have done a better job.
- Do you take points off for spelling?
- (One week before project is due)—I can't find any articles in the library. Can I change my topic?
- I didn't know there was a test today. I wasn't in class when you announced it, and I never look at my syllabus. Do I have to take it now?
- Do class presentations count toward my final grade?
- I hope this class ends on time.
- Which of the assigned readings will be on the test?
- I can't make it to class today. I'm working on a paper for another class and it's due tomorrow.
- That's not what Professor Smith said about that.
- (During the week before finals)—What can I do to get an "A" in this class?

Table 7.3: Student Behaviors to Avoid In and Out of the Classroom (Or, What Professors Don't Want to Hear From Their Students) (continued)

- Did the syllabus really say that?
- Does my paper have to have a reference section?
- Does the paper have to be typed? Why? Are you sure?
- I missed the last class meeting; did we do anything important?
- Will we be responsible for *everything* covered in the book and in the class?
- Why did I have to read all this if it wasn't going to be on the test?
- (After the exam is handed out)—I don't feel good. Can I take a make-up exam?
- I forgot the time of the exam. Can I take it now?
- I'm not doing well in this class. Can I do some extra credit work?
- There is nothing written on the subject. I looked for a book in the library and couldn't find one.
- I missed class last week. Can you tell me what happened?
- It's not fair. I wasn't in class when you gave the assignment.

Note. From "Doc Whiz's 40 Ways to P.O. the Prof," by D. Whiz, 1995, [online], retrieved September 8, 1998, at http://monster.educ.kent.edu/docwhiz/poprof.html.

Again, please remember that the listing in Table 7.3 consists of statements and questions that professors do *not* want to hear from their students.

Dilbert / By Scott Adams

DILBERT reprinted by permission of United Feature Syndicate, Inc.

Chapter 8
ETHICAL ISSUES FOR UNDERGRADUATE PSYCHOLOGY STUDENTS

In this chapter, we'll discuss ethical issues from two different perspectives: ethics as a student enrolled in a college or university (whether you are a psychology major or not), and ethics from the perspective of an undergraduate researcher. As covered in Chapter 4, serving as a research assistant for a professor in the psychology department allows you to gain valuable skills/abilities and a potentially strong letter of recommendation. However, the opportunity to serve as a research assistant carries additional responsibilities, such as the guarantee that you will interact ethically with your research study participants. The latter portion of this chapter reviews the guidelines and principles for ethical behavior as a psychologist.

Before we address those principles specific to psychology, however, a broader topic involves your ethical behavior as a person. How do you treat other people? Do you treat everyone you encounter with dignity and respect? Do you show respect for the laws of the land and the rules that your institution imposes on the student body? It is clearly difficult to legislate ethical behavior amongst people—in fact, some people split hairs between actions and behavior that are probably unethical but not technically illegal. Of course, the authors would encourage you to seek the higher moral and ethical plane—some people behave in a certain way because they don't think they'll be caught; whereas others know the difference between right and wrong and do what's right, even if they could get away with what's wrong.

As an undergraduate psychology major, you should have exposure to ethical concepts and ideas, hopefully in a number of classes that you take in the major. It is clear from the literature that education in ethics is valuable for undergraduate students (Lamb, 1991; Mathiasen, 1998) and that students can be taught ethical behavior and beliefs (LaCour & Lewis, 1998). For instance, student researchers working with Institutional Review Boards (more on this topic later in this chapter) became more serious about the research process (Kallgren & Tauber, 1996).

THE ETHICS OF BEING A STUDENT

What are the ethical responsibilities of being a college student? Most colleges and universities address this topic with respect to cheating and academic dishonesty. Much of the work in this area has been done by one of the authors of this book, Stephen Davis (Davis, 1997; Davis, Grover, Becker, & McGregor, 1992; Davis & Ludvigson, 1995; Davis, Pierce, Yandell, Arnow, & Loree, 1995). In a series of studies conducted across the nation, 40%–60% of college students self-report that they have cheated at least once during their college career, and over 50% of that number report cheating on a regular basis. Although many colleges and universities have academic dishonesty policies, students still cheat—again, it is hard to legislate ethical behavior.

It is fair to ask, "So what if a student cheats on an exam?" Thinking back to Chapters 2 and 3, if you have a career in psychology, at some point someone is going to expect you to know about your major and the discipline. Cheating is a short-term solution that leads to bigger problems—it will probably become apparent at some point post-graduation that you did not "know your stuff," and that lack of knowledge may create some significant employment issues for someone who has cheated. Additionally, it makes your institution look bad, because "we" are graduating students who do not "know their stuff." This perception lowers the value of a degree of other graduates from your institution, and specifically those graduates in your major. Think of it this way—do you want a surgeon operating on you who cheated his or her way through medical school? Do you want a lawyer protecting your legal interests who cheated his or her way through law school? Do you want someone who is having serious psychological problems to see a psychologist who cheated his or her way through school? The bottom line is that someone someday is going to expect you to know about and understand the principles of psychology—why not just learn the material and complete the projects rather than spending an enormous amount of time and effort in schemes based on cheating?

It may be of interest to you to see how different schools address this issue of academic dishonesty. In Table 8.1, we present the academic dishonesty policies of Emporia State University (the school of Stephen F. Davis) and Boise State University (the school of R. Eric Landrum). Although the words are different, the theme of ethical behavior comes through in both statements.

Table 8.1: Academic Dishonesty Policies From Two Universities

Emporia State University

Academic dishonesty, a basis for disciplinary action, includes but is not limited to activities such as cheating and plagiarism (presenting as one's own the intellectual or creative accomplishments of another without giving credit to the source or sources).

The faculty member in whose course or under whose tutelage an act of academic dishonesty occurs has the option of failing the student for the academic hours in question. The division chair should be advised of any action taken by the faculty member regarding academic dishonesty.

The faculty member may consent to refer the case to other academic personnel for further action. Divisions, schools, and colleges may have provisions for more severe penalties than are set forth above. Emporia State University may impose penalties for academic dishonesty up to and including expulsion from the university.

The student has the right to appeal the charge of academic dishonesty in accordance with the university's Academic Appeals policy and procedure as set forth in section 9A-04 of the Faculty Handbook.

Table 8.1: Academic Dishonesty Policies From Two Universities (continued)

Boise State University

The University community expects all members to live by the following standards designed for its general well-being. Any violations of these University policies may result in disciplinary action and/or legal action.

Academic dishonesty. Cheating or plagiarism in any form is unacceptable. The University functions to promote the cognitive and psychosocial development of all students. Therefore, all work submitted by a student must represent his/her own ideas, concepts and current understanding. In an attempt to promote these ideals, dishonesty in the University can be defined generally as cheating or plagiarism in any form. The following are examples which can be used as a guide to the student in interpreting the above general definition, but is not meant to be an exhaustive list:

    a. buying or in any way using a term paper or other project that was not composed by the student turning it in

    b. copying from another exam paper either before or during the exam

    c. using crib notes or retrieval of information stored in a computer/calculator outside the exam room

    d. having someone else take an exam or taking an exam for someone else

    e. collaboration on take-home exams where it has been forbidden

    f. direct copying of another term paper, or

    g. failure to give proper credit to sources.

The course instructor is responsible for handling each case of dishonesty in the classroom except where a major or repeated offense is involved. In a proven case of cheating, a student will be dismissed from the class and a failing grade issued. If the instructor and the department chair concur that a case ought to be referred for further University action (which could include suspension or expulsion from the University), the dean, or his/her designee, of the college in which the student is majoring will appoint a special hearing board consisting of three faculty and three students. The dean, or his/her designee, will preside over any hearing and will accord due process. The Academic Grievance and Academic Dishonesty Board would be the appropriate appeal body in such an instance. If there are additional alleged violations of the Code of Conduct, a separate complaint should be filed according the Judicial Procedures in this Handbook. If a student feels s/he has been unjustly dismissed from class and given a failing grade, the Academic Grievance and Academic Dishonesty Board should be utilized as in any other case of an academic grievance.

As you can see, the consequences can be serious, including failure on the assignment, failure in the class, and suspension or expulsion from the university. It's clear there are ethical responsibilities to being a student, but what about the special responsibilities of being a student researcher? The remainder of this chapter is devoted to that topic.

THE ETHICS OF RESEARCH

Ethics is a commonly used term that has broad applications in psychology. For example, we might question the ethics of a particular researcher, whether or not a procedure is ethical, or if measuring a participant's behavior can be done in an ethically prudent way. Ethics generally refer to a code of honor in science that proper procedures are followed and that the subject of our investigation (in psychology, whether that be human or animal) be treated properly. As you might expect, psychologists trained in research methods occasionally disagree as to what is proper. Fortunately, the APA has developed a set of rules and regulations of ethical behavior (first adopted in 1953 with major revisions in 1982 and 1992).

In doing psychological research, the overriding consideration is the analysis of cost versus benefit. The researcher is required to weigh this decision carefully in any situation involving the participation of humans. Do the potential benefits that might be derived from a research study outweigh the potential harms (or costs) to the participant? This decision is not taken lightly. One method to minimize the costs or harms to a participant (at least a human participant) is to fully inform the person about the nature of the research. Thus, if there are potential harms from placing the participant at risk, then the participant can make an informed judgment about whether to participate or not. This judgment is typically called *informed consent*. Formally speaking, informed consent "is a procedure in which people are given an explicit choice about whether or not they would like to participate in the research *prior* to participation but *after* they have been fully informed of any harmful effects of the research and made aware that they are completely free to withdraw from the research at any time" (Jones, 1985, pp. 35–36).

THE DEVELOPMENT AND USE OF APA ETHICAL PRINCIPLES

Although psychologists were self-motivated to generate a code of ethics on their own, events made public after World War II hastened the need for a written code of honor. In many of the Nazi concentration camps in Europe, prisoners were experimented on under horrible conditions and without regard for the sanctity of human life. Out of those events came the Nuremburg Code (Trials of War Criminals Before the Nuremberg Military Tribunals Under Control Council Law No. 10, 1949), from which much of the APA ethical guidelines are based. The ten-point Nuremburg Code is presented in Table 8.2.

Table 8.2: The Nuremburg Code
1. Participation of subjects must be totally voluntary and the subject should have the capacity to give consent to participate. Further, the subject should be fully informed of the purposes, nature, and duration of the experiment.
2. The research should yield results that are useful to society and that cannot be obtained in any other way.
3. The research should have a sound footing in animal research and be based on the natural history of the problem under study.
4. Steps should be taken in the research to avoid unnecessary physical or psychological harm to subjects.

Table 8.2: The Nuremburg Code (continued)
5. Research should not be conducted if there is reason to believe that death or disability will occur to the subjects.
6. The risk involved in the research should be proportional to the benefits to be obtained from the results.
7. Proper plans should be made and facilities provided to protect the subject against harm.
8. Research should be conducted by highly qualified scientists only.
9. The subject should have the freedom to withdraw from the experiment at any time if he (or she) has reached the conclusion that continuing in the experiment is not possible.
10. The researcher must be prepared to discontinue the experiment if it becomes evident to the researcher that continuing the research will be harmful to the subjects.
Note. From "Trials of War Criminals Before the Nuremberg Military Tribunals Under Control Council Law No 10," *Nuremberg Code,* 1949 (Vol. 2, pp. 181-182), Washington, DC: U.S. Government Printing Office.

As early as 1935 the APA formed a special committee to discuss ethical matters and make recommendations on how to resolve complaints. By 1948, this committee recommended that the informal procedure they had used for years be formalized into a code of ethics for psychologists. The Committee on Ethical Standards for Psychology was formed and used a unique method of forming and organizing the formal code of ethics. This committee surveyed thousands of members of the APA and asked them to describe any situation in which a psychologist would need to make an ethical decision. Based on the responses, the committee developed a code designed to encompass a large variety of ethics-type situations, which at that time condensed into six general categories: responsibility to the public, the relationship between therapist and client, teaching, research, publishing, and professional relationships (Crawford, 1992). After input was received from the membership, this code was published as the *Ethical Standards of Psychology* by the APA in 1953. This basic code has been revised several times, and the general principles are presented in Table 8.3. For more on the ethical standards related to teaching, training supervision, research, and publishing (Ethical Standard 6), see Appendix C at the back of the book.

Table 8.3: General Principles From *Ethical Principles of Psychologists and Code of Conduct*
PRINCIPLE A: COMPETENCE
Psychologists strive to maintain high standards of competence in their work. They recognize the boundaries of their particular competencies and the limitations of their expertise. They provide only those services and use only those techniques for which they are qualified by education, training, or experience. Psychologists are cognizant of the fact that the competencies required in serving, teaching, and/or studying groups of people vary with the distinctive characteristics of those groups. In those areas in which recognized professional standards do not yet exist, psychologists exercise careful judgment and take appropriate precautions to protect the welfare of those with whom they work. They maintain knowledge of relevant scientific and professional information related to the services they render, and they recognize the need for ongoing

Table 8.3: General Principles From *Ethical Principles of Psychologists and Code of Conduct* (continued)

education. Psychologists make appropriate use of scientific, professional, technical, and administrative resources.

PRINCIPLE B: INTEGRITY

Psychologists seek to promote integrity in the science, teaching, and practice of psychology. In these activities psychologists are honest, fair, and respectful of others. In describing or reporting their qualifications, services, products, fees, research, or teaching, they do not make statements that are false, misleading, or deceptive. Psychologists strive to be aware of their own belief systems, values, needs, and limitations and the effect of these on their work. To the extent feasible, they attempt to clarify for relevant parties the roles they are performing and to function appropriately in accordance with those roles. Psychologists avoid improper and potentially harmful dual relationships.

PRINCIPLE C: PROFESSIONAL AND SCIENTIFIC RESPONSIBILITY

Psychologists uphold professional standards of conduct, clarify their professional roles and obligations, accept appropriate responsibility for their behavior, and adapt their methods to the needs of different populations. Psychologists consult with, refer to, or cooperate with other professionals and institutions to the extent needed to serve the best interests of their patients, clients, or other recipients of their services. Psychologists' moral standards and conduct are personal matters to the same degree as is true for any other person, except as psychologists' conduct may compromise their professional responsibilities or reduce the public's trust in psychology and psychologists. Psychologists are concerned about the ethical compliance of their colleagues' scientific and professional conduct. When appropriate, they consult with colleagues in order to prevent or avoid unethical conduct.

PRINCIPLE D: RESPECT FOR PEOPLE'S RIGHTS AND DIGNITY

Psychologists accord appropriate respect to the fundamental rights, dignity, and worth of all people. They respect the rights of individuals to privacy, confidentiality, self-determination, and autonomy, mindful that legal and other obligations may lead to inconsistency and conflict with the exercise of these rights. Psychologists are aware of cultural, individual, and role differences, including those due to age, gender, race, ethnicity, national origin, religion, sexual orientation, disability, language, and socioeconomic status. Psychologists try to eliminate the effect on their work of biases based on those factors, and they do not knowingly participate in or condone unfair discriminatory practices.

PRINCIPLE E: CONCERN FOR OTHERS' WELFARE

Psychologists seek to contribute to the welfare of those with whom they interact professionally. In their professional actions, psychologists weigh the welfare and rights of their patients or clients, students, supervisees, human research participants, and other affected persons, and the

Table 8.3: General Principles From *Ethical Principles of Psychologists and Code of Conduct* (continued)
welfare of animal subjects of research. When conflicts occur among psychologists' obligations or concerns, they attempt to resolve these conflicts and to perform their roles in a responsible fashion that avoids or minimizes harm. Psychologists are sensitive to real and ascribed differences in power between themselves and others, and they do not exploit or mislead other people during or after professional relationships. PRINCIPLE F: SOCIAL RESPONSIBILITY Psychologists are aware of their professional and scientific responsibilities to the community and the society in which they work and live. They apply and make public their knowledge of psychology in order to contribute to human welfare. Psychologists are concerned about and work to mitigate the causes of human suffering. When undertaking research, they strive to advance human welfare and the science of psychology. Psychologists try to avoid misuse of their work. Psychologists comply with the law and encourage the development of law and social policy that serve the interests of their patients and clients and the public. They are encouraged to contribute a portion of their professional time for little or no personal advantage.
Note. From *Ethical Principles in the Conduct of Research With Human Participants*, 1992, Washington, DC: American Psychological Association, Committee for the Protection of Human Participants in Research. Copyright © 1992

THE ROLE OF INFORMED CONSENT AND THE INSTITUTIONAL REVIEW BOARD

In terms of ethical behavior, one of the fundamental concepts that emerges from examining both the Nuremburg Code and the *Ethical Principles* of the American Psychological Association is that participants must be told, at some time or another, about the nature of the research project. In most cases, it is preferable to accomplish this objective prior to the onset of the experiment. Why? First, it allows participants to make a judgment about whether they want to participate. Second, it informs participants about the general nature of the tasks required giving the subject more information. Third, telling participants about the general nature of the research prior to onset allows the experimenter to obtain informed consent. Informed consent means that participants have some idea about the research study and have given their permission not only to participate, but that the experimenter may collect data.

Who decides whether an experiment (minimal risk, informed consent, or deception) meets the ethical standards of the APA? Although experimenters are required to always consider the ethical practices in their research, most colleges and universities also have a standing committee called the *Institutional Review Board (IRB)* (this committee is sometimes called the Human Subjects Committee). The IRB is typically composed of faculty members from various disciplines and individuals from the community; it is charged with one major function: to protect the rights of persons who participate in research. Any college or university that receives federal funding for research is required to have such a committee. Gone are the days when a researcher might design a new experiment in the morning and actually administer that experiment to participants (i.e., "run subjects") that afternoon. The hypotheses, research methodology, and participant recruitment and treatment all come under scrutiny of the IRB. Only after the approval of this board may researchers go forward with their research. The IRB screens research projects so that no or minimal harm occurs to persons who participate. If minimal harm may occur, the IRB certifies that the proper informed consent procedures are in place. Experiments involving deception come under the close scrutiny of the IRB, especially in weighing the risk of the deception against the potential benefits of the outcomes. For more information about the role and status of IRBs, see Chastain and Landrum (1999) or Rosnow, Rotheram-Borus, Ceci, Blanck, and Koocher (1993).

Although the chief function of the IRB is the protection of the participant population, other advantages occur from its use. The IRB also serves as a screening device for the university in knowing what kinds of activities are taking place. If the IRB feels that a particular research project may involve too much risk (risk to the participant as well as risk to the university), it may reject a project. Another advantage of the IRB is for the protection of the researchers. Often the IRB may have procedural suggestions to make and offer improvements.

The decision to conduct psychologically sound research is not a light one. There are a number of factors that must be carefully considered in making this decision—only a handful of those factors have been discussed here. In Table 8.4 we present a listing of the rights and responsibilities of research participants. This listing echoes the sentiments of the Nuremburg Code and the APA *Ethical Principles*. Although we have focused on your responsibilities as a researcher, the participant also has responsibilities in this process. The dual benefit that accrues from student participation in research is that it allows psychologists to study human behavior and collect data to further the human condition; this opportunity gives students a firsthand learning experience with the research process. To read about research in a textbook or journal article is one way to learn it; a very different experience is to be an active participant in actual "live" research.

Table 8.4: Rights and Responsibilities of Research Participants

Rights of Research Participants

1. Participants should know the general purpose of the study and what they will be expected to do. Beyond this, they should be told everything a reasonable person would want to know in order to decide whether to participate.

2. Participants have the right to withdraw from a study at any time after beginning participation in the research. A participant who chooses to withdraw has the right to receive whatever benefits were promised.

3. Participants should expect to receive benefits that outweigh the costs or risks involved. To achieve the educational benefit, participants have the right to ask questions and receive clear, honest answers. When participants do not receive what was promised, they have the right to remove their data from the study.

4. Participants have the right to expect that anything done or said during their participation in a study will remain anonymous and confidential, unless they specifically agree to give up this right.

5. Participants have the right to decline to participate in any study and may not be coerced into research. When learning about research is a course requirement, an equivalent alternative to participation should be available.

6. Participants have a right to know when they have been deceived in a study and why the deception was used. If the deception seems unreasonable, participants have the right to withhold their data.

7. When any of these rights is violated or participants object to anything about a study, they have the right and the responsibility to inform appropriate university officials, including the chairperson of the Psychology Department and the Institutional Review Board.

Responsibilities of Research Participants

1. Participants have the responsibility to listen carefully to the experimenter and ask questions in order to understand the research.

2. Be on time for the research appointment.

3. Participants should take the research seriously and cooperate with the experimenter.

4. When the study has been completed, participants share the responsibility for understanding what happened.

5. Participants have the responsibility for honoring the researcher's request that they not discuss the study with anyone else who might be a participant.

Note. From "Students' Roles, Responsibilities, and Rights as Research Participants," by J. H. Korn, 1988, *Teaching of Psychology, 15*, pp. 74-78.

Actually conducting research is a complicated enterprise, not only from the methodological perspective, but also from an ethical perspective. As undergraduate student researchers, you have a responsibility to protect the health and welfare of your research participants, and at the same time pursue research that enables you to test worthy hypotheses. A psychologist must never take lightly the consideration of using humans or animals for research purposes, and the potential benefits from such research enterprises must always outweigh any potential costs or harm to the participant.

Chapter 9
MAJORING IN PSYCHOLOGY AND OTHER OPTIONS

If you've read every chapter of this book up to this point, you know that we've covered a myriad of topics. We opened with details about majoring in psychology, and what psychology majors can do with a bachelor's degree and higher degrees. Opportunities outside of the classroom play a considerable role in your success during your undergraduate years of study. We then refocused on some of the skills and abilities that you'll need for success in almost any major, but particularly in psychology: locating prior research, tips for writing in APA format, and tips for doing well in classes in general. Following that, the ethics of being a college student and also doing research in psychology were presented. We now try to bring this journey full circle by addressing issues related to the psychology major, and other disciplines related to psychology that you might not have considered, and by directing you toward some self-reflection and assessment. This chapter is not designed to talk you "in to" or "out of" the psychology major—rather, we think it's best for you to consider all of your options.

Readers of this book are either psychology majors or seriously considering the major. Given that situation, it would be interesting to know how our profession is regarded, especially in the context of other professions (such as psychiatrists, physicians, counselors, teachers, and scientists). Webb and Speer (1986) asked various samples of students and their parents to rate the six different professions (the five listed above plus psychology). The results were interesting—each profession was rated on a variety of dimensions that yielded mean scores. Webb and Speer found that "compared to the five other professions, psychologists scored above the group means on rich, patient, inquisitive, understanding, psychological, and helpful. Scores were below the group means on unappreciated, scholarly, dedicated, alienated, and arrogant" (p. 7). The authors concluded from these data that the public image of psychologists is favorable, confused with the role of psychiatrists, clinically biased, and based on limited information. It seems that there were no negative attitudes about psychology; this finding is good news for students planning to major in psychology!

THE PSYCHOLOGY MAJOR

In this section, we would like to briefly present three topics of interest. First, why do students major in psychology? Although not much work has been done in this area, the results are interesting. Second, what are the factors that lead to success in the major? Various sections of this book are designed to lead you to success—what else does the available research say?

Third, how satisfied are students with the psychology major and how prepared are they for careers in psychology?

Why do students choose to major in psychology? Gallucci (1997) surveyed students at a variety of locations, including conferences that were held in different parts of the country (see Table 9.1). Students rated the reasons on a 1–5 scale, with 1 indicating *not a reason*, and 5 indicating a *very important reason* for majoring in psychology.

Table 9.1: Reasons for Choosing Psychology as an Undergraduate Major		
Reason	*Mean*	*SD*
I have a very strong interest in the subject matter of psychology.	4.59	0.71
I want to become a professional psychologist.	3.89	1.17
Psychology is a good undergraduate degree to prepare me for a graduate or professional (e.g., MD, JD) degree.	3.73	1.43
A bachelor's degree in psychology will prepare me for a job.	3.21	1.41
I want to become an academic psychologist.	2.74	1.47
Psychology is a good undergraduate degree to prepare me for teaching.	2.45	1.39
I want to figure myself out.	2.31	1.34
I want to become a professional social worker.	1.62	1.26
I want to become an industrial or organizational psychologist.	1.35	0.87
Psychology is an easy major.	1.27	0.68
Note. From "An Evaluation of the Characteristics of Undergraduate Psychology Majors," by N. T. Gallucci, 1997, *Psychological Reports, 81*, pp. 879-889.		

Gallucci (1997) concluded that "these results indicated that the most important reason for choosing psychology as an undergraduate major was a very strong interest in the subject matter of psychology. Career concerns were also salient, as undergraduates rated preparation for graduate study in professional psychology, other graduate or professional study, and employment as important reasons for selecting the psychology major" (p. 886). The lowest rated item is also of interest: "Psychology is an easy major." Clearly, psychology majors do not select psychology because they think it is easy. This result provides some good truth in advertising about the major and what to expect from it—don't choose it because you think it will be easy.

In another interesting study, Meeker, Fox, and Whitley (1994) studied the predictors of academic success for undergraduate psychology majors. Specifically, they looked at high school grades, college admission scores, and college grades to determine the best predictors of psychology GPA in college. They examined the number of semesters of classes taken in high school (e.g., English), average high school grades in certain areas (e.g., average grades in math classes), high school demographics (GPA, class rank, class size), Scholastic Aptitude Test (SAT) scores, college grades in core/general studies courses (e.g., history, speech), grade in introductory psychology, applied statistics, and research methods. The strongest factor that emerged to predict college psychology GPA was performance in core/general studies classes, such as research methods, mathematics, English, history, and science.

Interestingly, in the Meeker et al. (1994) study, grade in the introductory psychology course was not a strong enough variable to be included in any of the three factors that emerged as predictors of psychology GPA and success in the major. Because many students become attracted to psychology through the introductory course, the results can be interpreted to mean that the grade in the introductory course alone should not drive the decision to major in the discipline. Considering that we have some information about why students choose the major and what leads them to be successful in their psychology courses, what about student satisfaction with the major? If they had it to do all over again, would psychology graduates (i.e., alumni) select the same major? Kressel (1990) conducted a survey of social science (including psychology) alumni and asked a series of questions about degree satisfaction and job satisfaction. It should be noted that other studies similar to this one have been conducted (Braskamp, Wise, & Hengstler, 1979; Finney, Snell, & Sebby, 1989; Keyes & Hogberg, 1990; McGovern & Carr, 1989). Kressel found that 39% of the respondents said they would probably select the same major. The strongest predictor of degree satisfaction was the job-relatedness to the major. The factors that lead to higher satisfaction with the psychology degree include having a higher degree, being female, more course enjoyment, more course difficulty, income satisfaction, and job satisfaction.

Kressel (1990) suggests that based on his research, there are several strategies that can be used to enhance degree and job satisfaction of social science graduates. His suggestions were to (a) improve instructor and advisor education about career options in psychology, (b) implement career development courses for undergraduate majors, and (c) incorporate business training into psychology curricula. Clearly, the use of this book can help achieve two of these goals. Psychology instructors who read this book will be up to date on the latest information related to job opportunities; Chapters 2 and 3 are devoted to job opportunities. Second, we wrote this book for career development courses, whether the course is an "Introduction to the Psychology Major" for undergraduate students or "The Professional Psychologist" for the new graduate student. Students attracted to studying psychology are from diverse backgrounds with varied interests. This diversity provides for a valuable learning experience; psychology, by its very nature, is a discipline that strives to understand human behavior—all human behavior.

DIVERSITY IN PSYCHOLOGY

You can think about diversity in many ways. A person can have number of diverse experiences, or receive their education at a diverse collection of schools. Typically, however, we think of diversity as in cultural diversity or ethnic diversity. There have been some dramatic demographic shifts in psychology in the past 25 years or so. For instance, considering gender diversity, the number of women receiving their bachelor's degree in psychology has increased from 46% of all degrees in 1971 to 73% of all bachelor's degrees in 1993. With respect to graduate school enrollments, in 1977 women comprised 47% of graduate students in psychology, and in 1997 that number had risen to 71%. In 1976, women received 33% of the new doctorates awarded in psychology, and in 1996 that number was 69%. Finally, among Ph.D.'s in the workforce, women accounted for 20% in 1973, and 44% in 1997 (APA, 1998l).

When considering people of color, there have also been a number of changes, but not nearly as dramatic a shift as in gender diversity. For example, the percentage of people of color receiving bachelor's degrees went from 11.6% of all degree recipients in 1976 up to 16.0% in 1993. When considering graduate enrollments, people of color comprised 11.8% of all graduate enrollments in psychology in 1980, and in 1997 that number had risen to 17.0%. When considering the number of new doctorates awarded, people of color received 7.5% of all new doctorates in psychology in 1977, and in 1997 that percentage was 13.9%. Finally, considering the percentages of people of color in the workforce with Ph.D.'s in psychology, that percentage went from 2.0% in 1973 to 8.5% in 1997 (APA, 1998l).

Diversity seems to be an important component of higher education. Why? We think this is a fair question to ask. In a civilized society, sometimes the qualities that are aspired to are hard to pinpoint, and for some, hard to justify. In February 1999, 67 learned societies banded together to publish a statement titled "On the Importance of Diversity in Higher Education" (Chronicle of Higher Education, 1999). While we can't provide the entire statement below, here are some of the key points:

Many colleges and universities share a common belief, born of experience, that diversity in their student bodies, faculties, and staff is important for them to fulfill their primary mission: providing a high quality education. The public is entitled to know why these institutions believe so strongly that racial and ethnic diversity should be one factor among the many considered in admissions and hiring. The reasons include:

- Diversity enriches the educational experience. We learn from those whose experiences, beliefs, and perspectives are different from our own, and these lessons can be taught best in a richly diverse intellectual and social environment.
- It promotes personal growth—and a healthy society. Diversity challenges stereotyped preconceptions; it encourages critical thinking; and it helps students learn to communicate effectively with people of varied backgrounds.
- It strengthens communities and the workplace. Education within a diverse setting prepares students to become good citizens in an increasingly complex, pluralistic society; it fosters mutual respect and teamwork; and it helps build communities whose members are judged by the quality of their character and their contributions.
- It enhances America's economic competitiveness. Sustaining the nation's prosperity in the 21st century will require us to make effective use of the talents and abilities of all our citizens, in work settings that bring together individuals from diverse backgrounds and cultures. (p. A42)

If you believe in the values of diversity as outlined above, then you can be confident that psychology as a profession seems to be headed in a good direction. Given the emphasis of understanding human beings and the study of individual differences, it is hard to think of someone who would not value diversity *but* be truly interested in understanding human behavior.

OTHER RELATED OPTIONS

The bulk of our efforts has been to address psychology and students choosing to major in it. There are a number of related disciplines that we want to discuss briefly to make the picture complete. A common response students give when they are asked, "Why are you majoring in psychology?" is "Because I want to help people." Although this is a noble reason, it is also broad and vague. Many disciplines also strive to help people—in this section we'll focus on anthropology, criminal justice, political science, social work, and sociology. We do not present this information to talk you out of psychology but to make you aware of the full palette of possibilities available in the social sciences. Even though you may feel *strongly* that psychology is the major for you, we would be remiss if we didn't mention, at least in passing, that there are other opportunities for careers that help people. Our ultimate goal is for *you* to be satisfied in your choice of major and career. Table 9.2 presents some brief descriptions of the disciplines we mentioned above. It is extremely difficult to convey the essence of any discipline in a single paragraph or two. Psychology is included in the table for comparison purposes.

Table 9.2: Related Options to Psychology: Disciplines in the Social Sciences

Anthropology

From the American Anthropology Association (1998): Anthropology is the study of humankind. The word anthropology itself tells the basic story—from the Greek *anthropos* ("human") and *logia* ("study")—it is the study of humankind, from its beginnings millions of years ago to the present day. Nothing human is alien to anthropology. Indeed, of the many disciplines that study our species, Homo sapiens, only anthropology seeks to understand the whole panorama—in geographic space and evolutionary time—of human existence. Its subject matter is both exotic (e.g., star lore of the Australian aborigines) and commonplace (e.g., the anatomy of the foot). Its focus is both sweeping (the evolution of language) and microscopic (the use-wear of obsidian tools). Anthropologists may study ancient Mayan hieroglyphics, the music of African Pygmies, and the corporate culture of a U.S. car manufacturer. A common goal links these vastly different projects: to advance knowledge of who we are, how we came to be that way—and where we may go in the future.

Criminal Justice

From the University of Wisconsin-Milwaukee (1997): Study in the field of criminal justice examines the component parts of criminal justice—police, courts and corrections—and seeks to gain an understanding of the interdependencies between these separate parts of the criminal justice system. Courses emphasize the role of criminal justice agencies in society, particularly in relation to the impact of alternative criminal justice policies on society and social problems.

From San Diego State University (1998): The nature and control of crime are important social phenomena that affect all of our lives. The criminal justice program provides an in-depth analysis of this subject to students. Students who choose this major will study the development, functions, and structure of the criminal justice system. They will examine the roles of law enforcement agencies, the courts, correctional agencies, and private agencies that aid in the prevention and control of crime and delinquency. The in-depth study of pertinent justice issues is designed to foster the capacity for balanced and critical evaluation of criminal justice problems. The criminal justice administration major will appeal to undergraduates who are interested in preparing for a career in criminal justice, law, or a related field; to persons currently employed in the criminal justice community; and to individuals who are generally interested in studying how public policies about crime and its control, as well as deviance and its treatment, are created and implemented.

Table 9.2: Related Options to Psychology: Disciplines in the Social Sciences (continued)

Political Science

From Harvard University (1998a): Political science is by far the oldest of the social sciences and was invented when Socrates, it is said, first called Philosophy down from heaven and placed her in cities. In its oldest definition, political science was called the master science. More modern definitions are less comprehensive, but of the social sciences, political science has perhaps the least definite boundaries and the widest concerns. If political science is not the imperious master of other disciplines, it is their pliable servant and the most receptive to the data and methods of its neighbors and rivals. Almost anything that is not politics can be made relevant to politics, and a political scientist is almost never heard to say modestly "That is a non-political question."

From Mt. San Jacinto College (1998): Political science is the study of the acquisition and use of public power and authority. Politics and government affect everyone's life and impinge on activities in many fields.

From Marietta College (1998): Political science is the study of political behavior and the groups and institutions through which power is exercised. Students examine the purposes and problems of politics and evaluate many of the controversial issues of political life. They examine different viewpoints about the world community, analyzing political issues and relating them to ethical decisions.

Psychology

From Harvard University (1998b): Psychology is the scientific study of thought and behavior, and as such is an extremely broad discipline. To understand the events, internal and external, that lead us to behave as we do, we need to know a number of things. We must look at the biological basis of behavior, such as the nervous system, the endocrine system, and genetic influences. We also need to consider the role of learned behaviors acquired through experience and about the roles of sensation, perception, memory and cognition. We have to address individual differences, such as the characteristics that distinguish the individual from every other. We also need to consider the effects of social interaction, for people live among others and are influenced by their contacts and communications with other people. Because people change over time, we also need to know something about developmental processes. Understanding the roles of these various factors in the production of thought and behavior is a complex task, and therefore psychology is a complex and fascinating discipline. Psychologists share the common goal of understanding behavior through empirical investigation.

Social Work

From the Occupational Outlook Handbook (1998e): Social work is a profession for those with a strong desire to help people. Social workers help people deal with their relationships with others; solve their personal, family, and community problems; and grow and develop as they learn to cope with or shape the social and environmental forces affecting daily life. Social workers often encounter clients facing a life-threatening disease or a social problem requiring a quick solution. They also assist families that have serious conflicts, including those involving

Table 9.2: Related Options to Psychology: Disciplines in the Social Sciences (continued)
child or spousal abuse. Social workers practice in a variety of settings, including hospitals, in schools, mental health clinics and psychiatric hospitals, and in public agencies. Through direct counseling, social workers help clients identify their concerns, consider solutions, and find resources. Social workers typically arrange for services in consultation with clients, following through to assure the services are helpful.
Sociology
From Harvard University (1998c): Sociology is the study of society, of the social frameworks within which we live our lives. It is a study of social life at every level, from two-person relationships to the rise and fall of nations and civilizations. More than any other discipline it is a meeting place of the social sciences, combining its own ideas and methods with insights from history, anthropology, economics, political science, and psychology in an extended examination of the ways societies work—or fail to work.

Clearly, there are a variety of methods that you can use to help people—Table 9.2 just samples some of the disciplines related to psychology. In addition, the undergraduate degree is good preparation for graduate work in many of the disciplines mentioned above. This is a career path that students sometimes overlook. Don't limit your horizons and career choices.

SELF-REFLECTION AND SELF-ASSESSMENT

Our focus of this book has been to provide information that we feel is critical for you to be a successful psychology major. That goal rests on the notion that you want to be a psychology major. In the previous section, we reviewed several options that share some similarity with psychology. In this section we explore career interest tools. In particular, we focus on the Self-Directed Search (SDS), a career planning tool developed by John L. Holland (1994). The SDS developed out of Holland's theories of vocational choice (1958, 1959). According to Holland (1973), four working assumptions drive the theory:

1. In this culture, most persons can be categorized as one of six types: realistic, investigative, artistic, social, enterprising, or conventional.
2. There are six kinds of environments for a person: realistic, investigative, artistic, social, enterprising, and conventional.
3. People search for environments that will let them exercise their skills and abilities, express their attitudes and values, and tackle agreeable problems and roles.
4. A person's behavior is determined by an interaction between his or her personality and the characteristics of his or her environment.

The basic notion of this theory is that people are happier and more successful in a job that matches their interests, values, and skills. Scoring of the SDS is linked to occupational codes and titles. Thus, by determining your preferences for styles or types, the SDS gives you some indication of the jobs that you might like and would make the most of your skills and interests. The fundamental idea is that people and work environments can be classified according to Holland's six types; thus, if you know your own type and understand the types that are associated with particular careers, you can find a match.

Holland's SDS (1994) is a relatively straightforward inventory to take and complete. There is even an Internet version (http://self-directed-search.com/taketest.html), which, for a small fee, you can take on your computer and receive a personalized report with your results. According to the publisher, Psychological Assessment Resources (1998a), the SDS Form R is an easy-to-use, self-administered test that helps individuals find the occupations that best suit their interests and skills. Individuals answer questions about their aspirations, activities, competencies, occupations, and other self-estimates, and then add up their scores. These scores yield a three-letter Summary Code that designates the three personality types an individual most closely resembles. With this code, test-takers use the Occupations Finder to discover those occupations that best match their personality types, interests, and skills. This comprehensive booklet lists over 1,300 occupational possibilities—more than any other career interest inventory. The Occupations Finder also provides the educational development level each occupation requires and the associated *Dictionary of Occupational Titles* code. Although it's not possible for you to take the SDS here, we describe the six personality types and examples of corresponding careers in Table 9.3. If you are interested in taking the SDS, you might want to contact your campus Counseling and Testing Center or Career Center. There may be a small fee for this service, but the insight and self-reflection gained from the SDS is worth it.

Table 9.3: Types and Occupations of the Self-Directed Search

Realistic		*Investigative*	
Type	*Occupations*	*Type*	*Occupations*
• Have mechanical ability and athletic ability? • Like to work outdoors? • Like to work with machines and tools? • Genuine, humble, modest, natural, practical, realistic?	• Aircraft controller • Electrician • Carpenter • Auto mechanic • Surveyor • Rancher	• Have math and science abilities? • Like to explore and understand things and events? • Like to work alone and solve problems? • Analytical, curious, intellectual, rational?	• Biologist • Geologist • Anthropologist • Chemist • Medical technologist • Physicist
Artistic		*Social*	
Type	*Occupations*	*Type*	*Occupations*
• Have artistic skills and a good imagination? • Like reading, music, or art? • Enjoy creating original work? • Expressive, original, idealistic, independent, open?	• Musician • Writer • Decorator • Composer • Stage director • Sculptor	• Like to be around other people? • Like to cooperate with other people? • Like to help other people? • Friendly, understanding, cooperative, sociable, warm?	• Teacher • Counselor • Speech therapist • Clergy member • Social worker • Clinical psychologist

Enterprising		Conventional	
Type	*Occupations*	*Type*	*Occupations*
• Have leadership and public speaking ability? • Like to influence other people? • Like to assume responsibility? • Ambitious, extroverted, adventurous, self-confident?	• Manager • Salesperson • Business executive • Buyer • Promoter • Lawyer	• Have clerical and math abilities? • Like to work indoors? • Like organizing things and meeting clear standards? • Efficient, practical, orderly, conscientious?	• Banker • Financial analyst • Tax expert • Stenographer • Production editor • Cost estimator

Note. From "Welcome to the Self-Directed Search®, Psychological Assessment Resources, 1998, [online], retrieved January 4, 1999, at http://self-directed-search.com.

The SDS presents some interesting options for persons thinking about a career. Although you haven't taken the SDS, you can look at the six different types and realize that perhaps one or two of them fit you very well. The idea here is to not be afraid of some self-exploration; it is important for you to figure out what you would like to do for a career. College is a great time for career exploration; if you put some work into it, you will enjoy the rewards you reap.

MORE RESOURCES

We designed this entire book to include a listing of valuable resources for you. Be sure to take advantage of the references section (which lists everything we have referenced). As you can tell from our citations, the Internet is becoming a valuable resource for information about psychology; we recommended some specific Web sites in Chapter 5. For more information, especially about careers, you might want to check out some of the resources listed below. Lloyd and Dewey (1998) made some of these suggestions.

- Appleby, D. (1997). *The handbook of psychology*. Reading, MA: Longman.
- DeGalan, J., & Lambert, S. (1995). *Great jobs for psychology majors*. Lincolnwood, IL: VGM Career Horizons.
- Field, S. (1992). *100 careers for the year 2000*. New York: Prentice Hall.
- Keith-Spiegel, P. (1991). *The complete guide to graduate school admission: Psychology and related fields*. Hillsdale, NJ: Erlbaum.
- Morgan, B. L., & Korschgen, A. J. (1998). *Majoring in psych? Career options for psychology undergraduates*. Boston: Allyn & Bacon.
- Reingold, H. (1994). *The psychologist's guide to an academic career*. Washington, DC: American Psychological Association.
- Sternberg, R. J. (Ed.). (1997). *Career paths in psychology: Where your degree can take you*. Washington, DC: American Psychological Association.
- Super, C. M., & Super, D. E. (1994). *Opportunities in psychology careers*. Lincolnwood, IL: VGM Career Horizons.

- United States Bureau of Labor Statistics. (1998). *Occupational outlook handbook.* Washington, DC: Author.

We have previously mentioned many of these resources. Keep them in mind as you make your career plans. Knowledge is power; so we hope you will gather all the information you can and then make intelligent decisions.

Psychology is an exciting profession, and one with a positive, growing future. The complications of current lifestyles and choices make understanding behavior even more important and imperative. Behavioral problems and difficulties are all the more commonplace nowadays. Compared to other sciences, psychology is a relatively young science, with many frontiers still to be blazed, and a number of behavioral phenomena yet to be explored or understood. We do have a bias, however—we think that psychology is inherently fascinating, and when you are passionate about a topic such as this, it's natural to want to share that feeling and hope it is infectious. We hope that you come away from this book feeling more positive and more informed about what psychology has to offer, and how you can do well in the psychology major. As we discussed in Chapter 1, the choice of psychology as a discipline to study and as a career can take many different directions and occur in many different settings. We hope that your use of this book will be a continual one as you journey through the major—at different times you may need to refer to different sections of the book.

What can be more interesting than understanding human behavior? Many psychologists have found that attempting to answer that question can make for a pleasant and rewarding career choice.

REFERENCES

American Anthropology Association. (1998). What is anthropology? [Online]. Retrieved January 4, 1999, at http://www.ameranthassn.org/anthbroc.htm.

American Psychological Association, Committee for the Protection of Human Participants in Research. (1992). *Ethical principles in the conduct of research with human participants.* Washington, DC: Author.

American Psychological Association. (1992). Starting salaries for full-time employment positions: 1992 baccalaureate recipients in psychology. [Online]. Retrieved November 20, 1998, at http://research.apa.org/95survey/table7.html.

American Psychological Association. (1994). *Publication manual of the American Psychological Association* (4th ed.). Washington, DC: Author.

American Psychological Association. (1996). *Psychology: Careers for the twenty-first century.* Washington, DC: Author.

American Psychological Association. (1997a). Employment activities of 1992 baccalaureate recipients in psychology. [Online]. Retrieved November 20, 1998, at http://research.apa.org/bac10.html.

American Psychological Association. (1997b). A guide to getting in to graduate school. [Online]. Retrieved November 28, 1998, at http://www.apa.org/ed/getin.html.

American Psychological Association. (1998a). *Graduate study in psychology* (31st ed.). Washington, DC: Author.

American Psychological Association. (1998b). Skills (that may be) obtained during graduate study in psychology. [Online]. Retrieved March 30, 1998, at http://www.apa.org/science/skills. html.

American Psychological Association. (1998c). Data on education and employment – master's. [Online]. Retrieved November 28, 1998, at http://research.apa.org/mas2.html.

American Psychological Association. (1998d). Data on education and employment – master's. [Online]. Retrieved November 28, 1998, at http://research.apa.org/mas1.html.

American Psychological Association. (1998e). Data on education and employment – master's. [Online]. Retrieved November 28, 1998, at http://research.apa.org/mas4.html.

American Psychological Association. (1998f). Data on education and employment – master's. [Online]. Retrieved November 28, 1998, at http://research.apa.org/mas5.html.

American Psychological Association. (1998g). Data on education and employment – doctorate. [Online]. Retrieved November 28, 1998, at http://research.apa.org/doc1.html.

American Psychological Association. (1998h). Data on education and employment – doctorate. [Online]. Retrieved November 28, 1998, at http://research.apa.org/doc9.html.

American Psychological Association. (1998i). Data on education and employment–doctorate. [Online]. Retrieved November 28, 1998, at http://research.apa.org/doc5.html.

American Psychological Association. (1998j). Acceptance and enrollment rates in the fall of 1996 in U.S. graduate departments of psychology by degree level and program area. [Online]. Retrieved November 28, 1998, at http://research.apa.org/inserttable4.html.

American Psychological Association. (1998k). Attrition rates of students enrolled full-time in U.S. and Canadian doctoral and master's programs: 1996–97. [Online]. Retrieved November 28, 1998, at http://research.apa.org/inserttable10.html.

American Psychological Association. (1998l). Data on education and employment—general. Demographic shifts in psychology. [Online]. Retrieved April 11, 1999, at http://research.apa.org/gen1.html.

Appleby, D. (1997). *The handbook of psychology*. Reading, MA: Longman.

Appleby, D. (1998a, August). The teaching-advising connection: Tomes, tools, and tales. G. Stanley Hall lecture, American Psychological Association meeting, San Francisco.

Appleby, D. (1998b, August). *Professional planning portfolio for psychology majors*. Indianapolis, IN: Marian College.

Appleby, D. C. (1990). Characteristics of graduate school superstars. [Online]. Retrieved September 28, 1998, at http://www.psychwww.com/careers/suprstar.htm.

Banerji, A. (1998, June 5). College degree is not necessary for economic success, U. of Michigan study finds. [Online]. Retrieved June 8, 1998, at http://www.chronicle.com/daily/98/06/9806506n.shtml.

Benjamin, L. T., Jr., Cavell, T. A., & Shallenberger, W. R., III. (1984). Staying with initial answers on objective tests: Is it a myth? *Teaching of Psychology, 11*, 133–141.

Bloom, L. J., & Bell, P. A. (1979). Making it in graduate school: Some reflections about the superstars. *Teaching of Psychology, 6*, 231–232.

Bloomquist, D. W. (1981). *A guide to preparing a psychology student handbook*. Washington, D.C.: American Psychological Society.

Boise State University Department of Counseling. (1998). BSU Counseling and Testing Center paraprofessional program. [Online]. Retrieved January 7, 1999, at http://www.boisestate.edu/counsel/workshop/parapro.htm.

Bordens, K. S., & Abbott, B. B. (1988). *Research design and methods: A process approach*. Mountain View, CA: Mayfield Publishing Co.

Boring, E. G. (1950). A history of experimental psychology (2nd ed.). Englewood Cliffs, NJ: Prentice Hall.

Brandeis University. (1998). Library research guides—psychology. [Online]. Retrieved October 27, 1998, at http://www.library.brandeis.edu/resguides/subject/psycguide.html.

Braskamp, L. A., Wise, S. L., & Hengstler, D. D. (1979). Student satisfaction as a measure of departmental quality. *Journal of Educational Psychology, 71,* 494–498.

Buckalew, L. W., & Lewis, H. H. (1982). Curriculum needs: Life preparation for undergraduate psychology majors. *Psychological Reports, 51,* 77–78.

Bureau of Labor Statistics. (1998, September 9). Employment and total job openings, 1996-2006, and 1996 median weekly earnings by education and training. [Online]. Retrieved on September 20, 1998, at http://www.bls.gov/news.release/ecopro.table5.htm.

Butler, D. L. (1997, May 7). Getting a job with an undergraduate degree in psychology. [Online]. Retrieved March 30, 1998, at http://www.bsu.edu/psysc/what/ujob.html.

CareerMosaic. (1997). Resume writing tips. [Online]. Retrieved September 28, 1998, at http://www.careermosaic.com/cm/rwc/rwc3.html.

Carmody, D. P. (1998). Student views on the value of undergraduate presentations. *Eye on Psi Chi, 2,* 11–14

Cashin, J. R., & Landrum, R. E. (1991). Undergraduate students' perceptions of graduate admissions criteria in psychology. *Psychological Reports, 69,* 1107–1110.

Chastain, G., & Landrum, R. E. (Eds.). (1999). *Protecting human subjects: Departmental subject pools and institutional review boards.* Washington, DC: APA Books.

Chicago Editorial Staff. (1993). *The Chicago manual of style: The essential guide for authors, editors, and publishers* (14th ed.). Chicago: University of Chicago Press.

Chronicle of Higher Education. (1998a). Demographics. [Online]. Retrieved on August 27, 1998, at http://www.chronicle.com/free/almanac/1998/nation/nation.htm.

Chronicle of Higher Education. (1998b). Attitudes and characteristics of freshmen, Fall 1997. [Online]. Retrieved on August 27, 1998, at http://www.chronicle.com/weekly/almanac/1998/facts/3stu.htm.

Chronicle of Higher Education. (1998c). Psychology. [Online]. Retrieved on August 27, 1998, at http://www.chronicle.com/weekly/almanac/1998/facts/9stu.htm.

Chronicle of Higher Education. (1999, February 12). *On the importance of diversity in higher education* [Advertisement]. Chronicle of Higher Education, p. A42.

Clay, R. A. (1998). Is a psychology diploma worth the price of tuition? [Online]. Retrieved December 1, 1998, at http://www.apa.org/monitor/sep96/tuition.html.

Conners, F. A., Mccown, S. M., & Roskos-Ewoldsen, B. (1998). Unique challenges in teaching undgergraduate statistics. *Teaching of Psychology, 25,* 40–42.

Coxford, L. M. (1998). How to write a résumé. [Online]. Retrieved September 28, 1998, at http://www.aboutwork.com/rescov/resinfo/cosford.html.

Crawford, M. P. (1992). Rapid growth and change at the American Psychological Association: 1945 to 1970. In R.B. Evans, V.S. Sexton, & T.C. Cadwallader (Eds.), *The American Psychological Association: A historical perspective* (Chapter 7, pp. 177–232). Washington, DC: American Psychological Association.

Davis, S. F. (1995). The value of collaborative scholarship with undergraduates. *Psi Chi Newsletter, 21,* 1, 12–13.

Davis, S. F. (1997). "Cheating in high school is for grades, cheating in college is for a career": Academic dishonesty in the 1990s. *Kansas Biology Teacher, 6,* 79–81.

Davis, S. F., Grover, C. A., Becker, A. H., & McGregor, L. N. (1992). Academic dishonesty: Prevalence, determinants, techniques, and punishments. *Teaching of Psychology, 19,* 16–20.

Davis, S. F., & Ludvigson, H. W. (1995). Additional data on academic dishonesty and a proposal for remediation. *Teaching of Psychology, 22,* 119–122.

Davis, S. F., Pierce, M. C., Yandell, L. R., Arnow, P. S., & Loree, A. (1995). Cheating in college and the Type A personality: A reevaluation. *College Student Journal, 29,* 493–497.

DeGalan, J., & Lambert, S. (1995). *Great jobs for psychology majors.* Lincolnwood, IL: VGM Career Horizons.

Diehl, J., & Sullivan, M. (1998). Suggestions for application for graduate study in psychology. [Online]. Retrieved Septmeber 28, 1998, at http://psych.hanover.edu/handbook/gradapp2.html.

Dodson, J. P., Chastain, G., & Landrum, R. E. (1996). Psychology seminar: Careers and graduate study in psychology. *Teaching of Psychology, 23,* 238–240.

Educational Testing Service. (1998a*). Graduate Record Examinations® 1998–1999 information and registration bulletin.* Princeton, NJ: Author.

Educational Testing Service. (1998b). *Graduate Record Examinations®: Guide to the use of scores.* Princeton, NJ: Author.

Educational Testing Servide. (1998c). *Graduate Record Examinations®: Writing assessment.* Princeton, NJ: Author.

Edwards, J., & Smith, K. (1988). What skills and knowledge do potential employers value in baccalaureate psychologists? In P. J. Woods (Ed.), *Is psychology for them? A guide to undergraduate advising.* Washington, DC: American Psychological Association.

Erdwins, C. J. (1980). Psychology majors in the paraprofessional role. *Professional Psychology, 11,* 106–112.

Field, S. (1992*). 100 careers for the year 2000.* New York: Prentice Hall.

Finney, P., Snell, W., Jr., & Sebby, R. (1989). Assessment of academic, personal, and career development of alumni from Southeast Missouri State University. *Teaching of Psychology, 16,* 173–177.

Gallucci, N. T. (1997). An evaluation of the characteristics of undergraduate psychology majors. *Psychological Reports, 81,* 879–889.

Garavalia, L. S., & Gredler, M. E. (1998, August). Planning ahead: Improved academic achievement? Presented at the American Psychological Association, San Francisco.

Gibaldi, J., & Achtert, W. S. (1988). *MLA handbook for writers of research papers* (3rd ed.). New York: Modern Language Association of America.

Harvard University. (1998a). Government. [Online]. Retrieved January 4, 1999, at http://www.registrar.fas.harvard.edu/handbooks/student/chapter3/government.html.

Harvard University. (1998b). Psychology. [Online]. Retrieved January 4, 1999, at http://www.registrar.fas.harvard.edu/handbooks/student/chapter3/psychology.html.

Harvard University. (1998c). Sociology. [Online]. Retrieved January 4, 1999, at http://www.registrar.fas.harvard.edu/handbooks/student/chapter3/sociology.html.

Hayes, L. J., & Hayes, S. C. (1989, September). How to apply to graduate school. [Online]. Retrieved September 28, 1998, at http://psych.hanover.edu/handbook/applic2.html.

Hayes, N. (1996, June). The distinctive skills of a psychology graduate. [Online]. Retrieved March 30, 1998, at http://www.apa.org/monitor/jul97/skills.html.

Holder, W. B., Leavitt, G. S., & McKenna, F. S. (1958). Undergraduate training for psychologists. *American Psychologist, 13,* 585–588.

Holland, J. L. (1958). A personality inventory employing occupational titles. *Journal of Applied Psychology, 42,* 336–342.

Holland, J. L. (1959). A theory of vocational choice. *Journal of Counseling Psychology, 6,* 35–45.

Holland, J. L. (1973). *Making vocational choices: A theory of careers.* Englewood Cliffs, NJ: Prentice Hall.

Holland, J. L. (1994). Self-Directed Search® (SDS®) Form R (4th ed.). [Instrument]. Odessa, FL: Psychological Assessment Resources.

Hopper, C. (1998a). Ten tips you need to survive college. [Online]. Retrieved on September 28, 1998, at http://www.mtsu.edu/~studskl/10tips.html.

Hopper, C. (1998b). Time management. [Online]. Retrieved on September 28, 1998, at http://www.mtsu.edu/~studsk1/tmt.html.

Idaho Department of Labor. (1998, October). Job application tips. Meridian, ID: Author.

Institute for Scientific Information. (1998). *Social sciences citation index.* Philadelphia: Author.

Instructions in Regard to Preparation of Manuscript. (1929). *Psychological Bulletin, 26,* 57–63.

Jessen, B. C. (1988). Field experience for undergraduate psychology students. In P. J. Wood (Ed.), *Is Psychology for Them? A Guide to Undergraduate Advising.* Washington, DC: American Psychological Association.

Jones, R. A. (1985). *Research methods in the social and behavioral sciences.* Sunderland, MA: Sinauer Associates.

Kallgren, C. A., & Tauber, R. T. (1996). Undergraduate research and the institutional review board: A mismatch or happy marriage? *Teaching of Psychology, 23*, 20–25.

Keith-Spiegel, P. (1991). *The complete guide to graduate school admission: Psychology and related fields*. Hillsdale, NJ: Erlbaum.

Kennedy, J. H., & Lloyd, M. A. (1998, August). *Effectiveness of a careers in psychology course for majors*. Poster presented at the meeting of the American Psychological Association, San Francisco.

Kerckhoff, A. C., & Bell, L. (1998). Hidden capital: Vocational credentials and attainment in the United States. *Sociology of Education, 71*, 152–174.

Keyes, B. J., & Hogberg, D. K. (1990). Undergraduate psychology alumni: Gender and cohort differences in course usefulness, postbaccalaureate education, and career paths. *Teaching of Psychology, 17,* 101–105.

Korn, J. H. (1988). Students' roles, responsibilities, and rights as research participants. *Teaching of Psychology, 15*, 74–78.

Kressel, N. J. (1990). Job and degree satisfaction among social science graduates. *Teaching of Psychology, 17,* 222–227.

LaCour, J., & Lewis, D. M. (1998). Effects of a course in ethics on self-rated and actual knowledge of undergraduate psychology majors. *Psychological Reports, 82*, 499–504.

Lamb, C. S. (1991). Teaching professional ethics to undergraduate counseling students. *Psychological Reports, 69*, 1215–1223.

Landers, A. (1997, June 18). Job hunters should be aware of rules. *The Idaho Statesman*, Section D, p. 3.

Landrum, R. E. (1998, April). *Career opportunities in research, industry, & consulting*. In "Good Jobs for B.A.'s in Psychology" symposium, Midwestern Psychological Association, Chicago.

Landrum, R. E., & Chastain, G. (1995). Experiment spot-checks: A method for assessing the educational value of undergraduate participation in research. *IRB: A Review of Human Subjects Research, 17 (4)*, 4–6.

Landrum, R. E., Jeglum, E. B., & Cashin, J. R. (1994). The decision-making processes of graduate admissions committees in psychology. *Journal of Social Behavior and Personality, 9*, 239–248.

Landrum, R. E., & Muench, D. M. (1994). Assessing students' library skills and knowledge: The Library Research Strategies Questionnaire. *Psychological Reports, 75*, 1619–628.

Lefton, L. A. (1997). *Psychology* (6th ed.). Boston: Allyn & Bacon.

Library of Congress. (1990). *LC classification outline*. Washington, DC: Author.

Lloyd, M. A. (1997a, August 28). Exploring career-related abilities, interests, skills, and values. [Online]. Available at http://www.psych-web.com/careers/explore.htm.

Lloyd, M. A. (1997b, September 23). Entry-level positions obtained by psychology majors. [Online]. Retrieved on March 30, 1998, at http://www.psych-web.com/careers/entry.htm.

Lloyd, M. A., & Dewey, R. A. (1998, February 16). Books on careers for psychology majors. [Online]. Retrieved March 30, 1998, at http://www.psych-web.com/careers/books.htm.

Lloyd, M. A., Kennedy, J. H., & Dewey, R. A. (1997, August 28). Suggested courses to develop skills that prospective employers want. [Online]. Available at http://www.psych-web.com/careers/suggest.htm.

Lore, N. (1997). How to write a masterpiece of a resume. [Online]. Retrieved September 28, 1998, at http://www.his.com/~rockport/resumes.htm.

Lunneborg, P. W. (1985). Job satisfaction in different occupational areas among psychology baccalaureates. *Teaching of Psychology, 12*, 21–22.

Lunneborg, P. W., & Baker, E. C. (1986). Advising undergraduates in psychology: Exploring the neglected dimension. *Teaching of Psychology, 13*, 181–185.

Marietta College. (1998). Political science. [Online]. Retrieved January 4, 1999, at http://www.marietta.edu/~poli/index.html.

Martin, D. W. (1991). *Doing psychology experiments* (3rd ed.). Pacific Grove, CA: Brooks/Cole.

Mathiasen, R. E. (1998). Moral education of college students: Faculty and staff perspectives. *College Student Journal, 32*, 374–377.

Maxwell, S. E., & Delaney, H. D. (1991). *Designing experiments and analyzing data*. Belmont, CA: Wadsworth.

McConnell, K. (1998). Study skill checklist. [Online]. Retrieved September 28, 1998, at http://wwwmc.nhmccd.edu/elc/reading_writing_area/studycl.html.

McGovern, T. V., & Carr, K. F. (1989). Carving out the niche: A review of alumni surveys on undergraduate psychology majors. *Teaching of Psychology, 16, 52–57.*

McGovern, T. V., Furumoto, L., Halpern, D. F., Kimble, G. A., & McKeachie, W. J. (1991). Liberal education, study in depth, and the arts and sciences major—psychology. *American Psychologist, 46*, 598-605.

Meeker, F., Fox, D., & Whitley, Jr., B. E. (1994). Predictors of academic success in the undergraduate psychology major. *Teaching of Psychology, 21, 238–241.*

Menges, R. J., & Trumpeter, P. W. (1972). Toward an empirical definition of relevance in undergraduate instruction. *American Psychologist, 27*, 213–217.

Merriam, J., LaBaugh, R. T., & Butterfield, N. E. (1992). Library instruction for psychology majors: Minimum training guidelines. *Teaching of Psychology, 19*, 34–36.

Morgan, B. L., & Korschgen, A. J. (1998*). Majoring in psych? Career options for psychology undergraduates*. Boston: Allyn & Bacon.

Mount Saint Vincent University. (1998). Benefits to the co-op student. [Online]. Retrieved on December 1, 1998, at http://serf.msvu.ca/coop/st_ben.htm.

Mt. San Jacinto College. (1998). Mt. San Jacinto College political science. [Online]. Retrieved January 4, 1999 at http://www.msjc.cc.ca.us/degrees/courseindex/polysci.html.

Murray, B. M. (1998). Bachelor's graduates seek greater challenges. Is psychology for them? A guide to undergraduate advising. Retrieved March 30, 1998, at http://www.apa.org/monitor/jul97/jobs.html.

National Science Foundation. (1995). Selected characteristics of 1994 psychology baccalaureate recipients. [Online]. Retrieved November 20, 1998, at http://research.apa.org/bac1.html.

Occupational Outlook Handbook. (1998a, January 15). Social and human service assistants. [Online]. Retrieved September 20, 1998, at http://www.bls.gov/oco/ocos059.htm.

Occupational Outlook Handbook. (1998b, August 31). Table 1. Fastest growing occupations and occupations having the largest numerical increase in employment, projected 1996–2006, by level of education and training. [Online]. Retrieved September 20, 1998, at http://www.bls.gov/oco/ocotjt1.htm.

Occupational Outlook Handbook. (1998c, January 15). Counselors. [Online]. Retrieved September 20, 1998, at http://www.bls.gov/oco/ocos067.htm.

Occupational Outlook Handbook. (1998d, January 15). Psychologists. [Online]. Retrieved September 20, 1998, at http://www.bls.gov/oco/ocos056.htm.

Occupational Outlook Handbook. (1998e). Social workers. [Online]. Retrieved September 20, 1998, at http://www.bls.gov/oco/ocos060.htm.

Perlman, B., & McCann, L. I. (1998a). *The most frequently listed courses in the undergraduate psychology curriculum*. Paper presented at the meeting of the American Psychological Association, San Francisco.

Perlman, B., & McCann, L. I. (1998b). *The structure of the psychology undergraduate curriculum*. Paper presented at the meeting of the American Psychological Association, San Francisco.

Pinkus, R. B. & Korn, J. H. (1973). The preprofessional option: An alternative to graduate work in psychology. *American Psychologist, 28*, 710–718.

Plous, S. (1998a). Advice on letters of recommendation. [Online]. Retrieved September 28, 1998, at http://www.wesleyan.edu/spn/recitips.htm.

Plous, S. (1998b). Tips on creating an academic vita. [Online]. Retrieved September 28, 1998, at http://www.wesleyan.edu/spn/vitatips.htm.

Plous, S. (1998c). Sample template for creating a vita. [Online]. Retrieved September 28, 1998, at http://www.weslyan.edu/spn/vitasamp.htm.

Psi Chi. (1998). Tips for paper/poster presentation. *Eye on Psi Chi, 2*, 35, 42.

Psychological Assessment Resources. (1998a). Self-Directed Search ® (SDS®) Form R: 4th edition. [Online]. Retrieved January 4, 1999, at http://www.parinc.com/career/sdsr98.html.

Psychological Assessment Resources. (1998b). Welcome to the Self-Directed Search®. [Online]. Retrieved January 4, 1999, at http://self-directed-search.com.

Quereshi, M. Y., Brennan, P. J., Kuchan, A. M., & Sackett, P. R. (1974). Some characteristics of undergraduate majors in psychology. *Journal of Experimental Education, 42*, 65–70.

Reingold, H. (1994). *The psychologist's guide to an academic career*. Washington, DC: American Psychological Association.

Rickard, H. C., Rogers, R., Ellis, N. R., & Beidleman, W. B. (1988). Some retention, but not enough. *Teaching of Psychology, 15*, 151–152.

Robinson, F. P. (1970). *Effective study* (4th ed.). New York: Harper & Row.

Rosnow, R. L., Rotheram-Borus, M. J., Ceci, S. J., Blanck, P. D., & Koocher, G. P. (1993). The institutional review board as a mirror of scientific and ethical standards. *American Psychologist, 48*, 821–826.

San Diego State University. (1998). SDSU criminal justice program. [Online]. Retrieved January 6, 1999, at http:/www.sdsu.edu/academicprog/crimjust.html.

Scheirer, C. J. (1983). Professional schools: Information for students and advisors. *Teaching of Psychology, 10,* 11–15.

Schultz, D. P., & Schultz, S. E. (1992). *A history of modern psychology* (5th ed.). Fort Worth, TX: Harcourt Brace Jovanovich.

Shepard, B. (1996, February 12). Employment opportunities for psychology majors. [Online]. Retrieved March 30, 1998, at http://www.cs.trinity.edu/~cjackson/employ.html#employ-top.

SilverPlatter Information Services. (1998). PsycLIT [CD-ROM]. Wellesley Hills, MA: Author.

Sternberg, R. J. (Ed.). (1997). *Career paths in psychology: Where your degree can take you*. Washington, DC: American Psychological Association.

Super, C. M., & Super, D. E. (1994). *Opportunities in psychology careers*. Lincolnwood, IL: VGM Career Horizons.

Taylor, R. D., & Hardy, C.-A. (1996). Careers in psychology at the associate's, bachelor's, master's, and doctoral levels. *Psychological Reports, 79*, 960–962.

TMP Worldwide. (1998). Action verbs to enhance your résumé. [Online]. Retrieved September 28, 1998, at http://www.aboutwork.com/rescov/resinfo/verbs.html.

Trials of War Criminals Before the Nuremberg Military Tribunals Under Control Council Law No. 10. (1949). *Nuremberg Code* (Vol. 2, pp. 181–182). Washington, DC: U.S. Government Printing Office.

Turabian, K. L. (1982). *A manual for writers of term papers, theses, and dissertations* (5th ed.). Chicago: University of Chicago Press.

United States Bureau of Labor Statistics. (1998). *Occupational outlook handbook*. Washington, DC: Author.

United States Department of Labor. (1991a). *What work requires of schools, A SCANS report for America 2000*. The Secretary's Commission on Achieving Necessary Skills. Washington, DC: Author.

United States Department of Labor. (1991b). *Tips for finding the right job*. Employment and Training Administration, Washington, DC: Author.

University of California–Berkeley. (1998). Taking tests—general tips. [Online]. Retrieved September 28, 1998, at http://www-slc.uga.berkeley.edu/CalREN/TestsGeneral.html.

University of California–Santa Cruz. (1998). Choosing a topic. [Online]. Retrieved October 27, 1998, at http://bob.ucsc.edu/library/ref/instruction/research/topic.htm.

University of Michigan at Dearborn. (1998). Benefits to the student. [Online]. Retrieved December 1, 1998, at http://www-personal.umd.umich.edu/~pdjones/benef_s.html.

University of Wisconsin–Milwaukee. (1997). Criminal justice undergraduate program info. [Online]. Retrieved January 6, 1999, at http://www.uwm.edu/Dept/CD/und_grad.htm.

University of Wyoming. (1998). Study distractions analysis. [Online]. Retrieved on September 28, 1998, at http://www.ucc.vt.edu/stdysk/studydis.html.

Vanderbilt University. (1996). How to select a research topic. [Online]. Retrieved October 27, 1998, at http://www.library.vanderbilt.edu/education/topic.html.

Waters, M. (1998, July). Naps could replace coffee as workers' favorite break. *American Psychological Association Monitor*, p. 6.

Watson, R. I., Sr., & Evans, R. B. (1991). *The great psychologists: A history of psychological thought* (5th ed.). New York: HarperCollins.

Webb, A. R., & Speer, J. R. (1986). Prototype of a profession: Psychology's public image. *Professional Psychology: Research and Practice, 17,* 5–9.

Weinstein, C. E., Palmer, D. R., & Schulte, A. C. (1987). *Learning and study strategies inventory*. Clearwater, FL: H&H Publishing Co.

Whiz, D. (1995). Doc Whiz's 40 ways to P.O. the prof. [Online]. Retrieved September 28, 1998, at http://monster.educ.kent.edu/docwhiz/poprof.html.

Wilson, D. W. (1998). It takes more than good grades. *Eye on Psi Chi, Winter,* 11–13, 42.

Wolfle, D. L. (1947). The sensible organization of courses in psychology. *American Psychologist, 2,* 437–445.

Woodworth, R. S. (1938). *Experimental psychology*. New York: Holt.

Woodworth, R. S., & Schlosberg, H. (1954). *Experimental psychology* (2nd ed.). New York: Holt.

Appendix A
BRIEF HISTORY OF PSYCHOLOGY

To look at the beginning of experimental psychology is to look at the beginning of psychology. The typical perception about psychology today is that it consists mostly of practitioners: clinicians, counselors, and therapists trained in the helping profession. Currently, that view is accurate: Over half of the members of the APA identify themselves as practitioners. However, the clinical and counseling areas of psychology did not emerge on a large scale until about 1945, at the close of World War II.

So how did psychology get its start? Wilhelm Wundt founded the first exclusive psychology laboratory in 1879; it was a laboratory that conducted experiments related to matters in experimental psychology. However, the study of, and interest in, human behavior has been with us probably since humans walked the earth. In fact, Hermann Ebbinghaus said it best in 1885, only six years after the founding of psychology, when he said, "Psychology has a long past but a short history." Our brief review of the history of psychology traces some of the antecedent influences leading psychology to its present status. As a psychology major, a better understanding of our historical roots will better equip you to evaluate and place current and future ideas in the appropriate context. Also, this chapter might come in as a handy review source if your college or university requires you to take a history and systems of psychology course or some sort of senior capstone course that includes historical information.

Why bother discussing the history of psychology in a book designed to be an introduction and overview of the psychology major? Watson and Evans (1991) note that there are a number of basic maxims (or beliefs) that govern the process of understanding behavior, and it is the ultimate goal of an experimental psychologist to understand behavior. Their historical maxims are presented here (Table A.1). Given the study of human behavior over the ages, a limited, common set of themes have emerged, and understanding the context and perspective of these themes hopefully helps us to understand behavior. Perhaps the most persuasive evidence for a psychologist to study the history of psychology comes from George Santayana, who once said, "Those who do not know history are doomed to repeat it." Whether this caution applies to prior research done in a particular area of experimental psychology or whether it applies to larger world events (e.g., the Holocaust), the implications are clear: Ignorance of the past is undesirable.

Table A.1: Some Historical Maxims

1. Remember that a written history is a mediated experience. The historian is always between you and the historical event. The historian's preconceptions, the selection of data, and other factors that a given history is *according to* some particular historian.
2. If an explanation of a complicated historical event seems to be too simple, chances are that it is. Historical events are seldom neatly packaged affairs.
3. Although it is important to understand what a particular writer had to say on a given topic, it is sometimes more important to know what those who were influenced by the person thought the writer said. The history of psychological thought is fraught with misreadings and misunderstandings.
4. Whether a given psychological theory in the past turns out to be true or false (from our historical perspective) is irrelevant here. What should be of importance to us is how a given school of thought or system influenced the thought of its own time, and how it deflected the course of psychological thought.
5. Ideas seldom, if ever, die. They may fade for a while, but they will almost always reemerge, perhaps with a different name and in a different context. None of the basic concepts on which modern psychology is based is new to this century or even to this millennium. It would be rash to say that a given idea originated with this psychologist or that philosopher.
6. Human thought, rather than being unlimited and eternally original, turns out to be surprisingly limited and repetitive. Only a few basic premises underlie psychological thought throughout history.

Note. From *The Great Psychologists: A History of Psychological Thought* (5th ed.), by R. I. Watson, Sr., and R. B. Evans, 1991, New York: HarperCollins.

ANTECEDENTS TO PSYCHOLOGY

In discussing the history of any science, there is always the issue of where to begin. With psychology one could begin with Wundt's laboratory in 1879 in Leipzig, Germany, but that would overlook many years of important, antecedent influences in the understanding of behavior. Where do we start then? We choose to begin our brief discussion with Descartes.

Descartes. Although there have been many potential contributors to the beginning of what is often called modern science, the ideas of the philosopher Rene Descartes (pronounced day-CART) are important to science but particularly to psychology. Descartes lived from 1596 to 1650 and worked to answer the question "Are the mind and body the same, or different?" His answer came to be known as Cartesian Dualism, which is the idea that mind and body are different, but that the mind can influence the body and the body can influence the mind. What was particularly important about this idea is that it allowed the emerging scientists of the Renaissance and the church to coexist. The church could still work to influence the mind of individuals, and the scientists of the day could study the body, each group having its own domain to some extent.

Descartes suggested that whereas the mind is the source of ideas and thoughts (which he correctly located in the brain), the body is a machine-like structure to be studied and understood. Descartes believed in both *nativism* and *rationalism*. A nativist believes that all knowledge is innate, inborn; whereas a rationalist believes that to gain knowledge one rationalizes or discovers the truth through experience and the operation of the mind. Descartes struggled to rationalize his own existence, trying to prove that he was real (in a philosophical way). His answer to the problem was to suggest "Cognito, ergo sum," meaning "I think, therefore I am."

Phrenology. Once the pursuit of science through sources other than philosophy was established, many disciplines and areas of study began to flourish. Two of these disciplines that had an impact on the beginning of psychology were phrenology and psychophysics. *Phrenology* was one approach to the mind-body problem studied by Franz Joseph Gall (1758–1828) and subsequently popularized by his student then colleague Joseph Spurzheim (1776–1832). The basic tenet of phrenology suggested that one could uncover and understand someone's personality by feeling and interpreting the bumps on the head. Although this idea may seem simplistic by today's standards, it was a popular idea at the time, and it was a concept that could be understood easily by common people. Phrenology assumed, however, that the skull was an accurate representation of the underlying brain, that the mind can be meaningfully divided and analyzed into 37 or more different functions, and that certain characteristics or qualities that we possess are found in certain precise locations in the brain. Therefore, by feeling someone's skull and noting the location of an abnormal bump (too much) or indentation (too little), an interpretation could be made as to whether someone possessed an overabundance or shortage of the corresponding trait.

Phrenology eventually ran its course, and skeptics ran phrenologists out of business, but phrenology contributed some important ideas to psychology. First, phrenology reemphasized that the brain is the organ of the mind, and if we are to understand the mind and behavior, the brain is a central area to understand. Second, the idea of localization of function (that different parts of the brain have certain specialties) is an idea that is still with us today. While the brain is not as easy to understand as some popular writers would have us believe (such as books for improving drawing skills by learning to use a particular side of your brain), particular brain structures do specialize in performing certain functions. Although phrenology's methods did not last, some of the assumptions of phrenology had great heuristic value.

Psychophysics. The area of psychophysics is probably the area of closest transition from philosophers studying behavior to psychologists studying behavior. Three researchers were key in the founding of psychology: *Hermann von Helmholtz*, *Ernst Weber*, and *Gustav Theodor Fechner*.

Hermann von Helmholtz (1821–1894) was interested in the general area of psychophysics. Psychophysics is the study of the interaction between the behavioral capabilities and limitations of the human perceptual system and the environment. In other words, how do we literally interpret the world we live in? For example, Helmholtz is famous for his extension and additions to a trichromatic theory of color vision (the Young-Helmholtz theory), explaining that the three basic colors of light—red, green, and blue—are represented in our visual system by three specialized cells in our retina (called cones). Helmholtz also worked on such topics as the speed of neuronal conduction and the perception of tones, both individually and in combination (such as in harmony or dissonance).

Ernst Weber (1795–1878) also shared this interest in psychophysics but studied the topic from a broader perspective. Weber was interested in all the sensory systems and how they worked. It was Weber who gave psychology the concept of just noticeable difference—that is, the smallest difference between two stimuli that can be noted by a person. This idea of *just noticeable difference* (jnd) could be applied to all sensory systems (sight, sound, taste, touch, smell), and in experimenting with various sensory systems Weber found that a constant equation emerged for each. That is, for each of the sensory systems, a consistent ratio emerged to detect a jnd. For the perception of lifting weight (the sense of touch), the ratio was found to be 1:40. That is, the average person can tell the difference between a 40- and a 41-pound suitcase, but cannot tell the difference between a 40- and a 40.5-pound suitcase. In this example, the just noticeable difference is 1 pound for every 40 pounds (hence 1:40). A jnd ratio was found for many of the sensory systems, and this general conceptualization has come to be known as Weber's law.

Gustav Fechner (1801–1887) was trained in both medicine and physics; he significantly expanded on the ideas of Weber. In fact, Fechner is said to be the founder of psychophysics, the science of the functional relationship between the mind and the body. Fechner has also been called the father of experimental psychology, and some historians (e.g., Boring, 1950) suggest that the founding of psychology could be accredited to Fechner in 1850 rather than Wundt in 1879. Why 1850? Fechner woke up from a long sickness on October 22, 1850, and recorded something in his journal like "the relative increase of bodily energy [is related to] the measure of the increase of the corresponding mental intensity." Fechner paved the path for psychology in making this important connection: *There is a direct relation between the stimulation received by the body and the sensation received by the mind.* Not only did Fechner make the explicit connection between mind and body, but he suggested that measurement is possible for both phenomena. For the first time in the study of thought the relationship between the mind and body could be measured and quantified, leading to the development of Fechner's law. Given the techniques from psychophysics to accomplish this task, later psychologists had the opportunity to measure behavior in much the same way as physical objects are measured. Although this quantitative link between mind and body may not seem striking today, it was revolutionary in its time and legitimized the work of later psychologists in trying to quantify all types of behaviors.

THE BEGINNING OF PSYCHOLOGY

Wundtian Psychology and Structuralism. Wilhelm Wundt (1832–1920) is credited with forming the first psychology laboratory (exclusively for psychological work) in Leipzig, Germany, in 1879. This starting date is rather arbitrary, and historians have argued that other dates (and people) are defensible. We might attribute the founding to Wundt in 1874, when he published *Principles of Physiological Psychology* (while physiological was the word used in the translation from German, a more appropriate translation would have been "experimental"), or perhaps the founding could be two years later in 1881, when Wundt began the first journal in psychology, *Philosophical Studies* (you might think that *Psychological Studies* would have been a better and less confusing title, but there already was a journal by that name that dealt primarily with psychic forces).

Wundt was interested in studying the mind and conscious experience. He believed that a rigorous program of *introspection* could be used to report the processes at work in the inner consciousness. Introspection was a technique used by researchers to describe and analyze their own inner thoughts and feelings during a research experience. Wundt and his colleagues carried out numerous research studies examining the contents of consciousness. Some of the better known results are Wundt's tridimensional theory of feeling and his work on mental chronometry. Thus, although mental processes themselves were not studied (they were unobservable), the time a mental process took was measurable and appropriate for study.

Wundt's contributions to psychology are briefly mentioned here. For the remainder of the 19th century, Wundt and his laboratory were the center of psychology, and anyone seriously interested in pursuing psychology traveled to Germany to study with Wundt. This situation changed rapidly by the beginning of the 20th century, when America took a stronghold on psychology. Perhaps Wundt's greatest influence was the mentoring of students: More than 160 students (an astounding number) received their Ph.D. under Wundt's supervision. One of those students was Edward Bradford Titchener (1867–1927), who studied with Wundt in Germany and then immigrated to Cornell University (Ithaca, NY) to promote his own variation of Wundtian psychology called structuralism.

Structuralism, the study of the anatomy of the mind, as a system of psychology shares some common characteristics with Wundt's ideas. Both systems were interested in the mind and conscious experience, and both used introspection. Structuralism departed from Wundt's ideas, however, in its application of introspection as the *only* method available for experimental inquiry and applied much more rigorous standards in its use. Titchener also spelled out quite clearly what structuralism was *not* interested in: applied problems, children, animals, individual differences, and higher mental processes.

Titchener's goal for structuralism was to use this rigorous introspective method to discover and identify the structures of consciousness, hence the title structuralism. Once the structures were understood, the laws of association could be verified, and then one could study the physiological conditions under which ideas and concepts become associated. The ultimate goal was to understand the workings of the mind. Titchener contributed significantly to the rapid growth of psychology in America by having 54 doctoral students complete their work under his direction at Cornell University; he also separated the psychology department from the philosophy department there. Although the pursuit of structuralism basically died with Titchener, he provided a concrete system of psychology that would later be the subject and focus of major changes in psychology, resulting in a alternative approach to psychology: functionalism.

Table A.2: Where Are the Women in the History of Psychology?

As you read about the history of psychology (whether it is in this brief appendix or in texts fully devoted to the topic), it is startling to notice the lack of women noted for their accomplishments and contributions to psychology. Why does this situation exist? Were women just not interested in psychology? Have historians of psychology been negligent in cataloging the contributions of women? Did societal forces preclude women from making contributions to

---

Table A.2: Where Are the Women in the History of Psychology? (continued)

psychology? The best evidence available indicates that general societal forces seemed to inhibit a woman's ability to receive training in psychology, hence limiting her contributions (Schultz & Schultz, 1992).

However, when looking at the late 1800s and the subsequent turn of the century, prohibition of women in the *sciences* was the status quo, not just in psychology. Although two women were elected as members of the APA in 1893 (the organization's second meeting ever), it wasn't until 1915 and 1918 that the American Medical Association and the American Bar Association admitted female members, respectively (Schultz & Schultz, 1992).

Three factors are identified as inhibiting the contributions of women during the early days of psychology. First, graduate programs were not very accessible to women. Women faced discrimination in their application to graduate school and, once admitted, sometimes had difficulty obtaining their rightfully earned degree. Second, there was a general discrimination held against women at the turn of the century. It was believed that women had innate deficits that hindered academic performance, and believing this, male graduate school professors did not want to "waste" educational opportunities on women. It was also believed that the rigors of graduate school were too much for a frail woman's physique. Third, even if a woman persevered through graduate school (gained admission, completed degree requirements, graduated), job availability for women was poor. Locked out of male-controlled faculty positions at universities, women often turned to more applied areas, such as clinical, counseling, and school psychology. Some of the most successful woemen from the early days of psychology include Margaret Floy Washburn, Christine Ladd-Franklin, Bluma Zeigarnik, Mary Whiton Calkins, and Karen Horney.

Functionalism. Functionalism is important to the history of American psychology, because it is a system of psychology that is uniquely American. Wundtian psychology and structuralism both have their roots in Germany, but functionalism is an American product. Three men were instrumental in promoting functionalism: William James, G. Stanley Hall, and James M. Cattell.

What was so different about functionalism that set it apart from Titchener's structuralism? Whereas structuralism focused on discovering the structure of consciousness and how its contents are organized and stored, functionalists were more interested in how the mind worked, what mental processes accomplish, and what role consciousness plays in our behavior. As you can see, these are two strikingly different approaches. The functionalist wanted to know how and why the mind works (as opposed to how is it structured).

William James (1842–1910) is noted in this transition period from structuralism to functionalism for his clarity of thought and strong opposition to Titchener. At Harvard University in 1875–76 he offered a course titled "The Relations Between Physiology and Psychology." In 1890, James published the two-volume *Principles of Psychology,* which was an impressive work written with brilliance and clarity. James supported more than just the introspective method, and felt that more experimental procedures as well as comparative studies (between species) were valuable approaches. James contributed his honorable reputation and standing to oppose the division of consciousness into structures, offering an alternative approach for studying the mind.

G. Stanley Hall (1844–1924) was a contributor to the founding of functionalism but probably would not be considered a functionalist. Hall is famous for his number of accomplishments in psychology (see Table A.3). Particularly important were (a) his founding the first American psychology laboratory at Johns Hopkins University in 1883; (b) his founding of the American Psychological Association in 1892; and (c) his bringing Sigmund Freud to America in 1909 (Freud's only visit to the United States). Hall was interested in a number of topics, including studying children and how they develop, and he founded developmental psychology and educational psychology. Hall's interests highlight the functioning of consciousness and how it allows us to adapt and survive in our environment.

Table A.3: G. Stanley Hall Firsts

- First American Ph.D. student in psychology
- First American student to study in the first psychology laboratory in the world in the first year that it opened (1879)
- Founded the first psychology research laboratory in the United States
- Founded the first U.S. journal of psychology
- First president of Clark University
- Organizer and first president of the American Psychological Association
- 11 of the first 14 American Ph.D.s in psychology were his students

---

James M. Cattell (1860–1944) was a student in G. Stanley Hall's laboratory course at Johns Hopkins University and went on to study with Wilhelm Wundt in Germany in 1883. Cattell was interested in studying human abilities and how they could be assessed and measured. Cattell brought this practical approach into the classroom, where he was the first psychologist to teach statistics and advocate their use in data analysis. In 1888, he was appointed a professor of psychology at the University of Pennsylvania; this type of appointment was the first in the world (at the time, all other psychologists held positions through a department of philosophy). Cattell's great contribution was his focus on a practical, test-oriented approach to studying mental processes rather than through introspective structuralism.

The transition from structuralism to functionalism reflects the rapidly changing times in psychology. In just the span of 20 years (1880–1900), the major focal point of psychology shifted from Germany to America. Multiple changes were taking place, and the work and influence of Charles Darwin was becoming better known (see Table A.4). In 1880, there were no American laboratories and no American psychological journals; by 1900, there were 26 U.S. laboratories and three U.S. psychology journals. In 1880, anyone wanting a respectable psychology education made the trip to Germany to study with the master, Wilhelm Wundt. By 1900, Americans stayed home to get a superior education in psychology. These changes seem revolutionary in that they occurred over a 20-year period, but the next system of psychology to come along was definitely revolutionary.

Table A.4: Contributions of Charles Darwin

The work of Charles Darwin (1809–1882) has influenced a number of scientific endeavors, including psychology. During a scientific voyage on the H.M.S. *Beagle* from 1831 to 1836, Darwin made some keen observations about the similarities and differences in the plant and animal life encountered in various regions of the world. Darwin discovered fossils and bones of animals that were no longer on earth. What could explain why some animals left traces of the past but were no longer present? In 1836, Darwin began considering a theory to explain the phenomena he had seen.

Twenty-two years later, in 1858, Darwin was pushed to publish his theory, and in 1859 *On the Origin of Species by Means of Natural Selection* was published. Darwin proposed a theory of survival of the fittest based on a few simple (parsimonious) ideas: (a) There is a degree of variation among members of a species; (b) this spontaneous variability is inheritable; (c) in nature, a process of *natural selection* works by identifying those organisms best suited for the environment. The best-suited organisms live and survive; those organisms not well suited are eliminated. Species must be adaptable and adjustable or else they die, ultimately through this process of natural selection. Darwin's practical approach to dealing with matters of survival greatly influenced the course of functionalism.

Darwin espoused the study of animals in addition to the study of humans. This viewpoint was accepted by the functionalists and subsequently made even stronger by the behaviorists. The subject matter of functionalism also fits quite well with the overall focus of the theory of natural selection: How does an organism function and adapt in its environment? Darwin's use of evidence from a number of fields of inquiry legitimized psychology's use of multiple approaches in studying functionalism, such as introspection, the experimental method, and particularly the comparative method. Lastly, Darwin's work focused on the individual differences between members of a similar species; today psychologists are still interested in understanding how we are different from one another.

Behaviorism and Neobehaviorism. In 1913, a functionalism-trained John B. Watson (1878–1958) literally declared war against the establishment by describing a totally new approach to psychology: behaviorism. The goals of this new behaviorism were to study only behaviors and processes that were totally objective and fully observable. In this new system there would be no introspection, no discussion of mental concepts, no study of the mind, and no mention of consciousness. Watson, in a pure scientific approach, wanted to study behavior, making no assumptions beyond what was available to the senses. Although behaviorism had a slow beginning, it took off in the 1920s and became (along with neobehaviorism) the dominant system of psychology for four decades. Any type of behavior was appropriate for study under Watson as long as it met the criteria of behaviorism. The methods of behaviorism were limited to observation and objective testing/experimentation.

Watson's views and behaviorism became quite popular both in psychology and to the general public. When studying and explaining behavior based on only what is observable, Watson did not depend on sexual overtones to explain behavior (this was a relief for many because Freudian ideas seemed to suggest that sex and sexual desires were the basis for just about everything we do). His message of behaviorism gave people hope in that they were not explicitly tied to their past or their heritage but could also be greatly influenced by their immediate environment. Watson's beliefs directly fed into the great American dream of the 1920s (freedom, liberty, hope).

Behaviorism as proposed by Watson defined a relatively narrow field of interest. While proposing a continuity between man and animals (so that animals are an appropriate avenue of study to understand humans), he also dictated that all mentalistic concepts were useless. For example, thinking, reasoning, and cognitive problem solving were not the subject matter of psychology, because they were not directly observable. Watson did not deny that those processes existed, but they were not studiable under a system of psychology that stressed the study of directly observable behaviors only. Watson also held a belief of extreme environmentalism, such that the situations and context that a person grows up in totally shape how the person behaves. Quite literally, Watson believed that the environment greatly controlled our behavior, and to understand how a certain environmental stimulus elicits a particular behavioral response—*that* was psychology. This theme was greatly expanded upon by B. F. Skinner (1904–1990) and his vast work in operant (instrumental) conditioning. Although the behaviorism approach literally attacked and demolished functionalism, some of the functionalist view survived. Behaviorists too were interested in how we adapt, survive, and function in our environment, but behaviorists had a vastly different approach to the study of these topics. This narrow approach of studying only directly observable behaviors troubled many, and eventually a new version of behaviorism called neobehaviorism developed.

Neobehaviorism continued much of the rigor of behaviorism while widening the scope of acceptable behaviors to study. Much of the distinction between behaviorism and neobehaviorism rests on the distinction between positivism and logical positivism (Maxwell & Delaney, 1991). Positivism is a system of evaluating knowledge based on the assumptions that (a) the only knowledge considered valuable is that which is objective and undebatable, (b) the only knowledge one can be sure of is that which is observable, and (c) empirical observations should be the basis for the acquisition of knowledge. Positivism in this sense means that knowledge is based on the presence of something; the basis for knowledge must physically exist, be objective, and be undebatable. Logical positivism allows for the study of unobservable phenomena as long as these hypothetical constructs and ideas are defined in such a way that they can be logically inferred. Behaviorists were strict positivists, only studying what was directly observable and undebatable.

What would be an example of the distinction between positivism and logical positivism? I like to use the concept of hunger. To a strict positivist, hunger is probably not a subject that can be studied by psychology. Can we directly observe hunger? No, because hunger is a hypothetical construct. For the logical positivist, hunger is an appropriate topic of study if and only if it can be operationally defined in directly observable terms. For example, we might operationally define hunger as the number of hours since last consuming food, or the decibel level of a growling stomach (at this point, we won't debate whether these definitions are any good). The logical positivist can study *any topic* in psychology as long as it could be operationally defined in observable, measurable terms.

Neobehaviorists, however, wanted to study somewhat mentalistic concepts like learning, memory, and problem solving, but at issue was the inability to observe behavior directly. Neobehaviorists found a solution by adopting logical positivism. That is, theoretical concepts that are not directly observable may be studied if these concepts are defined in terms of directly observable behaviors. Logical positivism hastened the need for operational definitions.

In neobehaviorism, any theoretical construct could now be studied (even ones that were directly unobservable) as long as the actual behavior measured was observable. What? Consider this example: A neobehaviorist is interested in doing a memory study. To a strict behaviorist, memory is not an acceptable subject to study, because a person's memory is not directly observable. In neobehaviorism, memory is an acceptable concept as long as it is defined in observable terms. In this case, memory could be defined as the number of items recalled from an original list of 25 items. The concept of memory has now been defined in terms of its operations (what happens), and number of items verbally recalled is an observable behavior. Neobehaviorism widened the focus of behaviors acceptable for study in psychology, and this combined approach of behaviorism and neobehaviorism dominated psychology for approximately 40 years (1920–1960).

Cognitive Psychology. In the field of experimental psychology in general, cognitive psychology seems to be the dominant area currently. Cognitive psychologists study how mental processes work and how knowledge is formed and used. The topics are wide ranging: Subjects such as attention, memory, problem solving, reasoning, logic, decision making, creativity, language, cognitive development, and intelligence are some of the many areas of interest in cognitive psychology. Cognitive psychology grew out of and as a reaction to neobehaviorists who tried to limit the acceptable topics of study (e.g., if you were interested in memory when neobehaviorism was still in, you were a "verbal learner"; nowadays you are a cognitive psychologist). Cognitive psychology is not quite yet a system of psychology, but it is probably the most popular approach in experimental psychology today.

Appendix B:
MORE VITA TIPS, WITH EXAMPLE VITAE FROM SENIOR-LEVEL PSYCHOLOGY MAJORS

Reprinted from the May 1989 issue of the **APS Observer.** Used with permission of the American Psychological Society.

For Students:

Writing Your Vita

by Steven C. Hayes and Linda J. Hayes

Your vita is a document you will get to know well. Regardless of your goals, you will be asked for it many times. It is a record of what you have done and a ticket allowing you to do more.

The topic of vita development can have a negative quality. Some people fall into vita building just for the sake of personal aggrandizement. Some scientists focus more on the quantity of the work than its quality; more on the notoriety of the work than its substance. But don't let these attitudes blind you to the importance of a good record, professionally presented. Your vita can give you access to good jobs where you can do good things; and considering what goes into a vita can help you focus your efforts and maintain your professional growth.

There are two aspects to a vita: doing and telling. That is, both form and substance are important. This article will describe what kinds of things go into a vita and how to present them.

The Sections of a Vita

Personal History

Usually the first things mentioned in a vita are items of personal history. Who are you? Where are you from? Are you married? These are the questions answered in this section. One good way to arrange these items is as follows:

Vita

Your Name   Date

A. Personal History

Business Address: Department of Psychology
                      University of London
                      London, England

Phone: (123) 456-7890
Home Address: 123 St. Norbert Cross
                      Flat #34
                      London, England

Phone: (123) 987-6543
Birthdate: August 24, 1965
Citizenship: USA
Marital Status: Single

You should line up the information in an attractive manner. Double space between items. You may wish to leave out marital status and/or birthdate. Some feel this information is irrelevant and could be used in a discriminatory fashion. You should not include such items as religion, hobbies, or items of that kind. They are unnecessary and unprofessional.

Educational History

Here you simply list each post secondary school you have attended. For each school, list your major, minor, degree (type and date), any honors you received there, and titles of theses or dissertations (and the chairs of your advisory committees). The entries should either go from first to last or last to first. First to last is more traditional. You may wish to put the dates flush right so that they stand out. Here's an example:

B. Educational History

1. University of California at Los Angeles, Los Angeles, California

Major: Psychology
Minor: Philosophy
Degree: B.A., Cum Laude   1980
Honors: California State Scholar: 1976–1979
                          Honors Program: 1977–1980

Honors Thesis: A comparison of response prevention and shaping in the reduction of avoidance
        behavior in rats (Chairperson: Ima Psychologist, Ph.D.)

Professional Positions

The next section is usually professional positions. Like the schools attended, professional positions are usually ordered sequentially (either from first to last or vice versa). First to last is traditional.

This is the first section where you can be a little creative. You want to list all positions you held, even if not necessarily paid. Thus, a practicum appointment would usually fit here. Research assistantships would fit. What does not fit here are short, one-shot experiences (e.g., giving a lecture to a group). One-shot paid consultations may fit. Unpaid consultations would probably fit better in a later section, such as "Professional Activities."

For each item, list what your title was and the name and address of the agency. The city is usually a sufficient address for this purpose if the agency is known. You should also list the nature of the position (full-time; ½ time) and when you held it. List your duties and your supervisor. The duties list is important, especially for more applied jobs, because it allows you to show the fit between your background and your desired work setting. Think of all the jobs you actually did and list them. This is often hard to remember, which is why you should get ready for vita writing long before you have much to put into one. Keep a file of your professional positions and add to it as new duties are fulfilled.

Here is an example: Note the consistency of style, both within this section, and between sections (e.g., note the flush right date).

C. Professional Positions

1. Psychology Trainee, Veteran's Administration Hospital, Palo Alto, California. Full-time
    Summer position.   1983
    Duties: Consultation to kidney dialysis unit; group behavior therapy; program development on a token economy ward.
    Supervisor: George Doright, Ph.D., Unit Psychologist

2. Research Assistant, Brown University, Half-time position.   1985–1986
    Duties: Assist in research on priming effects on memory. Analyze data using SPSS-X and SAS. Program in BASIC and PASCAL.
    Supervisor: H. D. Science, Ph.D.

There are many places where you can tailor your description of your duties. For example, if you want to make it clear that you take a cognitive perspective, use cognitive terms to describe your work. Try to think of who will read the document, then describe yourself honestly, but in the most favorable light. Don't offend people needlessly. If you use philosophically loaded words (e.g., "radical behaviorism," Mentalistic," "mechanical models") to describe your work you will please only the like-minded. This is something you should probably avoid, unless it would be a real disaster to work with folks not completely comfortable with your preferred manner of describing yourself.

Membership and Professional Associations

List all of them. Note whether you are a member, associate, or student member. Here is an example:

D. Membership in Professional Associations

American Psychological Society (Student Associate)

Society for Research in Child Development (Student Member)

Professional Activities

This is the place where you list all the projects you started, neat things you did, committee memberships you held (don't forget departmental committees. They count.), in-service training programs you conducted, important guest lectures you presented, etc. You can be creative here (but see later section on "padding"). You can subdivide this section as needed (e.g., Associations and Divisions, Administrative, etc.). Persons giving lots of workshops or colloquia may want a separate section for these. You may list items first to last or vice versa. An example:

E. Professional Activities

Associations and Divisions

1. Member of Program Committee, Nebraska Psychological Society, First Annual Convention, Lincoln, December 1988.

2. President, Psi Chi, University of Hawaii Chapter, 1984.

Administrative

1. Students' representative to the Departmental Training Committee, Department of Psychology, University of New Mexico.

Other

1. In service training, "Measuring change." Presented to the staff of the Piedmont Psychology Center, June 1985.

Editorial Activities

If you go to a lot of conventions, do a good deal of research, and get to know prominent people, you will probably be reviewing manuscripts before you get out of graduate school. Reviewing is a critically important activity for the field, and you should list it. If you review a MS sent to you, you usually list that as "Ad Hoc Editorial Consultant." Example:

F. Editorial Activities

1. Editor, **The Student Observer**, a student supplement to the **APS Observer**, 1989.

2. Ad Hoc Editorial Consultant, **Psychological Science**, 1989.

Grants

List the grants you have received. Some professionals include grants they had a significant role in, even if they were not the Principle Investigator. Many people list grants they wrote that were not funded. As a student or young professional that is probably fine, since if you even sent on in it is a good sign. Use your own sense in this area. Certainly a long list of "failures to fund," if not countered by several successes, could eventually hurt more than help. People may think you are a motivated incompetent. Here's an example of this section.

G. Grants

1. Small Grants Division, National Institute of Mental Health, #MH 36998-03, Social Skills Training for Sexual Deviants, $10,000, 1986–1987. E. Z. Dozit, Principle Investigator.

Papers Presented

List all the papers you presented at professional meetings. It seems to be common to list them by year starting with the most recent and working back. Some people number entries, but that seems to say that you are counting so it probably is not a good idea. Some people also put colloquia here; others put them in a separate section (e.g., in the "Professional Activities" section). List papers in regular APA format and double space between entries.

H. Papers Presented

1986

Dozit, E. Z. (August 1986). An experimental analysis of life, behavior, and the whole universe. Paper presented at the meeting of the American Psychological Association, Washington, D.C.

Dozit, E. Z. (August 1986). The role of response mediation in the formation of prototypes. Paper presented at the meeting of the International Society for Psychological Research, Lake Tahoe, NV.

Some people also list papers or talks presented to nonprofessional audiences (e.g., the PTA, radio talk shows). In general, this seems rather extreme, and might give an impression of padding. If you must list them, either create a special section (e.g., "Talks Presented to Non-professional Audiences") or put the most important ones in "Professional Activities."

Publications

When you have sufficient entries, organize them by year and by type (articles, chapters in books, books): It seems to be common to list them from the most recent to the oldest. That way, the current work (which is usually what you want folks to see) is seen first. List papers in regular APA format.

Do not put papers which are under submission or in preparation is this section. It will look as though you are padding (see section below). In press articles belong here. Invited articles which are in preparation probably belong since they will definitely be published. An example of this section:

I. Publications

a. Books

Tense, I. M. (1989). *Having fun with anxiety*. New York: Wierdo Publications.

b. Articles

1987

Tense, I. M. (1987). The relation between anxiety and performance is an inverted W, not a U. *Perceptual and Motor Skills, 112*, 445–446.

Papers Currently Under Submission

In this section, list your articles that are currently under submission. List only authors and title. It seems unnecessarily risky to say where you sent it. If it is turned down you have to change your vita and everyone knows that it was rejected. Listing the journal probably makes the listing more credible, however, so there is a trade-off. Once papers are on this list, keep them there until you give up resubmitting, or until they get accepted. When they get accepted, they go to the publications section, and are said to be "in press."

Project Underway

Use this section for manuscripts in preparation and for projects that are actually underway (e.g., experiments in progress). List as in the section on papers currently under submission. Both this section and the previous one (under submission) are optional; professionals with established reputations sometimes leave them off. Students often need these sections, however. Established researchers sometimes list articles in preparation just to make sure they will not forget the publication of a minor project when they update their vita.

Statement of Professional Interests

You may want to save some work by including a brief paragraph on your professional interests: research interests, applied interests, and teaching interests. Many vita of established professionals contain a brief outline of current or favorite research or other professional interests. You might want to start off with a general statement and then conclude with a specific listing.

Professional References

Finally, you need three to five professional references who will speak very highly of you. Don't ask for a reference simply because the person is well known, unless you are confident of the quality of the actual reference. Ask the person before you include his or her name on your vita if it is OK to do so, as a professional courtesy. List and number each reference, give their name, title, and address. Sometimes people leave this section blank, with a line such as "References Available on Request" appearing instead. The only advantage of this is that the best and most current references can then be used as needed. If the relationship with a former referee becomes strained, this would prevent their having an opportunity to speak in your behalf. This circumstance is rare, and it is more common to list the references.

Other General Considerations

This document is critical so prepare it carefully. Use a carbon ribbon or laser printer, not a cloth ribbon; use wide margins and white space in between items and sections; lay it out in an attractive and well organized fashion; proof the document carefully; put your name at the top of each sheet. For example:

E. Z. Dozit
Vita
3

Have the original printed or xeroxed on good paper on a very good machine. Staple each copy together.

Detail

Remember, you want to be honest, and you also want to impress. Provide sufficient detail to do so. For example, on papers presented, give the full reference on each. Such understatement as only listing the convention is needlessly modest (or it may be interpreted as lazy) and does not convey the important information. On the other hand, don't overburden the document with detail that is unimportant. Have some psychologists read it and get their feedback.

What Not to Put In

Don't try to overly personalize your vita—leave that for a separate letter or an interview. It is unprofessional to include your hobbies, the name of your dog, your high school activities, and the like. Occasionally, persons do foolish things like putting their favorite poem on the first page of his vita. That alone will kill any chance for many positions. Remember that if you are qualified, there are also a dozen others who are too. The slightest little stimulus could be reason enough to weed out your application. Poor attention to form, detail, content, or "what not to say" could be the stimulus.

Padding

One of the cardinal sins in vita writing is padding. Padding is defined when a reader reacts to the vita as more form than substance ("Who is he trying to kid?!") Thus, it refers to an audience reaction, not a specific vita writing behavior. The reaction is most likely when the importance or substance of the item is not obvious. This is especially true in the professional activities and projects underway sections. Make sure these sections are legitimate. For example, never list umpteen projects underway if you don't have any publications. People will never believe you even if it is true. Instead, if you are in that situation, list the most important projects underway. Similarly, don't list a zillion projects submitted, when you have no publications; it may not seem fair, but remember "padding" is an audience reaction, not a specific vita writing behavior.

Other signs of padding include listing conventions attended, journals subscribed to, articles you read over and edited for a friend, and projects you worked on in a non-professional role (e.g., secretary).

Vita Development

(a) Write up your vita now. No matter how puny. From acorns giant oaks grow, and you might as well begin. It will also get you thinking about your career development.

(b) Keep a vita development file. (If you aren't keeping any kind of files yet, start). Throw notes into this file regarding the kinds of things you are doing on your assistantships, special talks you gave, activities you performed that were noteworthy, committee assignments; papers presented, associations joined, everything you need to update your vita.

(c) Set goals for your career and work toward them. Design a reasonable strategy to reach those goals. Use the periodic updates of your vita as an opportunity to assess the development of your career.

(d) Revise your vita at least once a year or more often if the need arises.

(e) Have your advisor and others go over your vita before you send it out.

Good luck!

On the next two pages you will find two sample student vitae from students at Boise State University (used with their permission). These vitae represent years of work by these students to build their credentials. *If you are just starting out in psychology, your vita will not look like these samples.* It takes time to gain experience, so start as early in your career as you can. If you wait to do things like serving as a research assistant or teaching assistant until your last semester of college, those experiences will not be as valuable as they could have been had they occurred earlier.

KIMBERLY A. WIERSMA
1234 Main Street, Apt. #567
Boise, ID 83706 / (208) 555-1212
kimw@boisestate.edu

EDUCATION

INSTITUTION	DEGREE	RECEIVED	MAJOR FIELD
Boise State University	B.S. *Magna cum laude* GPA 3.85 Major 4.0	May 1998	Psychology
Boise State University	Non-Matriculated Graduate Coursework	N/A	Applied Psychological Research

RELEVANT EXPERIENCE

1997–*present* Project Supervisor, Annual Student Drinking Assessment Undergraduate Research Initiative, College of Social Sciences and Public Affairs, Boise State University.

1997 – *present* Project Supervisor, Parent Education in College Binge Drinking Research. Psychology Department, Boise State University.

1996–1997 Research Assistant, Prevention of Adolescent Skin Cancer Research Program. Psychology Department, Boise State University.

1996–1997 Research Assistant, Medical Volunteers in Haiti Research Program, Psychology Department, Boise State University.

1995–1996 Research Assistant, Traumatic Brain Injury Program, Idaho Neurological Institute, St. Alphonsus Regional Medical Center.

SCIENTIFIC PUBLICATIONS: *PAPERS AND PRESENTATIONS*

Wiersma, K. & Turrisi, R. Examination of judgments of drunkenness, binge drinking, and drunk driving tendencies in teens with and without a family history of alcohol abuse. Alcoholism: Clinical and Experimental Research, under review.

Turrisi, R. & Wiersma, K. The buffering effect of parent communication on consequences of college student binge drinking. Journal of Studies on Alcohol, under review.

Wiersma, K. & Turrisi, R. (1998). Judgment processes in individuals with a family history of alcoholism. Paper presented at the Research Society on Alcoholism, Hilton Head, SC.

Wiersma, K. & Turrisi, R. (1998). An analysis of college student binge drinking Final Report, Undergraduate Research Initiative Annual Student Drinking Assessment, Boise State University.

Turrisi, R., Wiersma, K., & Jaccard, J. (1998). Parent education in college binge drinking. Paper presented at the Research Society on Alcoholism, Hilton Head, SC.

Wiersma, K. A., Seibert, P.S., Basom, J., & Zimmerman, C. (1996). Greater windows of opportunity using memory notebooks during acute care. Paper presented at the Rocky Mountain Psychological Association, Park City, UT.

GRANT & SCHOLARSHIP AWARDS

YEAR	SOURCE	AMOUNT OF AWARD
1995-1998	Psychology Departmental Scholarship, Boise State University	Approximately $1,700 Annually
Spring 1996	Research Travel Award Idaho Neurological Institute	Accommodations @ the Annual Meeting of the Rocky Mountain Psychological Association
Summer 1998	Research Travel Award, Undergraduate Research Initiative College of Social Sciences & Public Affairs, Boise State University	$600
Fall 1998	Research Award, Undergraduate Research Initiative College of Social Sciences & Public Affairs, Boise State University	$1,000

TEACHING & ADVISEMENT

Spring 1998	Advanced Statistical Methods, Teaching Assistant
Fall 1997	Life-Span Development II, Teaching Assistant
Fall 1995	Statistical Methods, Teaching Assistant & Paid Tutor
Spring 1995	General Psychology, Teaching Assistant
1996-1997	Psychology Department Academic Peer Advisor

HONORS

1994-1998	Dean's List
1995-1998	Member of the Honors Program
1995-present	Member of Psi Chi, Psychology National Honor Society (Secretary 97-98)
1995-1996	Boise State Ambassador
1997-present	Member of Phi Kappa Phi, National Honor Society
1998	Who's Who Among Students in American Colleges and Universities

PROFESSIONAL MEMBERSHIPS & COMMUNITY WORKSHOPS

1998-present	Research Society on Alcoholism
1996	Rocky Mountain Psychological Association
1998	Parent-Teen Communication Workshops, Idaho PTA

SPECIAL TRAINING

SPSS, LISREL VII, Microsoft Word, Excel, Power Point

REFERENCES

Dr. Robert Turrisi, Associate Professor, Department of Psychology; Director, Undergraduate Research Initiative, Boise State University.

Dr. Eric Landrum, Associate Professor and Chair, Department of Psychology, Boise State University.

Dr. Mark Snow, Professor, Department of Psychology, Boise State University.

KIMBERLY D. OTTER

1234 Cherry Lane
Boise, ID 83702
(208) 555-1212 (home)
(208) 555-2121 (work)
Kim@aol.com (e-mail)

EDUCATION

BA Psychology (5/99 Expected)	Cumulative GPA 2.7/4.0*
Boise State University	Psychology GPA 3.4/4.0*
Boise, Idaho	Last two years GPA 3.5/4.0*
	*(As of 12/98)

CAREER GOALS

I aspire to obtain a Ph.D. in Developmental or Experimental Psychology so that I may pursue a career in academia and conduct research based on sound theoretical principles and research design. Specifically, I would like to focus on research areas that promote a better understanding of the influences that peers, teachers, and family have on the educational, emotional, and social development of children and adolescents.

PAPERS AND PRESENTATIONS

Otter, K., Moody, K., & Amato, S. (April 1998). Homes, cars, parks: Where does sexual abuse occur? Poster presentation at the annual meeting of the Western Psychological Association and the Rocky Mountain Psychological Association, Albuquerque, New Mexico.

Otter, K. Norton, R. E., & Amato, S. (April 1999). From the perpetrator's perspective: Abuse characteristics as a function of abuse location. Submitted to the annual conference of the Midwestern Psychological Association for presentation.

Otter, K., Honts, C. R., & Amato, S. (April 1999). Spontaneous Countermeasures. Submitted to the annual conference of the Rocky Mountain Psychological Association for presentation.

SPECIALIZED TRAINING

Software packages- SPSS, PowerPoint, Word, and FrontPage Editor (web page software)

Communication Skills- I have developed a broad range of communication skills through working with adolescents and children as a mentor and with adults through working as a teaching assistant and project leader. I feel that these experiences have enabled me to develop a strong sense of leadership and authority that only could be obtained and maintained through effective communication

Organizational Skills- I have the ability to apply organization to all aspect of my academic and professional career. I create and maintain an orderly process of the projects I undertake as a facilitator, advisee, and co-worker

---

KIMBERLY D. OTTER VITAE   PAGE 2

RESEARCH AND TEACHING ASSISTANT EXPERIENCES

Fall 1997

- Title: Research Assistant
  Study: Sane Solutions: Sexual offender treatment effectiveness, recidivism rates
  Supervisor: Dr. Susan Amato
  Research description:
      S.A.N.E is a non profit facility that treats sexual offenders. The goal of this research was to establish some level of treatment effectiveness for the program. We made inquires regarding the recidivism rates between offenders that had completed the program and offenders who had not completed the program
  Responsibilities included:
      I was responsible for archival data collection and encoding

Spring 1998

- Title: Research Assistant
  Study: Applied Cognition Research Institute: Automated Polygraph Examination (APE)
  Supervisor: Dr. Susan Amato and Dr. Charles R. Honts
  Research description:
      Paid position - federally funded project assessing the differences of human examiner verse automated examiner reliability of polygraph examinations
  Responsibilities included:
      Creation and application of the pre-polygraph interview questions and post-polygraph exam debriefing, participant recruitment and scheduling, facilitation of the participants through the experiment, data collection from the pre and post interviews, polygraph chard editing, and data encoding and analysis using SPSS

- Title: Research Assistant
  Study: Sane Solutions: Location and prevalence of child sexual abuse
  Supervisor: Dr. Susan Amato
  Research description:
      Independent research conducted at a facility that treats sexual offenders. The goal of this research was to address the public's misconception regarding the location of child sexual abuse. This study showed that the two most common locations of child sexual abuse were the offender's home and the victim's home. The results of this project were presented at the annual conference of the Rocky Mountain Psychological Association (RMPA)
  Responsibilities included:
      Hypothesis construction; project facilitation; and archival data collection, encoding, and analysis, primarily using SPSS

- Title: Teaching assistant
  Course: Psychology P-101 (General Psychology)
  Professor: Dr. Susan Amato
  Duties included:
      Maintained three office hours weekly to be available to students for tutoring; graded extra credit papers, essays, and tests; maintenance of over 300 student's grades; and served as a class supervisor during exams and in the professors absence

---

KIMBERLY D. OTTER VITAE   PAGE 3

Fall 1998

- Title: Research Assistant
  Study: Applied Cognition Research Institute: Outside Issue Question (OIQ)
  Supervisor: Dr. Susan Amato and Dr. Charles R. Honts
  Research description:
      Paid position - federally funded project assessing the construct of outside issue questions regarding polygraph examinations.
  Responsibilities included:
      Creation and application of the pre-polygraph interview questions and post-polygraph exam debriefing, participant recruitment and scheduling, facilitation of the participants through the experiment, data collection from the pre and post interviews, polygraph chart editing, and data encoding and analysis using SPSS

- Title: Research Team Leader
  Study: Sane Solutions: Secret-keeping methods as a function of location
  Supervisor: Dr. Susan Amato
  Research description:
      Independent research, that addressed the function of location as it pertains to the secret-keeping methods employed by child sexual offenders.
  Responsibilities included:
      Hypothesis construction; project facilitation; recruitment and coordination of research assistants; served as a liaison between the research assistants, Dr. Amato, and the Sane Solutions staff and therapists; and data collection, encoding, and analysis, using SPSS

- Title: Teaching Assistant
  Course: Research Methods P-321 (Experimental Design)
  Professor: Dr. Anne K. Gordon
  Duties included:
      I held three office hours a week for tutoring, attended class daily, took copious notes, offered supplemental detail based on research experiences for in class examples, and graded student's paper for adherence to APA format

Spring 1999

- Title: Research Assistant
  Study: Applied Cognition Research Institute: Outside Issue Question (OIQ)
  Supervisor: Dr. Susan Amato and Dr. Charles R. Honts
  Research description:
      Paid position - federally funded project assessing the construct of outside issue questions regarding polygraph examinations.
  Responsibilities included:
      Creation and application of the pre-polygraph interview questions and post-polygraph exam debriefing, participant recruitment and scheduling, facilitation of the participants through the experiment, data collection from the pre and post interviews, polygraph chart editing, and data encoding and analysis using SPSS

- Title: Research Team Leader
  Study: Sane Solutions: Sexual offender treatment effectiveness, pro-social measures
  Supervisor: Dr. Susan Amato, Ph.D.
  Research description:
      This project is an undertaking to establish standardized measures of treatment effectiveness for funding purposes.

KIMBERLY D. OTTER VITAE   PAGE 4

  Responsibilities included:
      Hypothesis construction, project facilitation, recruitment and coordination of research assistants, liaison between the research assistants, Dr. Amato, the Sane Solutions staff and therapists, and the Advisory Board and data collection, encoding, and analysis, using SPSS

- Title: Research Assistant
  Study: Perception
  Supervisor: Dr. Garvin Chastain
  Research description:
      Visual perception reaction time as it pertains to familiar vocabulary
  Responsibilities included:
      Facilitation of participants through the visual perception tasks, consent, and debriefing

VOLUNTEER EXPERIENCES

Boise Family YMCA

- YMCA summer camp (1989-1992)
  Title: "Y" Camp Counselor
  Experience:
      I worked with YMCA summer camp as a counselor for six years. As a counselor I was responsible for six to eight children at one time, both boys and girls. The camps were created with the intention of growth in three areas of a child's life: mind, body, and spirit. It was my job to encourage growth in all of those areas through lesson plans dealing with educational and spiritual growth, physical activity, and facilitation of group interaction

- Teen-night (1990-1997)
  Title: Co-Facilitator
  Experience:
      I served as a Co-Facilitator for Teen-night for several years. The purpose of YMCA teen-nights was to provide a safe environment for teens to work on social issues and hanging-out. Typical activities included basketball, air hockey, swimming, educational lectures, sleepovers, movies, and spiritual seminars. I was responsible for the facilitation of all the aforementioned activities and I served as a mentor. As a mentor I worked with females providing guidance through the facilitation of group discussions and sharing personal experiences

PROFESSIONAL MEMBERSHIPS AND HONORS

Awarded the Research Excellence Award from PSI CHI (RMPA, 1998)
Member of Boise State University Psychology Club (98-99 Vice President)
President's (Dean's) List, Spring 1998 and Fall 1999
Student Member of the American Psychological Association
Student Member of the Rocky Mountain Psychological Association
Student Member of Division 7 of the American Psychological Association (Developmental Psychology)

REFERENCES

Dr. Susan Amato, Assistant Professor, Department of Psychology, Boise State University
Dr. Garvin Chastain, Professor, Department of Psychology, Boise State University
Dr. Charles Honts, Professor, Department of Psychology, Boise State University

Appendix C
PRINCIPLE SIX OF APA'S ETHICAL PRINCIPLES AND CODE OF CONDUCT

AMERICAN PSYCHOLOGICAL ASSOCIATION—ETHICAL PRINCIPLES OF PSYCHOLOGISTS AND CODE OF CONDUCT

Effective date December 1, 1992. Copyright © 1992 American Psychological Association. Reprinted with permission.

TEACHING, TRAINING SUPERVISION, RESEARCH, AND PUBLISHING

6.01 Design of Education and Training Programs. Psychologists who are responsible for education and training programs seek to ensure that the programs are competently designed, provide the proper experiences, and meet the requirements for licensure, certification, or other goals for which claims are made by the program.

6.02 Descriptions of Education and Training Programs.

(a) Psychologists responsible for education and training programs seek to ensure that there is a current and accurate description of the program content, training goals and objectives, and requirements that must be met for satisfactory completion of the program. This information must be made readily available to all interested parties.

(b) Psychologists seek to ensure that statements concerning their course outlines are accurate and not misleading, particularly regarding the subject matter to be covered, bases for evaluating progress, and the nature of course experiences. (See also Standard 3.03, Avoidance of False or Deceptive Statements.)

(c) To the degree to which they exercise control, psychologists responsible for announcements, catalogs, brochures, or advertisements describing workshops, seminars, or other non-degree-granting educational programs ensure that they accurately describe the audience for which the program is intended, the educational objectives, the presenters, and the fees involved.

6.03 Accuracy and Objectivity in Teaching.

(a) When engaged in teaching or training, psychologists present psychological information accurately and with a reasonable degree of objectivity.

(b) When engaged in teaching or training, psychologists recognize the power they hold over students or supervisees and therefore make reasonable efforts to avoid engaging in conduct that is personally demeaning to students or supervisees. (See also Standards 1.09, Respecting Others, and 1.12, Other Harassment.)

6.04 Limitation on Teaching. Psychologists do not teach the use of techniques or procedures that require specialized training, licensure, or expertise, including but not limited to hypnosis, biofeedback, and projective techniques, to individuals who lack the prerequisite training, legal scope of practice, or expertise.

6.05 Assessing Student and Supervisee Performance.

(a) In academic and supervisory relationships, psychologists establish an appropriate process for providing feedback to students and supervisees.

(b) Psychologists evaluate students and supervisees on the basis of their actual performance on relevant and established program requirements.

6.06 Planning Research.

(a) Psychologists design, conduct, and report research in accordance with recognized standards of scientific competence and ethical research.

(b) Psychologists plan their research so as to minimize the possibility that results will be misleading.

(c) In planning research, psychologists consider its ethical acceptability under the Ethics Code. If an ethical issue is unclear, psychologists seek to resolve the issue through consultation with institutional review boards, animal care and use committees, peer consultations, or other proper mechanisms.

(d) Psychologists take reasonable steps to implement appropriate protections for the rights and welfare of human participants, other persons affected by the research, and the welfare of animal subjects.

6.07 Responsibility.

(a) Psychologists conduct research competently and with due concern for the dignity and welfare of the participants.

(b) Psychologists are responsible for the ethical conduct of research conducted by them or by others under their supervision or control.

(c) Researchers and assistants are permitted to perform only those tasks for which they are appropriately trained and prepared.

(d) As part of the process of development and implementation of research projects, psychologists consult those with expertise concerning any special population under investigation or most likely to be affected.

6.08 Compliance With Law and Standards. Psychologists plan and conduct research in a manner consistent with federal and state law and regulations, as well as professional standards governing the conduct of research, and particularly those standards governing research with human participants and animal subjects.

6.09 Institutional Approval. Psychologists obtain from host institutions or organizations appropriate approval prior to conducting research, and they provide accurate information about their research proposals. They conduct the research in accordance with the approved research protocol.

6.10 Research Responsibilities. Prior to conducting research (except research involving only anonymous surveys, naturalistic observations, or similar research), psychologists enter into an agreement with participants that clarifies the nature of the research and the responsibilities of each party.

6.11 Informed Consent to Research.

(a) Psychologists use language that is reasonably understandable to research participants in obtaining their appropriate informed consent (except as provided in Standard 6.12, Dispensing With Informed Consent). Such informed consent is appropriately documented.

(b) Using language that is reasonably understandable to participants, psychologists inform participants of the nature of the research; they inform participants that they are free to participate or to decline to participate or to withdraw from the research; they explain the foreseeable consequences of declining or withdrawing; they inform participants of significant factors that may be expected to influence their willingness to participate (such as risks, discomfort, adverse effects, or limitations on confidentiality, except as provided in Standard 6.15, Deception in Research); and they explain other aspects about which the prospective participants inquire.

(c) When psychologists conduct research with individuals such as students or subordinates, psychologists take special care to protect the prospective participants from adverse consequences of declining or withdrawing from participation.

(d) When research participation is a course requirement or opportunity for extra credit, the prospective participant is given the choice of equitable alternative activities.

(e) For persons who are legally incapable of giving informed consent, psychologists nevertheless (1) provide an appropriate explanation, (2) obtain the participant's assent, and (3) obtain appropriate permission from a legally authorized person, if such substitute consent is permitted by law.

6.12 Dispensing With Informed Consent. Before determining that planned research (such as research involving only anonymous questionnaires, naturalistic observations, or certain kinds of archival research) does not require the informed consent of research participants, psychologists consider applicable regulations and institutional review board requirements, and they consult with colleagues as appropriate.

6.13 Informed Consent in Research Filming or Recording. Psychologists obtain informed consent from research participants prior to filming or recording them in any form, unless the research involves simply naturalistic observations in public places and it is not anticipated that the recording will be used in a manner that could cause personal identification or harm.

6.14 Offering Inducements for Research Participants.

(a) In offering professional services as an inducement to obtain research participants, psychologists make clear the nature of the services, as well as the risks, obligations, and limitations. (See also Standard 1.18, Barter [With Patients or Clients].)

(b) Psychologists do not offer excessive or inappropriate financial or other inducements to obtain research participants, particularly when it might tend to coerce participation.

6.15 Deception in Research.

(a) Psychologists do not conduct a study involving deception unless they have determined that the use of deceptive techniques is justified by the study's prospective scientific, educational, or applied value and that equally effective alternative procedures that do not use deception are not feasible.

(b) Psychologists never deceive research participants about significant aspects that would affect their willingness to participate, such as physical risks, discomfort, or unpleasant emotional experiences.

(c) Any other deception that is an integral feature of the design and conduct of an experiment must be explained to participants as early as is feasible, preferably at the conclusion of their participation, but no later than at the conclusion of the research. (See also Standard 6.18, Providing Participants With Information About the Study.)

6.16 Sharing and Utilizing Data. Psychologists inform research participants of their anticipated sharing or further use of personally identifiable research data and of the possibility of unanticipated future uses.

6.17 Minimizing Invasiveness. In conducting research, psychologists interfere with the participants or milieu from which data are collected only in a manner that is warranted by an appropriate research design and that is consistent with psychologists' roles as scientific investigators.

6.18 Providing Participants With Information About the Study.

(a) Psychologists provide a prompt opportunity for participants to obtain appropriate information about the nature, results, and conclusions of the research, and psychologists attempt to correct any misconceptions that participants may have.

(b) If scientific or humane values justify delaying or withholding this information, psychologists take reasonable measures to reduce the risk of harm.

6.19 Honoring Commitments. Psychologists take reasonable measures to honor all commitments they have made to research participants.

6.20 Care and Use of Animals in Research.

(a) Psychologists who conduct research involving animals treat them humanely.

(b) Psychologists acquire, care for, use, and dispose of animals in compliance with current federal, state, and local laws and regulations, and with professional standards.

(c) Psychologists trained in research methods and experienced in the care of laboratory animals supervise all procedures involving animals and are responsible for ensuring appropriate consideration of their comfort, health, and humane treatment.

(d) Psychologists ensure that all individuals using animals under their supervision have received instruction in research methods and in the care, maintenance, and handling of the species being used, to the extent appropriate to their role.

(e) Responsibilities and activities of individuals assisting in a research project are consistent with their respective competencies.

(f) Psychologists make reasonable efforts to minimize the discomfort, infection, illness, and pain of animal subjects.

(g) A procedure subjecting animals to pain, stress, or privation is used only when an alternative procedure is unavailable and the goal is justified by its prospective scientific, educational, or applied value.

(h) Surgical procedures are performed under appropriate anesthesia; techniques to avoid infection and minimize pain are followed during and after surgery.

(i) When it is appropriate that the animal's life be terminated, it is done rapidly, with an effort to minimize pain, and in accordance with accepted procedures.

6.21 Reporting of Results.

(a) Psychologists do not fabricate data or falsify results in their publications.

(b) If psychologists discover significant errors in their published data, they take reasonable steps to correct such errors in a correction, retraction, erratum, or other appropriate publication means.

6.22 Plagiarism. Psychologists do not present substantial portions or elements of another's work or data as their own, even if the other work or data source is cited occasionally.

6.23 Publication Credit.

(a) Psychologists take responsibility and credit, including authorship credit, only for work they have actually performed or to which they have contributed.

(b) Principal authorship and other publication credits accurately reflect the relative scientific or professional contributions of the individuals involved, regardless of their relative status. Mere possession of an institutional position, such as Department Chair, does not justify authorship credit. Minor contributions to the research or to the writing for publications are appropriately acknowledged, such as in footnotes or in an introductory statement.

(c) A student is usually listed as principal author on any multiple-authored article that is substantially based on the student's dissertation or thesis.

6.24 Duplicate Publication of Data. Psychologists do not publish, as original data, data that have been previously published. This does not preclude republishing data when they are accompanied by proper acknowledgment.

6.25 Sharing Data. After research results are published, psychologists do not withhold the data on which their conclusions are based from other competent professionals who seek to verify the substantive claims through reanalysis and who intend to use such data only for that purpose, provided that the confidentiality of the participants can be protected and unless legal rights concerning proprietary data preclude their release.

6.26 Professional Reviewers. Psychologists who review material submitted for publication, grant, or other research proposal review respect the confidentiality of and the proprietary rights in such information of those who submitted it.

Index